ELEMENTS

OF

MODERN ECONOMICS

PRENTICE-HALL ECONOMICS SERIES
E. A. J. JOHNSON, EDITOR

ELEMENTS

OF

MODERN ECONOMICS

by

ALBERT L. MEYERS, PH. D.

Principal Economist
Bureau of Agricultural Economics
United States Department of Agriculture

Revised Edition

NEW YORK
PRENTICE-HALL, INC.
1946

FIRST EDITION

First printing ....September 1937
Second printing ....January 1938
Third printing ....July 1939
Fourth printing ....May 1940
Fifth printing ....June 1940
Sixth printing ....October 1940

REVISED EDITION

Seventh printing..................August 1941
Eighth printing..................October 1941
Ninth printing...................February 1942
Tenth printing......................July 1942
Eleventh printing................August 1944
Twelfth printing..............November 1944
Thirteenth printing............December 1945
Fourteenth printing................April 1946
Fifteenth printing.................June 1946

Printed in the United States of America

To
MARJORIE CASTLE MEYERS

Preface to the Revised Edition

THE FIRST edition of this book enjoyed a reception that was far wider than I had anticipated. However, I owe a debt of gratitude to the multitude of economists whose constructive criticisms have resulted in this revised edition. Many of them, whose viewpoints differed from my own, were kind enough to criticize the book in the terms in which it was written.

I am most indebted to Elmer D. Fagan of Stanford, to Mabel Newcomer, Emily Brown, and Margaret Myers of Vassar, to E. C. Welsh of Ohio State, and to Billy E. Goetz of Armour Institute of Technology, all of whom were kind enough to write detailed criticisms of all or parts of the book.

Professor R. G. D. Allen of the London School of Economics devoted some time to reading and suggesting improvements to the new chapter on indifference curves. Unfortunately, I was unable to have him read the final draft; I hope that he will feel free to offer further criticism.

I am grateful to Professors Arthur D. Gayer of Queens College and W. W. Rostow of Columbia University who read the sections on money and banking.

My sincere thanks must also go to those many individuals who offered suggestions in casual conversations. I have in mind particularly the present and former members of the staff and the graduate students at Harvard University.

I sincerely hope that readers will continue to let me have their criticisms as they have in the past.

ALBERT L. MEYERS

Preface to the First Edition

THE PURPOSE of this volume is to reorient the beginning text in economics to conform to recent significant developments which have taken place in economic and monetary theory. While there is some pedagogical merit in a critical study of outmoded and partly fallacious doctrines, the place for it is not in the beginning course where the groundwork of the student's economic knowledge is to be laid. Although no text can hope to be free from occasional criticism, based on the more specialized knowledge of the individual instructor, the necessity for such criticism should be reduced to a minimum, since the spectacle of the instructor "having his daily quarrel with the text" can lead only to confusion for the beginner. It is hoped that this book will leave the instructor free to supplement, develop, and expound the principles stated and free him from the necessity of too extended contradictions of the text.

After careful experimental classroom use of this text, I am convinced that the use of the technique of monopolistic competition, wherever applicable, not only permits a closer approach to reality and a sounder theoretical analysis, but also makes the presentation of economic principles easier for the student to grasp. Knowledge of the conditions of monopolistic competition is not only a valuable theoretical tool in itself, but, by means of contrast, it also enables the student to form a clearer picture of the assumptions and the mechanism of pure competition than is obtained from the traditional presentation.

This book could not have been written without the monumental contributions to our knowledge which have been given us by Professor Edward Chamberlin and Mrs. Joan Robinson. To Chamberlin, in particular, my indebtedness is so great that to acknowledge it properly would unduly clutter the text with footnotes. I have therefore followed the expedient of footnoting the chapter headings. The articles devoted to the "Cost Controversy" in the *Economic Journal* by Young, Straffa, Shove, Harrod, Robertson, and Robbins have also been of great help in shaping the ideas both on costs and on the nature of competition.

I cannot allow an opportunity to pass without expressing my gratitude to my instructors at Harvard whose inspiring teaching has consciously and unconsciously permeated this book. I refer particularly to Professors J. A. Shumpeter, John D. Black, W. L. Crum, F. Machlup, and O. H. Taylor.

An especial debt of gratitude is due to Professor Fritz Machlup of the University of Buffalo, who read the entire manuscript and corrected many errors and made valuable suggestions for the improvement of the work.

I am also deeply indebted to my colleagues at Colgate University—Professors J. M. Shortliffe, H. D. Koontz, and C. F. Phillips—who read the manuscript, taught it experimentally in mimeographed form, and made valuable suggestions on the basis of their experience in teaching it. Professor Shortliffe has been particularly helpful and generous with his time in critical reading.

I am indebted to Professor Herman Aude of Colgate University for his help on the mathematical parts of the book, and to Professor E. Clare Bancroft for assistance on the banking chapter.

Drs. N. S. Buchanan and E. R. Rolph of the University of California have also given helpful criticism at various stages of the work.

The Economics Staff of the Department of Economics, Government, and History of the United States Military Academy has made many helpful suggestions that have been incorporated in recent reprints of the book.

A.L.M.

Contents

ELEMENTS

OF

MODERN ECONOMICS

CHAPTER I

The Nature of Economics

ECONOMICS is the science that deals with human wants and their satisfaction. We might also say that economics is the science that deals with those social phenomena arising from the wealth-getting and wealth-using activities of man. If each of us possessed an Aladdin's lamp which we had merely to rub in order to have any of our desires gratified immediately, there would be no economic problems and no need for a science of economics. Unfortunately, Aladdin's lamps exist only in Arabian fairy tales. In this real world of ours, the means of satisfying our wants exist in such limited amounts compared to our needs for them, and in such unsuitable forms and inconvenient places, that it requires human effort to obtain from nature the materials we want, to change them into suitable forms, and to deliver them at convenient places and convenient times for the satisfaction of our needs. We must either make this effort ourselves or find some method of inducing others to do so for us. Such inducement may take the form of coercion, as under slavery or serfdom; or it may take the form of the exchange of our own services for the goods and services of others; or we may offer in exchange for the things we want the goods or claims to goods which we have acquired in the past through our own labors, through inheritance, by fraud or theft, by begging or charity, or by gifts from others.

1

Primary Economic Problems

For most of us the goods we possess and the means of acquiring more are strictly limited. Consequently, any good or service that we acquire means that we must be content with less of something else which might have been obtained by the same effort or expenditure. We are confronted with the problem of determining what combination of goods and services will yield us the greatest amount of net satisfaction. This is an economic problem both for us as individuals and for society as a whole.

The primary economic problems of the production of wealth, the consumption of wealth, and the distribution of wealth will continue to be present regardless of either the economic or the political system under which we operate. Communism, Socialism, or Fascism, although essentially different attempts to solve these problems, would in actual practice eliminate none of them. Since it is the capitalist system under which we are living, we shall devote our attention to an attempt to understand how this system operates and the principles which explain its motivation.

Economics, being a social science,[1] is denied many of the means of experimentation and research which are open to the natural sciences. Human beings have wills of their own and resent being treated as guinea pigs for the purpose of social experimentation. The chemist and the physicist can perform their experiments in a vacuum at absolute temperature, and in sterile test tubes, thus reducing the extraneous elements to a minimum and confining attention to a single cause-and-effect relation. The economist, on the other hand, is forced to rely

---

[1] See Robbins, Lionel, *The Nature and Significance of Economic Science,* The Macmillan Co., New York, 1932, for a fuller discussion of this problem. This book also contains an excellent appraisal of the uses and limitations of the statistical method in economics.

very largely on the more indirect method of observing man's actions in society. Under these circumstances, when we wish to ascertain the effect of a single cause, we are forced to make a mental abstraction to allow for the influence of other causes in which we may not be interested at the moment, but which may be of great importance in producing the actual result which is under our observation. It is for this reason that we so often find economists making use of the phrase "other things being equal" although they recognize that in the actual world such things never are "equal."

Basic Assumptions of Economic Theory

The beginning student will save himself many hours of bewilderment if he takes special care to familiarize himself with the *assumptions* which underlie the formulation of economic principles by the economist. Failure to realize the significance of these assumptions gives rise to the loose misstatement, so often heard, that something "is all right in theory but all wrong in practice." Nothing that is wrong in practice is ever right in theory. If the conclusions of theory do not harmonize with apparent results in practice, either the theory itself is wrong, or we are attempting to apply the theory to practical conditions without recognizing the difference between actual circumstances and the *assumed conditions* which were postulated in the statement of the theory. For example, in economics we formulate the proposition that, other things being equal, people will buy more of the same product at a lower price than they will at a higher price. The proposition as stated is perfectly true; but let us examine some of the assumptions implicit in the phrase "other things being equal" that may or may not be fulfilled in practice. It is assumed: (1) that people's incomes remain the same; (2) that their tastes remain the same; (3) that the prices of other goods remain the same; (4) that people do not assume that this decline in price is a prelude to further decline; and (5) that the product is not one which depends upon its high price for "prestige value" (for instance, if anchovies should drop to $5.00 a ton in price, they would no longer confer any distinction upon the hostess who served them as *hors d'oeuvres,* and they would have to depend for their market upon those who actually liked them. Sales might actually be less than at the higher price. In any event, if sales did increase, they would probably not increase in proportion to the decline in price). We see, then, that in attempting to apply this proposition in practice and to predict whether a decline in a given price will increase the sale of a product, we must know the assumptions upon which the principle rests and the extent to which they are fulfilled by the practical situation. The failure of any one of these conditions to be fulfilled in practice necessitates a further study to ascertain how this will affect the final result.

The importance of assumptions in economic reasoning cannot be overemphasized. If an economist is not careful to keep them clearly in mind, he may very easily slip into a faulty chain of reasoning or apply his logical sequences to a situation which does not satisfy his original assumptions. You will also find that although they may be aware of their own assumptions and of the limitations which they impose, many writers on economics will neglect to state fully what their assumptions are. When an author's assumptions are implied rather than expressed, it will facilitate your understanding of his work if you will be very careful to ask yourself what assumptions are necessary to render his reasoning valid. This will not only help you to understand what the author is trying to say, but it will also help you to detect any errors that may be present in his reasoning; it will also help to save you from attempting to apply the reasoning to other conditions not warranted by the assumptions.

One of the most important assumptions underlying all economic reasoning is that of the rationality of human conduct. By this we do not mean that all individuals are highly intelligent or educated, nor that their actions will conform to the precepts of good conduct as laid down by the physician, the moralist, or the arbiter of social etiquette. All that we are implying by rational conduct from the viewpoint of economic science is that, given a choice among several lines of conduct, a rational individual will *try* to select that course of action which *seems to him* to promise either the greatest amount of satisfaction or the least amount of dissatisfaction. For example, if offered a choice between identically the same kind of articles (and knowing them to be the same) at different prices, the rational individual will choose the cheapest. Or, if offered a number of distasteful jobs all at the same rate of pay, the rational individual will choose that one which promises to be least distasteful (if accepting charity seems to be still less disagreeable, he will not work at all).

Obviously, if the economist were to try to explain the ultimate causes which motivate the rational action of an individual, he would be forced to duplicate the work which is at present being attempted by the psychologist. Why rational human beings desire to ornament themselves with diamonds is a matter for the psychologist to explain. But given the fact that they do desire them, and that diamonds are relatively scarcer to human wants than bread, the economist can explain why the price of diamonds is higher than that of bread under ordinary circumstances.

Of course, it must not be assumed that each individual goes through a lengthy process of reasoning every time he has an economic decision to make. *Habit* is a great saver of mental effort. Once an individual has found that a certain brand of coffee satisfies his taste and meets his requirements as to price, he is likely to continue to ask for that brand every time he requires more coffee, rather than to expend again the mental effort necessary in making a comparison of the various brands and prices of other coffees.   But the habit may persist long after the reason for it has passed.   The prices of better coffees may have dropped, or the coffee he has been using may have deteriorated in quality without his becoming aware of it.   The nauseous lengths to which the radio advertisers go in their efforts to get us to try a certain brand of product are an evidence of the persistence of the habits which they feel they must combat.   We shall have more to say about this important influence of habit later on.   For the present it is sufficient to remember that many economic phenomena may be explained only by the persistence of human habits.

Another very strong force which tends to modify or influence the economic conduct of rational individuals is *social habit* or *custom*.   It is not our purpose here to trace the rise and decline of social habits.   That is largely the task of the sociologist, even though economic motives have often played an important part in the formation and in the breakup of social habits.   Social customs are enforced by group opinion, by law, or by both law and opinion.   When an economically rational individual is confronted with a social custom that forbids a course of conduct which he desires to follow or which prescribes a line of conduct that he does not like, he has four possible alternatives to consider: (1) he may conform to the custom; (2) he may try to evade it; (3) he may openly defy it; (4) he may try to have the custom abolished or changed.   The alternative he chooses will depend both upon the intensity of his desire to do the forbidden act and upon the relative degree of dissatisfaction promised by the different alternatives.   Since the first alternative involves no effort or dissatisfaction except that of giving up the thing desired, it will be the usual course followed by most people, unless the attainment of the desired end appears so desirable as to outweigh the disadvantages of one of the other alternatives. The second alternative involves the individual's estimate of the chances of being caught and of the disagreeability of the penalties if he is found out. The third alternative involves an outright acceptance of the social disapproval and other penalties which may follow upon the given course of action. If the fourth alternative is chosen, the individual must have a considerable amount of altruism and believe that the change will benefit others as well as himself, or the personal gain from the change must be great enough to justify the effort required to persuade the community to change its custom.

We have perhaps strayed somewhat into the realm of sociology. Yet when we realize that prohibition provides an economic incentive for the bootlegger, that high taxes encourage evasion, and that styles and changes in styles can result in prosperity or bankruptcy for the businessman, then we may understand the importance of social habits, customs, and laws in influencing our economic actions.

The reader can easily see that if our science is to explain the economic life of a community, it must devote its main attention to the rational economic calculations of the average man. With the help of the psychologist, we might attempt to explain the economic decisions of the paranoiac or the cretin, but this would be of little help in explaining everyday economic affairs. It is equally true that economic laws based on the rational conduct of the average individual will not, without modification, explain fully the economic conduct of any one person. To the extent that the individual differs from the average, we must allow for personal idiosyncrasies. But if we have taken proper account of the rational actions of the average individual, we should be able to explain the economic actions of a group of persons and to predict under certain circumstances the way this group will react to different economic stimuli.

The Vocabulary of Economics

The beginner must be warned that he will have to master a technical economic vocabulary. Instead of coining new words, however, or using Latin or Greek terms as many of the other sciences do, economics has created its own vocabulary by taking words in ordinary everyday use and assigning special meanings to them. Unless the student is careful, this will be a source of confusion to him. For instance, "demand," "supply," "value," "utility," and other words have a far more restricted and exact meaning in economics than they do in common speech. Still more unfortunate from the student's point of view is the fact that not all economists always mean exactly the same thing when they use the same term. The only resource left to the student is to familiarize himself very carefully with the definitions of the book he happens to be reading in order to be sure to understand the author's meaning. The author of this book will try to use economic terms in their most usually accepted economic sense, and to define them as carefully as possible. The student must be alert, however, when reading other economic texts or articles on economic subjects in the public print, to detect different meanings assigned to the words used in this book.

Someone has said that economics is only common sense made difficult. To a great extent the statement is true. The student who will attempt to understand and apply the concepts he learns from this text will have made a start toward becoming an economist and toward understanding some of the economic questions which are agitating our country today. The student who merely attempts to memorize will have cluttered his mind with useless lumber.

CHAPTER II

Some Fundamental Economic Concepts

WE HAVE already said that economics deals with human wants and their satisfaction. The means by which human wants are satisfied are called *goods*.

A good is anything that satisfies a human want. The bread that I eat, the shoes that I wear, the house that I live in are all goods. It is not necessary that I in particular should want an article for it to be a good. I do not happen to care for artichokes, but as long as someone does, they are a good. Two conditions are necessary for the existence of a good: a human want, and a means that will satisfy that want.

Goods may be divided into two main classes, *free* goods and *economic* goods. *Free goods are those so plentifully supplied by nature that human effort is not required to obtain them. Economic goods are those that are so scarce relative to human wants that human effort is required to obtain them.* It will be obvious to the reader that whether a good falls in the classification of free goods or economic goods will depend upon circumstances. In certain thinly populated tropical islands untouched by navigation, bananas might be considered a free good. But when we consider the effort necessary to gather them and transport them, the bananas in New York City are an economic good. Probably the only goods which are free goods under nearly all circumstances are fresh air and sunshine. Even here, if we stop to consider air conditioning and ultra-violet-ray glass, we may raise some questions. If the reader wishes to test his grasp of this concept, let him ask himself whether free samples of corn flakes, free soup in soup kitchens, and free public libraries are free goods or economic goods, and why.

A service is any nonmaterial good. The acts of the cook who prepares my food, of the boy who mows my lawn, and of the orchestra which plays for my enjoyment are services. For many purposes, services need not be distinguished from other goods; but since we shall later have to make certain distinctions between the way in which the wages of free persons and the prices of goods are determined, we choose to draw this distinction now.

Utility

Utility is the quality or capacity of a good which enables it to satisfy a human want. Any good that is capable of satisfying my wants may be said to possess utility for me. It must be carefully noted that the good itself is not a utility. My desk itself is not a utility. It is a good; but its ability to serve as a support on which to write, as a place to hold my books, and whatever beauty of design it may have which pleases my eye constitute the qualities which give it utility for me.

The economic concept of utility carries with it no moral, esthetic, physiological, or any other kind of judgments or standards except those existing in the mind of the individual who desires the article. Utility is not synonymous with usefulness when we try to classify goods as being useful or harmful according to some abstract standards. Thus cocaine possesses utility for the dope fiend. Hideous paintings possess utility for those deficient enough in artistic taste to enjoy them. Poison possesses utility for the person who wants to commit suicide. As long as anything will satisfy any human want, it possesses utility. The economist, as an economist, can pass no judgment upon the merits of these wants. If all the paper in the country is used up in printing cheap magazines instead of great literature, this may be a cultural loss; but it cannot be considered an economic loss so long as the wants of the people are better satisfied by material which the English professor would say "panders to a degraded taste."

There are really four main kinds of utility:[1] *form* utility, *place* utility, *time* utility, and *ownership* utility. Form utility consists of the *physical form* or *structure* or of the *chemical composition* of a good which renders it capable of satisfying a human want. Thus the shoe manufacturer adds form utility to leather when he shapes it into shoes. The baker adds form utility to flour, salt, and yeast when he mixes and bakes them into bread. The florist adds form utility to a seed when he helps it grow into a flower.

Place utility, as its name implies, is the *presence* of a good in a *place* where it is able to satisfy a human want. Thus, the steamship companies, the railroads, and the retail stores are adding place utility to bananas by bringing them from the tropics and putting them in a place where one can buy them if one so desires.

Time utility is the *availability* of goods at a *time* when they are needed to satisfy human wants. Thus, the cold storage warehouse adds time utility to butter by keeping it from a time when it is overplentiful to a time when it is more needed. The retail store is adding time utility as well as place utility to goods by having them on its shelves so that one may obtain them immediately when he wants them instead of having to order them from the factory and wait for delivery.

Ownership utility consists in the *possession* of goods by those who desire them. Thus, the real estate agent adds ownership utility to houses by transferring their ownership from those who wish to get rid of them to those who wish to obtain them.

---

[1] This classification of kinds of utility is not necessary, nor is it fully inclusive or mutually exclusive. It may serve, however, to aid in understanding the concept.

Production

Production is the addition of utilities to goods or the rendering of services possessing utility. It may be readily seen that according to this definition all of the activities we have mentioned to illustrate the various kinds of utility are *productive* activities. Early economists used to consider only one kind of utility, form utility, when they spoke of production. Consequently they were forced into the untenable position of classing many kinds of human activity as *unproductive,* although at the same time they were forced to recognize these activities as useful and even necessary. The reader will realize, after careful consideration, that there are very few kinds of human employment which could be classed as unproductive under our definition.

Karl Marx and his followers were fond of hurling the stigma of "unproductive labor" at a great many types of human activity. This was because Marxists regarded as productive only those activities which led to the physical "creation" of physical goods. When we remember that the only reason we desire goods is for the utility which they are capable of giving, it must be obvious that any activity which increases utility must be productive. If I happen to desire to hear violin music more than I want to wear a new shirt, the efforts of Kreisler possess more utility for me and hence are more productive than those of Sadie the shirtmaker.

However, merely by saying that a certain kind of work is *productive* we do not necessarily mean that it is *desirable* by standards either of morality or of social welfare. Dope peddling is a productive enterprise, but it is a kind of production that most of us would like to see stamped out.[2]

---

[2] *Cf.* Taussig, F. W., *Principles of Economics,* Ch. II, Third Edition, The Macmillan Co., New York, 1921, for an excellent discussion of productive and unproductive labor.

Also, when we say that an activity is productive we do not necessarily imply that it is efficient. Many methods of production are extremely wasteful of both human and natural resources. The fact that some other method of production might be more efficient does not imply that a particular method is unproductive; it is merely inefficient.

When we say that a certain individual's activity is productive, we do not thereby justify the income which he receives for it. Real estate agents, stock brokers, movie actors, monopolists, and other persons may often receive far more than some people consider their services are worth; retail storekeepers may be making abnormal profits in times of rising prices; but none of this means that these individuals are unproductive.

Consumption

Consumption is the direct and final use of goods or services in satisfying the wants of free human beings. A distinction should be drawn here between consumption in the strict economic sense and the loose meaning which the word often has in popular speech. Consumption does not mean amount sold. The Federal Department of Commerce publishes figures of what it calls cotton "consumption" in the United States.[3] Actually, these figures are the *amounts* of raw cotton used by textile mills. Let us see what is really involved. Of the millions of pounds of cotton sold to the mills this year, some will be in the form of unsold or undelivered cotton thread or yarn. Some will be in the inventories of raw material or finished goods of knitting mills and weaving mills. Some will be in the hands of bleachers and dyers. Some will be in the form of unused cloth or finished goods in the dress and shirt fac-

---

[3] More recently many government bureaus have avoided this misuse by calling the figures: "apparent disappearance," "*mill* consumption," or other similar less confusing terms.

tories.   Some will be unsold goods on the shelves of wholesale and retail merchants.   And some will be unused sheets in an old maid's hope chest.   Of the stocks of raw cotton sold to the mills this year, probably only an infinitesimal part will be actually consumed during the year.   The cotton goods which we are consuming now belong largely to the production of last and previous years.[4]

Consumption does not mean the "using up" of a good unless such using is done by the ultimate consumer.   Coal is used up every day to generate power for the operation of machines in factories.   Economically speaking, however, such coal is not consumed until people use the goods which the machines have made.   The amount of wear and tear on a machine that occurs in making a single consumer's good may be said to be the consumption of the machine by the ultimate consumer as he uses up the product.   If businessmen would avoid the careless mental habit of considering everything they themselves have sold as being immediately consumed, and would try instead to find out what is actually happening to the goods, they would sometimes avoid producing for an already overstocked market.

Consumption is the final end and object of all economic activity.   If you were to ask the average manufacturer of machine tools why he was making them, his first answer would probably be: "Because I can sell them," or "Because I can sell them at a profit."   But a moment's reflection will show that unless those machine tools are capable of making consumer's goods which people want, or unless they are capable of making other tools which will in turn produce the consumer's goods which people want, the manufacturer will soon not only be unable to sell them at a profit, but will be unable to sell them at all.   At present it is only the *belief* that another manufac-

[4] For a clear picture of this phenomenon, see Taussig, F. W., *Wages and Capital*. The Macmillan Co., New York, 1896.

turer has that he in turn can sell the goods that the machine will make which induces him to buy the machine. Later, in the chapter on business cycles, we will see how such a belief can often be in error.

If at times we refrain from consuming all we might (in other words, if we *save*), the only rational motive for such conduct is that we believe that by so doing either we or our descendants may be able to have a greater quantity of goods, or an equal quantity of goods that will have greater utility in the future, or that more spending yields no more satisfaction.

The most important way in which the economic well-being of everyone in the community can be improved is by increasing the total amount of goods available for human consumption.[5] The only way in which the economic welfare of the individual can be improved is by an increase in the stock or the quality of goods which he can command for his own consumption. Often these two aims are in harmony with each other. Whenever an individual finds that by producing more goods his own income will be increased, he will be encouraged to make the effort, and both he and the community as a whole will benefit. Unfortunately this is not always the case. Robbery and fraud are ways of increasing the income of an individual without increasing the welfare of the community. Hence they may be condemned on economic as well as on moral grounds. There are also other ways in which the greatest well-being of the individual and that of society may diverge. For instance, assume that a union of bricklayers has a monopoly of its trade. If this union should find that it could command a greater income by laying only 1,000 bricks a day instead of 1,400 and should proceed to do so, its own welfare would be increased, but that of the community would suffer. Or, assume that a manufacturer

---

[5] Other possible ways might be a decrease in population with the same amount of goods, or an increase in quality of the goods. Whether *everyone* actually gained would also depend upon the distribution of the increased wealth.

has a monopoly of a certain product. If he finds that he can make a greater total income by producing a small quantity of articles, it will be to his own individual interest to do so, and his gain will be the community's loss. Fortunately the extent to which this is possible is somewhat limited. But the questions of monopolies and their consequences will continue to occupy a major portion of our attention throughout this book.

Property

Property is not goods but the right to the possession, use, enjoyment, and disposal of goods and services. Thus, the *right* which I have to the use of a house, either because I own it or because I am renting it, is property. So also are the *claims* of debts which I may have against someone, and the right to ride on a train after I have purchased a ticket.

The student should be careful to distinguish between *property* and *documents in evidence of property*. For example, my *right* of ownership of a house is property, but the deed to the house is merely a document in evidence of my right of ownership, a legal proof of ownership. If the deed should be lost or burned, the *right* of ownership which constitutes my property will be unimpaired, provided the deed has been recorded in the county clerk's office, or provided I can bring forward other proof that I own the house. Similarly, stock certificates, bonds, written records of contracts, and railroad tickets are not property. They are documents in evidence that property exists.

Factors of Production

The *factors of production* are land, labor, and capital. All three of these will be required in some proportion in any modern productive enterprise. It is possible to conceive of some exceedingly primitive productive processes being carried on with land and labor alone, entirely without capital goods. Such processes would be hunting or fishing with one's bare hands, or picking wild berries. But as soon as the hunter fashions a rude club, as soon as the fisherman makes a hook and line, and as soon as the berrypicker uses a pail, these producers will be making use of capital goods. Since any form of tool, no matter how crude, is a capital good, we shall be safe in stating that at least these three factors are involved in all modern productive enterprises.

Land in the economic sense means all of the natural resources used in the process of production. These include: the powers of the soil that are used for agriculture and forestry; mineral resources; water power and the uses of the surface of water for navigation; the fish and the minerals of the sea; and, finally, the use of land for sites or locations for productive enterprises. In other words, land in the economist's meaning includes all original non-human sources of energy and raw materials plus standing room.

Labor in the economic sense includes all human effort, either physical or mental, expended in the process of production. This definition is much broader than the popular concept of the term _labor_. Thus, not only the work of a carpenter, a machinist, and a ditchdigger is labor, but also the work of a musician in composing, of a corner grocer in buying and selling, and of a Henry Ford in managing his automobile factory. Any human effort which results in an increase of utilities is productive labor in the economist's meaning.

Capital may exist in the form either of capital goods or of money capital, or both, depending on the circumstances of the problem we are analyzing and the point of view of our analysis, as explained below.[6]

Capital goods consist of all produced goods used in the proc-

---

[6] Consult the article, "On the Meaning of the Marginal Product," by Fritz Machlup, in _Explorations in Economics_ (essays in honor of F. W. Taussig), McGraw-Hill Book Co., Inc., New York, 1936, pp. 250 ff., for a discussion of the nature of capital and the units in which it is measured.

ess of production. Land and labor are the *original means of production*. All of the tools, machinery, plant and equipment, and semifinished goods; in short, all of the material equipment used in production is merely the physical embodiment of the past services of land and labor. These material goods are called *intermediate* goods, or *capital* goods.

As an aid in production, land itself might be considered as one form of capital good; and for many purposes there is no significant difference between land and what we have called capital goods. However, since there are differences in the conditions of the supply of land and in the supply of intermediate goods, we have chosen to call land a separate factor of production, and we have ruled it out of the category of capital goods by the use of the phrase "produced goods" in our definition.

Money capital is the money funds available to an individual or firm for use in gaining command over the services of the original means of production. The command over these services may be obtained by hiring labor, by renting or purchasing land, or by purchase or hire of capital goods in which the past services of labor and land are embodied. The process of spending money capital for these services that are to be used in production is called *investment*. (The term *investment* is also used to mean the purchase of income-bearing assets, such as the stocks or bonds of different firms. But, unless specifically indicated, we shall not use it in this second meaning.) Money capital is available to a firm either through ownership or through borrowing.

When money capital is invested in such a way that the value represented will be fully recovered by selling the single unit of the product on which it is used, it is called *circulating capital*.[7] The wages paid to the laborers whose efforts are ex-

---

[7] In accounting terminology circulating capital is used to designate those investments which will be recovered within a given fiscal period (usually a year). This definition is more arbitrary than ours, but it may be more satisfactory to the accountant for his own purposes.

pended directly in making a unit of a product, the money spent for the raw material used to make the product, and the freight charges to send the good to market would all be examples of circulating capital.

When capital is invested in such a way that only a part of its value will be recovered by selling a unit of the product on which it is used, it is called *fixed capital*. The money spent for plant and equipment or for upkeep and repairs will be forms of fixed capital. The full cost of a factory will not be recovered in the selling price of one unit of a product which is made in that factory. But if the business succeeds, the price of the product will cover the entire cost of the circulating capital used in making each unit, plus a small amount which the owners of the business may take to reimburse them for the sum originally spent on the factory, or which they may reinvest to replace the plant equipment as it wears out. The value of fixed capital is thus recovered in installments by selling a number of successive units of the product.[8]

Management is really one kind of labor under the general definition given above. Because management is a *special* kind of labor, it is often classed as a separate factor of production. Management consists largely in the making of decisions. In the first place, the product to be manufactured or the business to be established must be determined. Then decisions must be made as to the proportions in which land, labor, and capital will be used and as to the methods by which they will be used. The amount of output will have to be decided upon, then the best size of plant or establishment to produce that output will have to be determined. Finally, there will be the labor of

---

[8] If we are thinking of the capital of a nation, we cannot consider paper money as capital, but must confine national capital to capital goods. An individual can obtain more command over the services of the original means of production by having more money with which to bid them away from other persons. But a nation cannot increase the sum total of available services merely by printing more paper money.

supervision to see that these decisions are carried out properly. The functions of management (that is, the labors of decision and supervision) may be performed by the owner or owners of a business, or they may be delegated in part to hired managers.

In actual life, the services of the various factors will not always be provided by separate individuals. Thus, a farmer may be a combination of landowner, laborer, capitalist, and manager. The same thing may be true of the owner of any small business. In fact, any two or three of these functions may be exercised by the same individual. But we should keep in mind that these are still separate functions, because, as we shall discover later, the incomes of these factors are determined differently.

The Marginal Concept

One of the most important concepts which the reader will have to master in order to understand economic literature is the concept of the marginal unit. *The marginal unit* of any factor of production, of any stock of goods, and of any output of goods *is the unit whose acquisition or loss* (or whose addition or subtraction) *is under consideration*. Whether the question is one of adding or subtracting will usually be apparent from the context. The marginal unit is not necessarily the last unit, although it may appear to be so on a diagram. In any stock or output of *identical* goods, or in any group of *identical* units of a factor of production, obviously any unit is a perfect substitute for any other unit; and thus the concept has reference to the addition or subtraction of any one unit without regard to which particular unit it may happen to be. For example, an employer who feels that he must lay off one man from a group of workmen of exactly similar kind and degree of skill may follow the policy of laying off the workman with the fewest dependents rather than the last one who was hired.

On the other hand, when we are considering firms in an

industry or farms in agriculture, the marginal firm or farm is the highest-cost firm or farm. In other words, it is the firm or farm which is just managing to stay in business and will be the first to leave the competition if the price of the product falls.

With this set of definitions thoroughly in mind, we can begin our exposition of economic activity. These definitions will be further explained, and other concepts will be defined as we proceed.

CHAPTER III
Utility and Value

Note: Chapter V presents an alternative approach, based on indifference curves, to the material in Chapters III and IV. Whichever approach is selected, it should be mastered thoroughly before any attention is paid to the other. After this study, the alternative approach may be used as collateral reading for comparison.

WE HAVE already defined utility as the quality or capacity of a good which enables it to satisfy a human want. A moment's reflection will convince the reader that his wants for different kinds of goods are of different intensity, and that consequently the goods which satisfy those wants will possess different degrees of utility for him. If you were given your choice of going without food for a week or not going to the movies for a week, even the best of shows would not be likely to induce you to give up eating. The utility of food is greater to you than that of movies. On the other hand, if your board bill has been paid for the coming month and you have just finished your dinner, the choice between eating another meal immediately and going to see your favorite screen star would probably be settled in favor of the latter. Obviously, under these circumstances the utility of a single movie is greater than that of a single meal. How can we explain this apparent contradiction?

Law of Diminishing Marginal Utility

The answer lies in the *law of diminishing marginal utility* which we shall now develop and explain. Given a large enough

22

quantity of any one good, our wants for that particular good will be completely satisfied, so that we desire no more of the article. Furthermore, after the first unit, each succeeding unit of a good acquired or consumed will yield us less satisfaction than the preceding unit.[1] A few examples will make this clear.

Let us assume that you are extremely fond of fresh strawberry sundaes, and that someone offers to buy you all you can eat at one sitting. The first one would taste delicious, the second one would give less satisfaction, the third still less, and so on until eventually you would reach a point where eating one more sundae would no longer give any satisfaction. In other words, the *utility* of each successive sundae has been *diminishing* with each one consumed until you have reached the point of zero utility. Even though your friend is still willing to buy more sundaes for you, you will not care to eat them. If he should now offer to give you a dollar for each additional one that you eat, you might try it for a while. But each sundae now would give you increasing discomfort and dissatisfaction (*disutility*) and you would soon reach a point where the disutility of eating another sundae was so great that a dollar would no longer compensate for it, and you would stop completely.[2]

In the preceding illustration, we have assumed that consumption occurs during one short period of time. However, the law of diminishing marginal utility applies also to the possession of a stock of goods of one kind which may be used at the pleasure of the owner. Let us assume that the commodity is suits of clothes. One suit of clothes will possess a high degree of utility for me, since it will protect me from the elements,

---

[1] The proof of this statement may be found in the fact that if marginal utility did not decrease with an increase in quantity, once one started to buy a commodity, he would never buy anything else.

[2] This illustration is somewhat more vivid than it is exact. If you were offered 10 or 12 sundaes, all at the same time, any one of them would not have much marginal utility regardless of whether you chose to down it first or last. See also Knight, Frank H., *Risk, Uncertainty and Profit,* Houghton Mifflin Co., Boston, 1931, Ch. 3.

will keep me from being arrested for indecent exposure, and will save me from the ridicule I would encounter from my friends should I go naked. A second suit will not be quite so important, but its utility will still be high because it will save me from having to go to bed while the other is at the cleaners. A third suit would provide an agreeable variety; and should I desire to dress differently for different occasions, additional suits would possess a high though diminishing degree of utility for me. The reader may here properly object that different kinds of suits are different commodities, although they are good substitutes for each other. I would be forced to agree. If our example is confined to the addition to our stock of more suits of the same cloth and cut as the first, the utility of each added suit would decline much more rapidly. However, if we agree that a person acquiring a wardrobe at the rate of one suit at a time will buy first those suits which have the most important uses for him, it is perfectly proper to speak of the diminishing marginal utility of suits in general as well as of a particular kind of suit.

The Marginal Unit

The reader will notice that we have been careful to speak of diminishing *marginal* utility. By the *marginal unit* we mean *any unit in a stock of goods which is used for the purpose of least utility.*[3] If the goods are identical in kind, the marginal unit will be the unit the acquisition or loss of which is under consideration in a given period of time. In any stock of goods, the marginal unit will be the one which the owner will part with most readily if he is forced by circumstances to give up something (for instance, if his salary is cut, he will give up the purchase of those units of goods which were marginal to him at his old salary level). In a stock of goods of identically the

---

[3] Note that marginal utility may be *negative*, as, for example, when we have so much of a commodity that we desire the storage space for something else.

same kind, *any* unit of the stock will be a perfect substitute for any other unit. Therefore, it is possible for us to say that in a stock of *identical* goods, any unit of the stock may be the marginal unit; and the utility of such a unit is the marginal utility of the stock of goods. This is true since, if we were forced to give up one unit in a stock of identical goods, we would abstain from using the good in that use in which it yielded us the least satisfaction. Thus, we might use salt for seasoning our food, for making pickles, or to scatter on our icy sidewalk. So long as we have enough salt for all three purposes, the marginal utility of salt to us will be only the utility of a pound of salt in its least important use, that is, for scattering on the sidewalk. If our stock of salt were not enough for sidewalks, without sacrificing some of that devoted to other uses, we would give up scattering it on our walks. If our stock of salt were still less, we would give up making pickles, and the marginal utility of salt would then be the high utility of a pound of it used for seasoning our food. So long as all pounds of salt are the same, no particular pound will have any more utility for us than any other pound. It is the amount which we possess that will determine the uses to which an article will be put; the marginal utility of the good will be the utility of a unit of it in its least important use. As our stock of the good increases and successive units of it satisfy less and less important wants, the marginal utility of the good diminishes.

Total Utility

We must be careful to distinguish between *marginal* utility and *total* utility. The *total* utility of a stock of a good is *the sum of the utilities of the various units considered as if the units were added to the stock one at a time.* Thus, if we had three suits of clothes, their total utility would be the high utility of one suit if we possessed it alone, plus the utility of the second suit if we possessed only two, plus the utility of the third suit when we have three. It may be seen that, although marginal utility is always decreasing as a unit is added to the stock, *total utility will increase at a decreasing rate until the point of zero marginal utility is reached.*[4] That is, we are adding to the total utility as we add the utility of each successive unit, but we are adding a smaller amount of utility each time.

We have now found the answer to the riddle of the first paragraph of this chapter. The total utility of food for a week would be greater than the total utility of movies for a week, in the first instance. In our second supposition, with meals for a month provided for, the marginal utility of a first movie is greater than that of a second immediate meal. A similar process of thought will enable us to explain why air, although necessary to sustain life, is a free good, while diamonds, although they satisfy nothing but vanity, are an expensive economic good. The total utility of air is infinite. If any monopolist could obtain complete control of all the supply and dole it out a little at a time, we would pay almost any price he asked rather than go without. Fortunately for us, this is impossible and, since each of us has absolutely all the air he wants, the marginal utility of air to everyone is zero. With diamonds, on the other hand, although their total utility is much less than that of air, bread, milk, or any one of a number of other goods, they are so scarce (both naturally, and artificially through control of a new supply by a syndicate) that their marginal utility is extremely high for those people who desire to possess them for their beauty or for their ostentatious use. The tradition of requiring diamonds in engagement rings has given them great marginal utility to women (being able to show the diamond saves them from feeling inferior), and in consequence many a struggling young clerk has given for a small diamond chip

---

[4] The mathematically minded reader may understand this better by recognizing that total utility is the integral of marginal utility.

the fifty dollars he desperately needed to help set up a household.

Measurement of Utility

Unfortunately, there is no scale or standard by which we can measure utility.[5] That is, utility cannot be measured in inches, pounds, gallons, or any other concrete standard with which we are familiar. The utility of a good, or of any unit of a good, can be measured only in terms of the degree of intensity of the want which the good is capable of satisfying. Since the want exists only in the mind of each individual and the want for the same good will differ in intensity from one individual to another, it is probably impossible to set up any standard unit in which utility can be measured. We can, of course, compare the utility of one good with that of another in our own minds. For instance, I can say that one melon will give me as much satisfaction as ten pears, but this will not indicate the utility of either in any absolute sense. The ratio of ten to one may hold either because of the high utility of melons to me or because of the low utility of pears, or because both are low in utility but pears are lower than melons. But we know from experience and observation that there is a law of diminishing marginal utility, although marginal utility decreases at different rates for different persons and for different goods.

A diagram may help to illustrate this law, even though the scale of utility units on such a diagram will have to be imaginary. In both figures of Diagram 1 the vertical distances measured along the OY axes indicate the amount of utility as shown by our imaginary scale. The distance along the horizontal or OX axes shows the number of units of the good that are possessed or consumed. The height of the rectangles in Figure 1 shows the utility of each successive unit. It will be

---

[5] It was precisely this difficulty which led to the indifference curve analysis given in Chapter V.

noticed that there is no top to the first rectangle. This is because in the case of a good capable of sustaining human life
the utility of a first unit of it may be infinite.[6]

The heights of the second, third, and fourth rectangles and
of successive rectangles decrease, indicating the diminishing
utility of each successive unit added to the stock. In the figure
the utility of the seventh unit would be zero. The possession
or consumption of more units of this good would then begin
to yield dissatisfaction or disutility, as is shown by the position
of the rectangles from here on below the zero (OX) line. At
any point where possession or consumption ceases, the utility
of the last unit is the *marginal utility* of the stock. Thus,
if our diagram illustrates the consumption of strawberry sundaes in the example five pages back, when we have eaten
four sundaes the marginal utility of sundaes will be the utility
of the fourth one, shown by the height of the fourth rectangle
in the diagram. The marginal utility of sundaes if we were

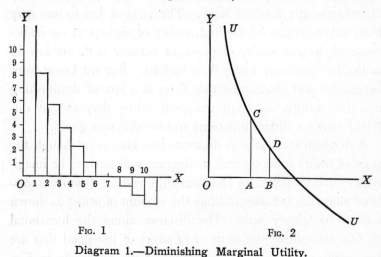

FIG. 1   FIG. 2

Diagram 1.—Diminishing Marginal Utility.

[6] This is on the assumption that there are no even remote substitutes for the
good. Where substitutes exist, we would close the top of the rectangle and join
the curve to the Y axis, although probably at a point higher than any shown in
the limits of the diagram.

to consume a fifth one is shown by the lesser height of the fifth rectangle, and so on.

Total utility is shown in Figure 1 by the total area enclosed in the number of rectangles up to whatever point possession or consumption stops. Thus the total utility of sundaes when three are consumed is the utility of the first, plus the utility of the second, plus the utility of the third. It will be seen that although marginal utility is decreasing with the consumption of each successive sundae, total utility increases to the point where zero marginal utility is reached. At the point of zero marginal utility, total utility is at a maximum. Further consumption beyond this point would necessitate the subtraction of the disutilities of more units from the sum total of utility.

If we choose small enough units of the good, the rectangles representing utility will be narrowed until they are vertical straight lines (for example, if, instead of the consumption of successive whole sundaes, we consider the consumption of successive spoonfuls). The tops of these lines may then be joined to form the curve *UU* as shown in Figure 2. This curve is known as the *curve of diminishing marginal utility*. The same principles apply to this curve as to the rectangles in Figure 1. Thus, when *OA* units of the good are consumed, marginal utility is represented by the height of the line *AC,* and total utility is represented by the area bounded by the lines *OA, AC, OY,* respectively, and that part of the curve *UU* which lies above the point *C*. When *AB* units of the good are consumed, marginal utility is represented by the height of the line *BD,* and so on.

Certain goods satisfy only one kind of want or desire. With this class of goods diminishing marginal utility is governed, as we have seen, by the extent to which the want becomes satiated with the possession or consumption of successive units of the good.

Utility of a Good with Several Uses

Other kinds of goods are capable of two or more uses. These goods, if our stock of them is limited, will be put to their most important use first (the use in which their utility is greatest). However, with the application of successive units of the good in its most important use, marginal utility will decline in that use, just as it does when there is only *one* use for the good. When marginal utility in the first use declines to the point where it is just equal to the utility of a first unit applied to another use, we will start using any further supply for the satisfaction of the second want as well as the first. Let us suppose that our stock of the good increases still further. When the marginal utilities of the good in its first and second uses have both declined to the point where they just equal the utility of a first application of the good to its third use, we will start using the good for its third purpose also. If we now think of the marginal utility of the good in general, as applied to all its uses, we will see that if a good has several uses, marginal utility will decline less rapidly than if the good has only one use. This principle may be more easily visualized if we think of a particular example. Let us consider a pioneer farmer with a limited stock of wheat and no possibility of buying more. His most important use for wheat will be as food for this year. The second use will be as seed for a crop next year. The third use might be to feed chickens. Obviously he will not starve to death in order to save seed wheat. But if he has any more wheat than enough to keep him alive, he will try to save some for seed to provide for next year, rather than eat all he possibly could. With a still greater stock, he will start feeding some to the chickens, rather than eat and plant the whole stock.

We are now prepared to draw a diagram to illustrate this principle. In each of the four figures of Diagram 2 the scale on the vertical or *OY* axis represents utility (measured in our imaginary units). The distances on the horizontal or *OX* axis in each figure represent quantity or number of units of the good, for example, bushels of wheat.

MU is the curve of diminishing marginal utility of the good in its first use.

M′U′ is the curve of diminishing marginal utility of the good in its second use.

M″U″ is the curve of diminishing marginal utility of the good in its third use.

M‴U‴ is the curve of diminishing marginal utility of the good in all three uses combined. It is found by adding the other three curves together.

Equal height of points on the three curves represents points of equal marginal utility in the three uses.

With any amount of the good less than *OA* (Figure 1) it

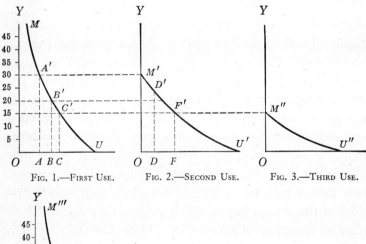

Fig. 1.—First Use.   Fig. 2.—Second Use.   Fig. 3.—Third Use.

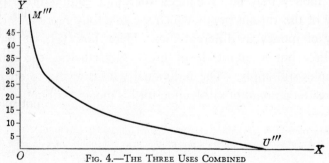

Fig. 4.—The Three Uses Combined

Diagram 2.—Marginal Utility of a Good with Three Uses.

will pay us to use the entire stock for use one because the marginal utility of *OA* units in use one is *A'A*, which equals 30, and no utility in the other uses is greater than 30.

The utility of the first unit used for the second purpose is 30; thus, from here on it will pay us to use the good for the second use as well as the first, if our stock is greater than *OA*.

Assume that the new stock increases to the amount *OB* (Figure 1); the new amount *AB* is equal to *OD* (Figure 2). The utility of the last unit in stock *OB* is *B'B*, or 20 (Figure 1). The utility of the last unit in stock *OD* is *D'D*, which is greater than 20 (Figure 2). Therefore, it would give greater utility to devote some of the increase *AB* to the second purpose rather than to use it all for the first want.

By a similar proof it can be shown that any amount greater than *OC* plus *OF* (Figures 1 and 2) should have part of the increase devoted to the third use to secure greatest utility.

It will be noticed that the extreme tops of the curves *MU* (Figure 1) and *M'''U'''* (Figure 4) do not touch their respective *OY* axes at any point. This is because, with any good that is a necessity of life, a very small quantity would have infinite marginal utility. Thus we may think of the curves as being extended upward indefinitely. We are concerned here only with that portion of the curves which we can measure.

This same type of analysis could well be applied to money.[7] Since money may be exchanged for other commodities, the utility of the various goods which we may buy represents the utility of money in different uses. Here, however, we have not three but a multitude of uses. Nevertheless, the same principles still apply. The individual who is trying to obtain the greatest amount of satisfaction for his money will not spend

---

[7] Where money, or any other good, is desired simply as a collector's item, or for the sake of personal aggrandizement, the marginal utility may increase for a while.

all of it on one product, but will try to obtain *equal marginal utility* for the last dollars spent upon various products. The student with five dollars of his monthly allowance left may spend two dollars for two neckties, two dollars for a shirt, and the remaining dollar for tickets to the movies. If you ask him why he did not buy five neckties instead, he might reply, "I would have liked to, but I could not afford them." Economically speaking, what he really means is that more neckties would still have some utility for him, but that the utility of the shirt and the movies was still greater; therefore, he divided his expenditures in the way which he thought would yield him the greatest amount of total satisfaction.

Marginal Utility and Apportionment of Expenditures

If the marginal utility doctrine is accepted, then the assumption of economically rational conduct on the part of the individual requires that he so apportion his expenditures that the marginal utility of all goods bought will be in proportion to their prices. Thus, if top hats are $10.00, neckties $1.00, and a pair of shoes $5.00, I will not buy a topper unless I consider that its utility for me would be equal at least to that of ten more neckties, or that of two more pairs of shoes. This relationship may be expressed by a simple equation, where *MU* represents marginal utility:

$$\frac{\text{Price of } A}{MU \text{ of } A} = \frac{\text{Price of } B}{MU \text{ of } B} = \frac{\text{Price of } C}{MU \text{ of } C} = \frac{\text{Price of } n}{MU \text{ of } n}$$

This equation will have as many terms as there are different goods whose purchase I am considering.

If this equation were followed exactly, then an increase in price of any one good would occasion a decrease in the purchase of that particular good and an increase in the purchase of other goods, until the proportions were again equal. Even if a person figured as exactly as this equation assumes, there are some reasons why exact proportions might not be capable of achievement. Certain durable consumers' goods are so high priced that an exact proportion of marginal utility to price for one good equal to the proportions for other goods may be difficult to achieve. This might apply to automobiles, refrigerators, electric stoves, and similar high-priced articles. Part of this difficulty may be overcome by installment plan buying, which, although it increases the actual price of the article (see chapter on "Interest"), may make the apparent burden of price less for those who do not stop to figure total cost accurately. Perhaps more important is the practice of driving a car a greater number of years to make the average cost of depreciation lower, or of purchasing a second-hand, rather than a new car in the first place.

A most important qualification is that such an equation be applicable only as long as the individual's tastes (relative marginal utilities) remain unchanged. Thus both prices and tastes must remain unchanged over a reasonable period of time for the individual to achieve that division of his expenditures which will yield him the maximum satisfaction from his purchases. In actual practice only a rough approximation is attained.

Value

After our inquiry into the nature of utility, we are now prepared to use the concept of utility as a tool to help explain the value and price of the goods we buy. *The value of any good is its power to command other goods in peaceful and voluntary exchange.* Thus, if I have a golf club which I am willing to trade for a dozen golf balls, and if you have a dozen golf balls that you would be willing to give me for the club, the value of the club may be said to be one dozen golf balls, or the value of the balls may be said to be one club. To measure accurately the value of any article, we should have to discover how much it would exchange for in terms of every kind of good in existence. To do this completely would be a fantastically difficult task. However, whenever exchange is carried on by barter, it is necessary to make at least a start on this problem in order to make the best possible trade. For example, I might have a horse which I wanted to trade for sheep. Someone offers me two sheep for the horse. But I find that I can trade the horse for a cow and that I can trade the cow for three sheep. Further effort might disclose a still better kind of trade. It may have been this kind of difficulty, among others, that induced people to give up barter systems and start using money as a medium of exchange and measure of values.

Value and Price

The price of anything is its value measured in terms of a standard monetary unit. In the United States the standard monetary unit is the dollar. Price gives us a great convenience in measuring values. At any particular instant of time we can say that the values of different goods are proportional to their prices. Thus, if a bushel of apples and a bushel of pears each sells for one dollar, we can say that they are equal in value. If a bushel of peaches sells for two dollars, we can say that its value is twice that of either apples or pears; and so on.

Yet this method of comparing the prices of various articles will give us their relative values only so long as all prices remain unchanged. If the price of one article alone should rise, while other prices remain the same, we could say that that article had increased in value in terms of other goods, or that all other goods had declined in value in terms of that article. When all prices, or a great number of them, are changing from one time to another, we cannot say whether an increase in the price of any one good represents an increase, a decline, or no change in its value unless we know what has happened to all other prices. To illustrate this simply, let us assume that there are only three commodities in existence: motor oil, butter, and eggs, and that the following table represents changes in their prices:

	1936 Prices	Assumed Prices After Inflation
Motor oil	25c qt.	$2.00 qt.
Butter	25c lb.	1.00 lb.
Eggs	25c dz.	.50 dz.

All three prices have gone up. The value of motor oil has risen. It will now exchange for twice as much butter and four times as many eggs as in 1936.

Butter has declined in its value in terms of motor oil, but has risen in value in terms of eggs. In terms of both together, it has not changed in value. One pound of butter will now buy half as much motor oil and twice as many eggs as before.

In spite of having risen in price, eggs have declined in value in terms of both butter and motor oil. One dozen eggs in the period after inflation will buy only half as much butter and only one quarter as much motor oil as it did in 1936.

We shall have more to say later about the general level of prices. However, this simple example should save us from confusing value and price. The changing price of an article, taken by itself, is not a good index of changing value in different times nor in different places. If wages (the price of labor) are higher in New York than in Chicago, we cannot say whether the value of labor is greater in New York unless we know the prices of all other commodities in both cities. In the discussion which follows in the next few chapters we shall assume, unless it is specifically stated otherwise, that the price of all goods other than the one we are examining remains unchanged. In this way we can properly consider changes in price of a particular article as being representative of changes in its value.

Use Value

Certain of the earlier economists were fond of attempting to distinguish between value in use and value in exchange. In doing this they drew so frequently upon the experiences of Robinson Crusoe that the term "Robinson Crusoe Economists" sprang up as a term of derision for them. The weakness of their arguments, such as it was, is to be found in the fact that marginal utility varies from one individual to another and also varies for the same individual in different circumstances. Thus, if Crusoe, instead of finding himself upon a desert island, had been set down in the middle of London in a rainstorm, a ride in a hansom cab would have had far more utility than the nails and ship's timbers which he valued so highly on the island.

Most of our economic activity is centered in highly developed economic systems where exchange is freely practiced. It is dangerous to consider the economic conduct of a group simply as a multiplication of the economic actions of an individual in isolation. The fact that the individual is in a group will alter both his economic motives and his freedom to exercise them.

CHAPTER IV

Demands for Goods

IF WE WISH to explain the price of any article, there are two questions which must be fully answered: First, why are people willing to pay the price which they do pay for it? Second, why do they have to pay what they do in order to obtain the article? When we have found the full answers to these two questions, we shall have explained *the law of supply and demand.*

Demand and Marginal Utility

If the total existing amount of a good is extremely small, the whole supply of it may be sold to those individuals who have both the greatest estimates of the marginal utility of the good and the greatest incomes; that is, to those people who would pay the highest prices rather than do without the good. If the amount in existence is greater, in order to dispose of it all either more units of it must be sold to the same people (in which case its marginal utility to them would be lower), or some of it must be sold to other people who have either lower incomes or lower estimates of the utility of a first unit of the good. In either event the price would have to be lower in order to induce the buyers to take the whole amount offered for sale. The question of what determines the amount which will be offered for sale will be reserved for the chapter on supply. At present we are concerned with the demand side of the market.

Demand Defined

The demand for a good is a schedule of the amounts that buyers would be willing to purchase at all possible prices at any one instant of time.[1] A thorough understanding of this definition will save the reader from many logical errors. Thus, by this definition, the only circumstances under which we can say that the demand for a good has increased are: (1) if people will buy more of the good at the same price, or (2) if they will pay a higher price for the same quantity. If people's tastes and incomes have not changed, the mere fact that they would buy more of the good at a lower price is not a change in demand. It is merely an increase in amount purchased in response to a lower price in the same demand schedule. If the conditions of demand remain the same, the only reason for a lower price would be an increase in the amount of which sellers were trying to dispose. To call the greater amount purchased at the lower price an increase in demand, under such conditions, would confuse the issue. What has really caused the lower price is an increase in the supply, which must be sold under the same demand conditions.

Demand Schedules and Demand Curves

The nature of demand will be more clearly understood if we attempt to construct a demand schedule for some product. Let us consider a list of the number of shirts I would be willing to buy at various prices. This schedule would depend upon both the marginal utility of shirts to me and the marginal utility of other ways in which I might spend the same sum of money. My schedule follows:

---

[1] Demand may also be considered as a *rate* of amounts that would be purchased during a given time period, such as a week, a month, or a year. The longer the period chosen, however, the greater the danger that the conditions of demand have changed, and that our observations represent not one demand curve but an average of the results of a perhaps unknown number of different demand curves.

Price of Shirts	Number that I Would Buy
$3.50	1
3.00	2
2.50	3
2.00	4
1.50	5
1.00	7

Now, if we could see into the minds of everyone, we might construct a demand schedule for shirts for the whole community. Some people with higher incomes or higher estimates of the marginal utility of shirts would be willing (if necessary) to pay much higher prices for one or two shirts rather than go without them. Others with lower incomes or with lower estimates of the marginal utility of shirts would not be willing to pay so much as I would. If the reader will attempt to draw up his own demand schedule of the amounts that he would buy at various prices, he will probably find them considerably different from mine. Now let us assume that we are mind readers so that we can find out the demand schedule for shirts of each person. By adding together the number of shirts that each person in a given city would buy at each price, we could construct a market demand schedule for shirts within that city. It might appear thus:

Price of Shirts	Number that Would Be Purchased
$10.00	200
9.00	300
8.00	400
7.00	600
6.00	800
5.00	1,200
4.00	1,600
3.00	2,400
2.00	4,800
1.00	5,600

We can plot these figures on a diagram to give us a demand curve (Diagram 1).

It should be noted that, except for one point on the demand

curve, all of the curve is imaginary. If the price does happen to be $2.00 and we notice that 4,800 shirts are actually sold, this will be one real point on the true demand curve for the product. How many more would be taken at a price of $1.00 or how many less would be bought at a price of $3.00 we have no way of knowing exactly, unless sellers should change their prices to those figures while conditions of demand remain the same. Certain economists have attempted to draw so-called statistical demand curves for certain products from amounts sold at prevailing prices in successive periods of time. In order to do this, they have to assume that conditions of demand have remained unchanged and that the only factor causing the changed price is the change in supply. Obviously this will seldom be the case, because from one time to another, while

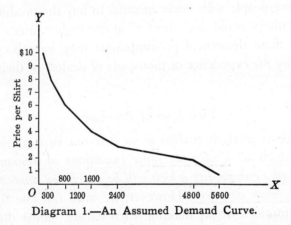

Diagram 1.—An Assumed Demand Curve.

the price of one product is changing, the prices of other goods may be changing, people's incomes may be changing, and even their tastes may be changing. Any of these factors would affect their demand for the product. However, even though they are inaccurate, these studies are probably closer approximations to the unknown points on the true demand curve than we could obtain by mere guessing.

Now, although we can know for a certainty only one point

on the demand curve, we can safely say that, *under the same conditions,* a smaller quantity of the article would be purchased at any price higher than that which now prevails in the market. This follows from the law of diminishing marginal utility and from the fact that people have different incomes. If the price is higher, the product can be sold only to those people whose estimates of its utility are high enough, or whose incomes are great enough, so that the utility of the last units which they buy will be great enough to offset their reluctance to spend money for this particular article rather than for other goods. A lower price than the one which prevails in the market would tend to offset the influence of diminishing marginal utility in the minds of the present buyers, and would thus act as an inducement for them to buy more. The lower price would also tend to influence those people with lower incomes to buy the product who felt that they "could not afford it" at the higher price. These are not mere theoretical presumptions; they have been confirmed by the experience of thousands of dealers in their price policies.

First Law of Purchase

The above analysis enables us to state our first law of purchase, which is: *Under the same conditions of demand, the amount of a commodity which will be purchased tends to vary inversely with its price.* However, we must not lose sight of the assumptions we are making when we say "under the same conditions of demand." We assume: (1) that people's incomes remain the same; (2) that their tastes remain the same; (3) that the prices of other goods remain the same; (4) that no new substitute for the product is discovered; (5) that people do not believe that this one change in price is a prelude to further changes; (6) that the product is not one which depends upon its high price for "prestige value" (for example, if diamonds were to sell for 10c a carat, the rich people might consider it "vulgar" to wear them and the poor, who ape the rich, might not buy them either). This last point, however, is perhaps already covered by our assumption of no change in tastes.

A change in any one of the six conditions mentioned above is a change in the conditions of demand and will give rise to a new demand curve. Our first law of purchase will then apply to the new curve for so long, and for so long only, as conditions of demand do not change again. It may help us to illustrate this principle by a diagram.

Let us assume the commodity to be butter. The solid curve *DD* represents the present demand. The point *P* is the only

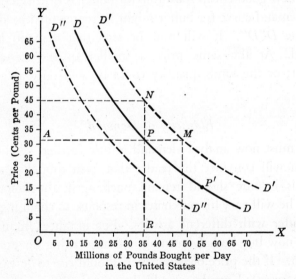

Diagram 2.—Changes in Demand.

point we actually know (we find that 35 million pounds are actually bought at 32c).

If the price should drop to 15c while all other conditions remain the same (and if our demand curve is accurate), 55 million pounds would be sold. The change, from point *P* to point *P'*, does not represent a change in demand, but a change in amount purchased in response to a lower price.

Now let us suppose that, with everything else unchanged, the price of bread should drop from 10c to 5c a loaf. Some people will buy more bread and want more butter to put on it. Those who do not buy more bread will have more money to buy butter for the bread that they do use. The new demand curve for butter might be represented by the dotted line $D'D'$. It will be noticed that at the same price a greater amount of butter will be purchased (the increase is from AP to AM); or for the same quantity a greater price would be paid (the increase is from RP to RN).

Now let us assume that, instead of the price of bread declining, a new good cheap substitute for butter is discovered. The new demand curve for butter might be represented by the dotted line $D''D''$. It will now be seen that demand has decreased. At the same price a smaller quantity would be bought; or the same quantity could be sold only at a lower price.

Elasticity of Demand [2]

We must now analyze demand a little further. A little reflection will convince the reader that even though his tastes and his income should remain unchanged, the amount by which he will vary his purchases in response to changing prices will differ with different articles. For instance, in my own case, I now buy both a morning and an evening newspaper at 3c each. If the price of newspapers should rise to 5c (a 66 per cent increase), I would very likely give up the evening paper rather than cut my consumption of cigarettes by one package a week. On the other hand, if the price of cigarettes should increase from 15c to 25c (also a 66 per cent increase), I would very likely give up the evening paper, an occasional trip to the movies, and whatever other petty economies were neces-

---

[2] To conform with our definition of demand, it might be better to call this *Elasticity of Purchase.*

sary in order to be able to smoke the same number of cigarettes. The economist would say that my demand for newspapers was more *elastic* than my demand for cigarettes, or that
my demand for cigarettes was very *inelastic* as compared to my
demand for newspapers.

The *elasticity of demand* is a measure of the relative change
in amount purchased in response to a relative change in price
on a given demand curve.[3]

Perfectly inelastic demand means that there would be no
change in amount purchased in response to any change in
price. This would be represented graphically by a vertical
straight-line demand curve. To express this in other words,
we can say that the elasticity of demand is equal to zero, indicating that there would be no change in number of units
purchased regardless of the change in price.

Perfectly elastic demand means that an infinite amount
would be purchased at the same price. This is represented
graphically by a horizontal straight-line demand curve. *Elasticity of demand equal to infinity* and *infinitely elastic demand*
are synonymous expressions for perfectly elastic demand.

For some purposes it is more convenient to think of elasticity
in terms of total amount spent for a product (that is, the price
per unit multiplied by the number of units purchased). In
these terms, if the total amount spent for a product remains the
same after a change in price, elasticity of demand is unity.
Unity of elastic demand is the dividing line between elastic
demand and inelastic demand.

If the total amount spent *increases* with a *decline* in price,
(or *decreases* with a *rise* in price), elasticity of demand is
greater than unity; the demand is elastic.

If the total amount spent *decreases* with a *decline* in price

---

[3] See Robinson, Joan, *Economics of Imperfect Competition*, Ch. 2, The Macmillan
Co., London, 1934, for a more thorough treatment of the geometry of elasticity.

(or *increases* with a *rise* in price), the elasticity of demand is less than unity; the demand is inelastic.

Diagrammatically, elasticity may be measured by changes in the area of a rectangle created by drawing perpendiculars from any point on a demand curve to the X and Y axes. The area of such a rectangle will represent total amount spent for the product.

In Figure 1 of Diagram 3 it can readily be seen that the elasticity of demand at the price point P is greater than unity. With a small decline in price, the area $RBOD$ is greater than the area $PAOC$. In other words, with a small decline in price the total amount spent on the product has increased.

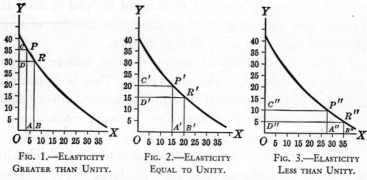

FIG. 1.—ELASTICITY GREATER THAN UNITY.   FIG. 2.—ELASTICITY EQUAL TO UNITY.   FIG. 3.—ELASTICITY LESS THAN UNITY.

Diagram 3.—Elasticity of Demand

In a similar manner it can be shown that the elasticity of demand at price *point P'* (Figure 2) is equal to unity for the same absolute decline in price. At price point P'' (Figure 3) the elasticity of demand is less than unity.

Note that all three price points, P, P', and P'', lie on identically shaped demand curves. The reader should recognize that it is not proper to speak of the elasticity of an entire demand curve unless the curve happens to be of uniform elasticity throughout its length. We may speak of the elasticity at price points on a curve, or of parts of the curve.

Ordinarily, however, when we speak of the elasticity of demand for a product, we are thinking of what change in the amount purchased would be occasioned by a small change from the existing market price. Thus we say briefly, if sometimes inaccurately, that the demand is elastic or that it is inelastic.

The elasticity of demand is a concept which is extremely important in helping us to explain prices; we shall make repeated use of it throughout the text.

Elasticity tends to be high when:

1. Substitutes are good and numerous.
2. Prices are relatively high.
3. There are many uses or users.

Elasticity tends to be low when:

1. The commodity is jointly demanded.
2. Quantities are relatively large and prices are low.
3. The good is almost a necessity—no good close substitutes are available.

CHAPTER V

Demand Explained by Indifference Curves[1]

Note: This chapter is intended as an alternative to the approach in the chapters on "Utility and Value" and "Demands for Goods." Both approaches may be used, but the author is of the impression that the material will be grasped more readily, particularly by the beginning student, if attention is confined to one or the other.

Defects of Utility Analysis

UNTIL quite recently, most economists have based their explanation of demand upon the concept of utility. Utility is defined as the quality or capacity of a good which enables it to satisfy a human want. Since utility is only an idea which is supposed to exist in the mind of an individual, it has so far proved to be incapable of measurement, and there is little chance that any scheme of measuring it will be devised in the future. This difficulty has led many people into logical pitfalls and has forced others who were more careful into awkward statements in order to avoid the pitfalls.[2]

Any one of us can say to himself, however: "I would just as soon have one more shirt as four more pairs of socks"; or, "I think I could enjoy one football game as much as I would enjoy five movies." This is equivalent to saying: "The utility of one more shirt for me is equal to the utility of four more pairs of socks"; or, "The utility for me of one football game is equal

---

[1] This entire chapter is based primarily on Hicks, J. R., *Value and Capital*, Oxford University Press, 1939; on Hicks, J. R., and Allen, R. G. D., "A Reconsideration of the Theory of Value," *Economica*, 1934; and on Allen, R. G. D., *Mathematical Analysis for Economists*, The Macmillan Co., London, 1938.

[2] See also Robinson, Joan, *Economics of Imperfect Competition*, Ch. III, pp. 211–215, The Macmillan Co., London, 1934.

to that of five movies." This is not at all the same thing, however, as saying, "The utility of a shirt is four times that of a pair of socks." The latter is an impossible statement. A little reflection will convince the reader that he cannot say to himself that he desires one article exactly two or three or four times as much as another.

A Scale of Preferences

Each of us, nevertheless, can have and probably does have a *scale of preferences* among different goods. We can convince ourselves of the existence of such a scale of preferences in several ways: by attempting to decide how much we would decrease our consumption of various goods if our income were decreased by a certain amount; by attempting to decide how much we would increase our purchases of various goods if our income were increased by a given amount; or by attempting to decide how we would react to a change in price of a particular good. Objectively, we may assure ourselves that others also have preferences among different goods by the fact that they actually do purchase some goods rather than others and do not stand forever undecided as to what to buy. (Often the most difficult decisions are those in which we are attempting to please another rather than ourselves—buying a gift for a friend, or choosing the meat for a husband's dinner.)

The careful reader may here object that we are using the concept of demand to explain demand. This is not the case. The fact that people do buy one or more units of one good in preference to the one or more units of some other good which they could purchase with the same amount of money is an observable and objective phenomenon which still remains to be explained. All the strain which is placed on the reader's imagination is simply to assume that a person making such a choice does make the choice which he happens to prefer at the moment, or, if you wish, that he makes the choice which he

thinks he prefers.[3]   At this point we can dismiss the concept
of utility.

An Indifference Schedule

As a first approximation to our problem, we may construct
an indifference schedule.   An *indifference schedule* may be
defined as *a schedule of various combinations of goods that will
be equally satisfactory to the individual concerned*.   To take
the simplest possible example, let us assume that there are only
two commodities in existence, apples and oranges.   Now
assume that I have 80 apples in my possession and no oranges.
Assume also that there is a man who has a barrel of oranges.
He tells me that I may take oranges from the barrel subject to
one condition.   I must replace the oranges I take with a number of apples that would yield me satisfaction equal to that
obtainable from the oranges I acquire, so that I will feel no
better and no worse off after any exchange I might make.   As
I start out in this imaginary experiment, I might leave 20 apples
for the first orange, 12 apples for a second orange, 8 for a third,
10 for the next two, and so on.   The result of a number of such
exchanges might indicate the following combinations of apples
and oranges as being equally satisfactory to me:

60 apples and	1 orange		12 apples and	17 oranges
48 apples and	2 oranges		10 apples and	21 oranges
40 apples and	3 oranges		8 apples and	27 oranges
30 apples and	5 oranges		6 apples and	37 oranges
24 apples and	7 oranges		5 apples and	45 oranges
20 apples and	9 oranges		4 apples and	57 oranges
16 apples and	12 oranges		3 apples and	77 oranges
15 apples and	13 oranges		2 apples and	117 oranges

1 apple and 237 oranges

This schedule refers to consumption over any given period of time
and not merely to stocks of the good.

---

[3] The problem of free will or predetermination may be left to the theologian
and the philosopher.

We can plot these points on a graph representing the number of apples on the vertical, or Y, axis and oranges on the horizontal, or X, axis. Connecting these points with a line, we obtain the curve shown in Diagram 1.

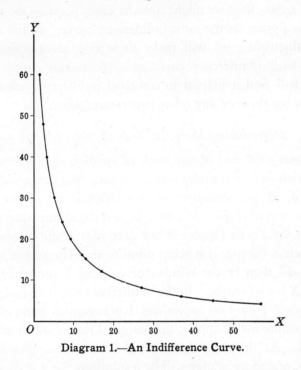

Diagram 1.—An Indifference Curve.

This curve is an indifference curve. Every point on it represents a combination of the two commodities that would be equally satisfactory to me. Note, however, that on this particular curve the only points having any significance are the points that we have actually plotted. The line between the points serves merely as "a convenient device to lead the eye from one point to the next."[4] In this case, to keep the illus-

4 Crum, W. L., "Rudimentary Mathematics for Economists and Statisticians," Supplement, Quarterly Journal of Economics, May, 1938.

tration simple, we have chosen only points which yield whole number values for X and Y. If it were convenient to divide apples and oranges into any desired fractions, and *if the intervening spaces followed the same mathematical law as the plotted points,* then we might consider every point on the whole curve as a point on the same indifference curve. In the subsequent discussion, we will make these two assumptions and regard each indifference curve as a continuous curve. The reader will find it helpful to construct indifference curves of his own for these or any other two commodities.

Diminishing Marginal Rate of Substitution

The *marginal unit* of any stock of goods is that unit whose acquisition or loss is under consideration. We can avoid confusion if, in the remainder of this chapter, we adhere to a common terminology. We shall regard the commodity measured on the Y axis (apples in our example) as the commodity for which X (oranges) is being substituted. The rate of substitution will then be the number of units of Y for which one unit of X is a substitute. In the indifference schedule two pages back, when I have 60 apples and 1 orange, one more orange is a substitute for 12 apples; the marginal rate of substitution is 12 to 1. At the next stage, when I have 48 apples and 2 oranges, one more orange will be a substitute for 8 apples, and the marginal rate of substitution is 8 to 1.

If, without changing our schedule or diagram, we wish to reverse this procedure and consider acquiring apples in exchange for oranges, we start at the bottom of the schedule and read up. Thus, when I have 1 apple and 237 oranges, one more apple would compensate me for the loss of 120 oranges; the marginal rate of substitution is 120 to 1. When I have 2 apples and 117 oranges, one more apple would compensate me for the loss of 40 oranges; the marginal rate of substitution is 40 to 1.

At the next stage the marginal rate of substitution is 20 to 1, and so on.[5]

One of the most important assumptions that has to be made in connection with the indifference curve analysis is that the marginal rate of substitution is always decreasing. In graphic terms this means that the slope of the indifference curve must always be decreasing as we move along it from left to right. A fairly general objective proof that this assumption is fulfilled in practice may be found in the observation of the conduct of the buyers on any market. If the marginal rate of substitution did not decrease, then, once a person started buying one commodity, he would continue to buy that commodity and no others until his entire purchasing power was exhausted. It is true that this is a rather negative sort of proof and is not sufficient grounds for claiming that the principle of diminishing marginal rate of substitution is universally true as applied to the purchase of all commodities by all people. Nevertheless, we are all familiar with the fact that under the stimulus of changing incomes or changing relative prices of goods, people are able to leave one position of equilibrium in their purchases of different goods and arrive at another position of equilibrium.

---

[5] In some respects it is much easier to treat this problem in terms of an *increasing* marginal rate of substitution, that is, in terms of an increasing amount of X necessary to compensate for the loss of one unit of Y. This was the treatment originally used by Hicks and Allen in the articles in *Economica*. It appeared, however, that this treatment was confusing to Marshallians, and accordingly Hicks uses the concept of a diminishing marginal rate of substitution in *Value and Capital*. It should be noted, nevertheless, that diminishing marginal rate of substitution and diminishing marginal utility are not the same thing. In Marshallian terms the indifference curve indicates constant total utility of the two commodities combined. Consequently, in Marshallian terms, the increase in marginal utility of the product which is decreasing in amount must compensate for any decrease in marginal utility of the stock which is increased sufficiently to keep total utility of the combined commodities at a constant level. All that we say, however, is that the number of units of the commodity acquired must be a satisfactory substitute for the number of units of the commodity given up. This proposition can be stated in terms of utility, but it is not necessary to do so.

All that our assumption requires is that the transition between these two points of equilibrium follows a fairly regular course. It is idle to deny that there will not be at least some small segments of the indifference curves of some people for some products which fail to follow the principle of diminishing marginal rate of substitution,[6] but when we begin to translate indifference curves into demand curves, and into demand curves for a whole community, the probable error from this source becomes extremely small.

The Limiting Case of Substitution

An indifference curve in the form of a straight diagonal line at a 45-degree angle would indicate a constant marginal rate of substitution of 1 to 1. This is a limiting case and is possible only when one good is a *perfect* substitute for the other. Such might be the case if you were indifferent to the blandishments of the advertisers and bought cornflakes as cornflakes; one brand would be a perfect substitute for another brand, and you would, of course, buy whichever was the cheaper.

I am indebted to Professor R. G. D. Allen for pointing out that this is not only a limiting case; it is also an impossible case. If one product is considered a *perfect* substitute for another product in the mind of a buyer, then the two are not different products but simply different lots of an identical commodity. The fact that the products are not differentiated in your mind merely means that you feel that you are buying the same product from whoever sells it the cheapest. This attempted product differentiation may, however, be effective with some other buyers, but in this case the marginal rate of substitution would not be 1 to 1.

---

[6] The best adverse examples would be the indifference curves of whiskey for drunkards, drugs for narcotic addicts, and, less seriously, that of stamps for the stamp collector. All of these people, however, generally eat at least occasionally, thus proving that their indifference curves for their favorite vice do not have an increasing marginal rate of substitution throughout their length.

Product Differentiation and the Rate of Substitution

On the other hand, even a slight degree of product differentiation might result in a constant marginal rate of substitution at some ratio other than 1 to 1. There may be, for example, some individuals who consume tea in very small quantities but who place a high premium on its freshness. Such individuals might always consider 3 one-quarter-pound packages as a satisfactory substitute for 1 one-pound package of tea. The marginal rate of substitution is ¾ to 1. In terms of money, these people would just as soon pay 75c for 3 one-quarter pound packages as 75c for one whole-pound package.

Complementarity

As the opposite limiting case to perfect substitution, we have the case of complete complementarity. Complete or *perfect complementarity* exists where one unit of one good requires a standard number of units of another good for the combination to be of any use whatever. Thus for most people one watch case requires one watch movement to go inside the case. Most people would not care for one more watch case without one more movement, and vice versa. In situations of this sort (other examples might be right and left shoes or right and left gloves), the indifference curves would be straight lines downward and turning at a right angle, the lines away from the turning point being parallel to each axis. In most cases where complementarity is as complete as this, dealers do not usually sell the article separately from its complement. In some other cases, as with cups and saucers, they may be sold separately or jointly, depending upon the practice of the individual store. Where they are sold separately, the housewife will buy saucers to replace broken ones, but will not buy more cups if her set of them is complete. Even if the price of saucers is lowered, she will seldom be interested in buying more saucers than the number necessary to complete the ratio of one cup to one saucer. (She cannot forecast which will break first.)

Substitutability and Complementarity—The Dividing Line

We have seen that perfect substitutability is represented by a straight diagonal indifference curve at a 45° angle, and that perfect complementarity is represented by an indifference curve parallel to each axis and bent at a 90° angle. We can generalize within these limits by saying that the flatter the indifference curve, the greater the degree of substitutability; and the more bent the indifference curve, the greater the degree of complementarity between the two goods. We cannot, however, draw an exact dividing line between the two conditions by geometry. Nor can we confine our attention to two commodities only. We must introduce a third, which we may call money or general purchasing power (with the assumption that the prices of all other goods except X and Y remain unchanged). Under these assumptions, if an increase of one unit of X requires that some substitution of money for Y take place in order to leave the individual no better off than he was before, then X and Y are substitutes for each other. (If X is a substitute for Y, then Y is also a substitute for X.) On the other hand, if the rate of substitution of Y for money is *increased* when one more unit of X is acquired, then X and Y are complementary.

A simpler example may make the proposition clearer. If I buy some new tires in order to drive more safely over slippery winter roads, then I am sure to drive the car more often in winter weather, and accordingly will buy more gasoline than I would buy if I had not bought the tires with new treads. (Tires and gasoline are complementary goods.)

On the other hand, if the strain of winter driving does not appeal to me, I will ride on the bus instead of driving my car in the bad spells. This means that I will spend more money on bus rides and less on tires. (Bus rides and tires are substitutes for each other.)

The Indifference Map

Diagram 1 was just one indifference curve based on the assumption that I started with 60 apples in my possession. Had I started with 50 or 70, or any other number, we would have other indifference curves based on the various combinations of apples and oranges that would be equally satisfactory to me. Each combination which is based on a greater number will lie on a higher indifference curve. Each point on a higher indifference curve indicates greater satisfaction than that on a lower indifference curve. Diagram 2 shows a family of such

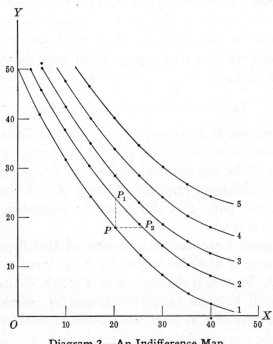

Diagram 2.—An Indifference Map.

curves, or, as we may call it, an *indifference map*. It will be noticed that the curves are numbered 1, 2, 3, and so on. This system of numbering has no particular significance. We might just as well have labeled the curves *A, B, C,* and so on.

At any point on an indifference curve, a movement either upward or to the right brings us on to a higher indifference curve. In Diagram 2, for example, a movement from P brings us to P_1 or P_2. The assumption behind this is that a greater quantity of either good accompanied by an unchanged quantity of the other good yields us a greater satisfaction. Note carefully that we do *not* say *how much* greater this satisfaction may be. Note also that the curves are not parallel. There is no need for them to be. Our only requirement is that one indifference curve must not touch another within the limits of our diagram. In any actual case the indifference curves would be much closer together than we have drawn them here, and there would be more of them. Our indifference curves are like the contour lines on a topographical map, showing only important changes.

Indifference, Income, and Purchase

We now come to a very useful property of indifference maps. If we know an individual's income, his indifference map, and the prices of the two commodities, we can determine directly from the indifference map the quantities of each commodity which he will buy. (We still retain the assumption of only two commodities.)

In Diagram 3, we assume an income of $140.00 per week. Given a price of $5.00 for commodity X, we measure the distance OQ, 28 units, as the amount of X which the individual could buy if he spent his entire income for commodity X. Given the price of Y as $4.00, we measure the distance OR, 35 units, as the amount of Y which the individual could buy if he spent his entire income for commodity Y.

The line RQ shows all possible combinations of the two commodities which the individual could purchase by dividing his

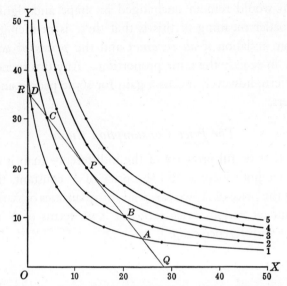

Diagram 3.—An Indifference Map Related to a Given Income
and a Price Ratio.

expenditures on the two goods in all the different ways that will
exhaust his total income.   Which combination will he choose?
The line RQ cuts a number of indifference curves at points
$A, B, C,$ and D.   None of these points, however, represents the
most preferred position, since, by moving along RQ in one
direction or another, we come on to a higher indifference curve.
At point P the line just touches (is tangent to) an indifference
curve.   This is the highest indifference curve which can be
reached by moving along the line RQ.   In other words, this is
the most satisfactory division of expenditure between the two
goods which can be achieved with the given income and the
given prices of the two goods and the given indifference map.

It may be instructive to note on Diagram 3 that if we doubled
the prices of the two goods and also doubled the assumed income, there would be no change in the diagram.   An income
of $280.00 and a price of $10.00 for X would again make OQ

equal to 28 units. An income of $280.00 and a price of $8.00 for Y would also make *OR* equal to 35 units, and the entire diagram would remain unchanged in shape and significance. The broader meaning of this is that there is neither gain nor loss from inflation if *all incomes* and the *prices of all goods* increase in *exactly* the same proportion. Any divergence from this pattern, however, means a gain for some people and a loss for others.

The Price Consumption Curve

A further useful property of the indifference map is the fact that, if we hold income and the price of Y constant, then, by varying the price of X, we can read the quantities of X that will be bought at various price ratios of X in terms of Y directly from the indifference map.

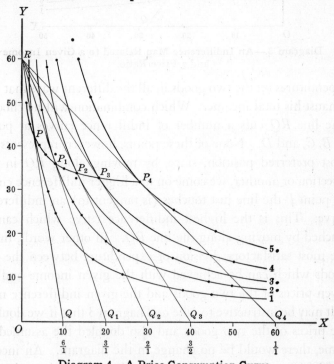

Diagram 4.—A Price Consumption Curve.

In Diagram 4 we assume a constant income of $60.00 per week and a constant price of Y of $1.00 per unit. Then, at a price of $6.00 per unit of X, the slope of the line RQ is 60 to 10; that is, $6.00 will buy 6 units of Y or 1 unit of X. At P, the point of tangency of the price ratio line with the indifference curve, we find that 3 units of X and 42 units of Y will be purchased. The following table summarizes the readings from the diagram:

Point	Price of X	Quantity of X Purchased (Units)	Price of Y	Quantity of Y Purchased (Units)	Total Spent for X	Total Spent for Y
P	$6.00	3	$1.00	42	$18.00	$42.00
P_1	3.00	8	1.00	36	24.00	36.00
P_2	2.00	13	1.00	34	26.00	34.00
P_3	1.50	18	1.00	33	27.00	33.00
P_4	1.00	28	1.00	32	28.00	32.00

Following the principles we developed in Diagram 3, we notice that each of the price-ratio lines is tangent to an indifference curve. These tangents occur at the points P, P_1, P_2, P_3, and P_4. The line which connects these points may be called a *price consumption curve*. The horizontal distances of the points from the OY axis indicate the amounts of X that would be purchased at various prices for X with the income, the price of Y, and the indifference map assumed constant.

The Individual Demand Curve

So far our indifference curves have generally had reference to only two commodities. This has been done for the sake of simplicity, but it is not necessary to confine ourselves in this way. If the *prices of all goods other than X are assumed to remain unchanged,* then, instead of calling Y a single commodity, we may call it general purchasing power. The indifference curves then represent the rates of substitution of X for all other goods in general (including, as one of the goods, the "cash balance" of the individual which may allow him to buy other goods at a later date rather than at present).

When Y is used to represent general purchasing power (with the prices of all goods other than X remaining unchanged), the price consumption curve is really a demand curve for X. We shall find it more convenient, however, to translate this curve into the demand curve more commonly used by economists.

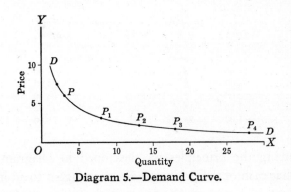

Diagram 5.—Demand Curve.

Diagram 5 shows the demand curve which is represented by the price consumption curve in Diagram 4. In Diagram 5 the vertical or OY axis represents the price of a commodity, and the horizontal or OX axis represents the quantity purchased. It may be noted that we have doubled both scales in order to enlarge the diagram and render it more readable. Columns 1, 2, and 3 of the table give the demand schedule or data which are represented by the curve DD. Diagram 5 is simply a location of these points on a price and quantity diagram. Several plotted points appear on the curve DD in Diagram 5 which are not located by curves and tangents in the price consumption curve of Diagram 4. These points, however, were actually computed and were omitted from Diagram 4 simply to avoid confusing the eye of the reader by too many curves and tangents drawn closely together.

Community Demand

If we could summarize the price consumption curves or the demand curves of an entire community, we would have a collective demand curve for the number of individuals involved. If all the people whose demand was summarized had exactly the same kind of indifference maps as is shown in Diagram 4, then the demand curve, or price consumption curve, would have exactly the same general shape as the demand curve shown in Diagram 5. If we chose to alter the horizontal scale to take account of the number of people who would purchase the article at each price (for example, to change the horizontal scale to 10,000, 20,000, 30,000, instead of 10, 20, 30, if there happened to be 1,000 people of similar tastes, having identical indifference maps) then the curve would be a community curve rather than an individual curve.

It is extremely unlikely, however, that the above situation would occur. Even if people's indifference maps were all identical, those with higher incomes would find that the point of tangency of the indifference curve and the price ratio line lies on a higher indifference curve than is the case for those with lower incomes. That is, those with higher incomes would buy more of commodity X at the same price than those with lower incomes and the same indifference maps. Furthermore, there is more evidence to cause us to believe that there is generally some difference, and often considerable difference, in the indifference maps of different people, regardless of differences in incomes. These differences may be the results of habits acquired in previous environment, or simply the result of keener tastes for one or more of the goods which are lumped in the category of "all other goods," whose prices are assumed to remain unchanged. The extent of the desire for social conformity (keeping up with the Joneses) may result either in close duplication of the indifference maps of the members or a marked grouping or stratification of these maps. Wherever the community consists largely of a single social group, and where the commodity is an article of "conspicuous consumption," the indifference maps tend toward uniformity. Where social classes are sharply stratified, we may expect considerable uniformity within each group, but there may be a wide divergence among the typical indifference maps of the different groups.

Demand and Time Periods

On page 42 appears a list of what we called the "conditions of demand." These were: (1) that incomes of individuals remain the same; (2) that their tastes remain the same; (3) that the prices of other goods remain the same; (4) that no new substitute is discovered for the product; (5) that individuals do not believe that one change in price is a prelude to further changes; (6) that the product is not one which depends upon its high price for "prestige value." Assumptions number (1) and (3) were also made in this chapter when we drew our price consumption curve. The other assumptions are covered when we assume that the indifference maps remain unchanged.

These assumptions, if adhered to rigidly, would in any practical case be almost certain to confine the application of the demand curve to a single instant of time. Your indifference map may undergo considerable change between the time you enter a movie and the time you leave it. What the actors have had to eat or wear in the picture may make a considerable difference in your scale of preferences. It is, however, often convenient to speak of a rate of demand for a given time period. The demand curve at any given moment may be called *instantaneous demand* or *immediate market demand*. We may also speak of the demand per day (a schedule or curve representing the amounts which people will purchase at all possible prices in a day), the demand per week, per month, or per year. The longer the period chosen, however, the greater the likelihood that the conditions which are assumed to remain constant will actually change during the demand period. For example, a demand curve for raincoats for a year might be drawn on the assumption (in addition to those given above) that the rainfall for the year would be average or "normal." Even if the normal amount of rainfall should occur, if it just so happened that all the storms came between the hours of 4:30 and 6:00 P.M., it might be found that a great many more raincoats are sold during the year than were indicated by the number at any given price on the assumed or computed demand curve. Clothing dealers are continually praying for what they call "seasonable" weather (that is, a cold winter and a hot summer, a spell of mild weather early in the spring, and a chill but not too cold autumn). This is because experience has taught them that they can sell more merchandise during a normal year at any given prices than when the winter is mild, so that people decide to make the old coat "do" for another year.

Regardless of the length of the demand period, we must bear one very important qualification in mind: *the points on a demand curve are alternative* and *not* successive. Your demand curve (or schedule) might indicate that you would buy 2 pairs of shoes at $9.00 a pair, or 3 pairs at $6.00, or 4 pairs at $5.00 during a given year. Assume now that the price at the beginning of the year should happen to be $9.00, and that you buy the 2 pairs. If, immediately after you made your purchase of 2 pairs at $9.00, the price should drop to $5.00, and the points on your demand curve are as indicated, you would not buy even one more pair. However, if the price had been $5.00 to begin with, you would have bought 4 pairs instead of the 2 pairs at $9.00 which you did buy. Apparently your "allowance" for shoes is about $20.00. You may regret that you did not wait for the "bargain," but, having 2 pairs already purchased at a total cost of $18.00, if your conditions of demand remain the same, you will probably not purchase another pair at any price greater than $2.00.

The qualification we have introduced in the above paragraph is another illustration of the difficulties involved in attempting to apply the demand curve to a period of time rather than an instant of time. Not only must the other conditions we have listed remain unchanged for the length of the demand period, but the price also must remain unchanged. Otherwise the original demand curve is not applicable, and we have a new demand curve which is influenced in some degree by the prices previously prevailing and the amounts purchased at those prices. This shows us a source of error always encountered (and not often recognized) by those who attempt to draw up statistical demand curves for agricultural products. These statisticians use the average prices and the amounts consumed each year, for a number of years, as points of observation for their estimated demand curve. They do, of course, attempt to correct for changes in income and such other factors as they believe to be influencing demand and are capable of measurement. Many of them do not, however, allow for the *variability* of prices *within* each year. This may be a considerable source of error even if proper allowance is made for all other conditions. For example: assume that there is one year in which the weighted average price of potatoes is 50c per bushel, resulting from a series of prices throughout the year which ranged from 45c to 55c. In another year of identical conditions, except for price, a weighted average price of 50c per bushel, resulting from prices which ranged between 25c and 75c, might result in either a greater or less total consumption of potatoes, depending upon the number of price changes, their duration, and the public reaction to them.

The Shape of Demand Curves

In most economics texts, demand curves will be found to be represented either as straight lines or as smooth curves which have no "kinks" (sudden changes in slope at particular points) in them. These curves are generally drawn smooth either to suit the convenience of the economist who is drawing them or to make the task of explanation to the reader somewhat easier. (Most of the demand curves in this book are so drawn.) If we should ever happen to have the good fortune to construct a demand curve which was absolutely accurate for a certain product, however, we should not be at all surprised to find some small kinks in the demand curves for a great many products, and some really sharp kinks in the demand curves for a few products.[7]

We can, nevertheless, lay down one fairly general principle about demand curves: With certain rare exceptions,[8] the demand curve will always be falling as we move from left to right along the curve. This is another way of saying that, in general, under the same conditions of demand, more units of a good will be bought at a lower price than at a higher price, or that a lower price is necessary to induce people to buy more units of a good.

There is still much to be said, however, for the contention that collective demand curves tend to smooth out many or most

---

[7] Certain preliminary studies that I have made of the demand for pork among Southern families with incomes of less than $500.00 per year indicate that at prices above 12c per pound, the demand curve has a very gentle slope, while at prices below this, the demand curve bends downward at almost a right angle, indicating that at some price around 11c they buy about all that they want, and that further declines in price are not much inducement to increase their purchases.

[8] The most likely exception is the case of an article which constitutes the major part of a family's expenditure and is considered an "inferior" good by them. For example, if a family were subsisting almost entirely on bread or potatoes, a fall in price might cause them to buy less bread or potatoes and spend the remainder of their income on goods which they could not afford before. *Cf.* Marshall, *Principles,* 8th Ed., p. 132.

of the "kinks" which are found in individual demand curves. The net incomes of individuals and families are not nicely stratified into the frequency tables so neatly drawn by statisticians and tax experts.[9] Within each arbitrarily chosen group, the individual or family incomes may change along the scale by very small amounts, perhaps by as little as $10.00, $5.00, or even $1.00. Thus, even if each individual demand curve had a kink in it, the fact that each indifference map may be based on a different income and that consequently the kink will be at a different price point means that a curve of collective demand made up of individual curves may result in the smoothing of the kinks so that the collective curve appears as a smooth curve or straight line.

The most important warning that we can take from the fact that there may be kinks is not to project an estimated demand curve beyond the points where we have at least some historical observations to guide us. A demand curve is most likely to be smooth in the middle portion, and more apt to have kinks at the extreme ends, particularly the lower end.

Elasticity of Demand

The elasticity of demand is a measure of the relative change in amount purchased in response to a relative change in price on a given demand curve. The reader will do well from the start to avoid making any connection between the shape or slope of the demand curve and the elasticity of demand, because elasticity depends *both* on the *slope* of the demand curve at any given price *and* on the *position* of the price and quantity point with respect to both the X and Y axes. Since elasticity is one of the most important concepts in economics, the reader should attempt to grasp it as thoroughly as possible.

There are three different mathematical properties of elasticity,

---

[9] For examples, see *Consumer Income in the United States* and *Consumer Expenditures in the United States*, published by the National Resources Committee.

any one of which may be used as the definition, and the others may be derived from it.[10]

Property No. 1. Let P represent price and Q quantity. Then PQ will represent total amount spent for the product. If PQ remains unchanged after a change in price, then elasticity of demand is equal to unity. Unity of elastic demand is the dividing line between elastic demand and inelastic demand. If the total amount spent *increases* with a *decline* in price, elasticity of demand is greater than unity; the demand is elastic (PQ increases in value). If the total amount spent *decreases* with a *decline* in price, elasticity of demand is less than unity; the demand is inelastic. (PQ decreases in value.) A diagrammatic representation is given on page 46 in Diagram 3.

This previous property gives us a criterion for determining whether elasticity is greater than unity, equal to unity, or less than unity (even this is a useful thing to know). It does not, however, give us a method of determining a numerical value for elasticity, except for the case where elasticity is unity. In this explanation the changes in total amount spent depend upon two things: the original price minus the per cent change in price, multiplied by the original quantity plus the per cent change in quantity. If we call the small letters p and q, the change in price and the change in quantity, respectively, the equation for unity of elasticity becomes:

$$(P - pP) \ (Q + qQ) \quad \text{or} \quad P(1 - p)(Q)(1 + q) = PQ$$

The equation solved for P yields $P = \dfrac{q}{1-q}$. This is the necessary relationship of the two percentages if PQ is to remain constant.

Property No. 2. This property is a geometrical concept. The definition is: Elasticity is the proportional change of the abscissa, divided by the proportional change of the ordinate, at any point on the curve, when the changes are small. To

---

[10] For the full derivation of these relationships, see Allen, R. G. D., *Mathematical Analysis for Economists*, pp. 255 ff.

illustrate this, assume a straight-line demand curve plotted on ordinary numerical scale graph paper (AB in Figure 1, Diagram 6).

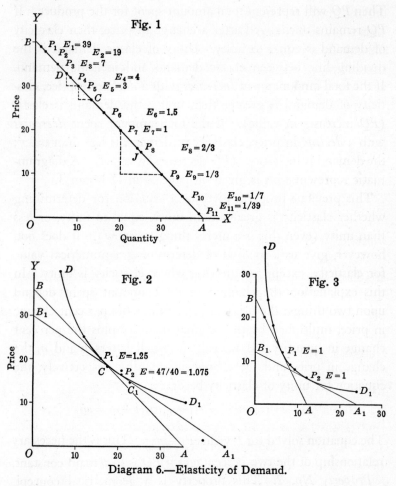

Diagram 6.—Elasticity of Demand.

Elasticity is then equal to the distance from A to any point P along the demand curve, divided by the distance from B to the same point. For example:

$$\frac{AP_5}{BP_5} = 3 \text{ and } \frac{AP_7}{BP_7} = 1,$$

and so on. The elasticity will be found to be high at the extreme left end of the demand curve. It drops to *unity* at the *midpoint* of the line; is less than unity and continually declining at all price and quantity points to the right of the midpoint. This condition is universally true for all *straight-line* demand curves * drawn on an ordinary numerical scale. On the diagram elasticity has been accurately computed for each of the points labeled P on the line. For example, at P_1, E_1 equals 39.

It may also be noted that, from any given price point, elasticity is the same in both directions. For example, at point P_5 the price is 30c and the quantity purchased is 10 units. A drop in price of 3c, or 10 per cent, brings us to point C, at which the quantity purchased has increased from 10 units to 13 units, a 30 per cent increase. $\dfrac{30\%}{10\%} = 3$, which agrees with $E_5 = 3$, as computed by the diagonal ratio division. A rise of 10 per cent in price from point P_5, on the other hand, brings us to point D, at which the amount purchased, 7 units, is 30 per cent less than the 10 units purchased at price point P.

Notice, however, that while elasticity is the same in both directions from a price and quantity point, it is *not reversible* from one price point to another. Thus, at point P_7, elasticity being unity, a 50 per cent decline in price brings us a 50 per cent increase in amount purchased, and we arrive at point P_9. If we had started out from point P_9 to increase the price by 50 per cent (from 10c to 15c), this would bring us back only to point J, at which the amount purchased has decreased by only 16.66 per cent (from 30 units to 25 units), or one third of 50 per cent, elasticity at point P_9 being $\frac{1}{3}$.

The most important lesson that we can learn from Figure 1 is to avoid considering the slope of a demand curve on a natural scale as an indication of elasticity. The slope of the line AB is constant at 1 to 1 throughout its length, but elasticity changes at every point on the line.

---

* Except for demand curve for individual seller under pure competition. See p. 110.

The reader can perform a very instructive exercise for himself by choosing other slopes and computing elasticity by $\frac{AP}{BP}$. It is suggested that a good ruler be used and the slope be chosen arbitrarily so that an inch mark hits on each axis. It will then be found, if units of one sixteenth of an inch are used, that whole number values of $\frac{AP}{BP}$ can be computed at certain points on the diagonal line.

The principles which we have developed about a straight-line demand curve on a natural scale may also be applied, with some limitations, to demand curves which actually do curve on the same scale. In Figure 2 of Diagram 6, the demand curve is indicated by the line DD_1. If we wish to determine the elasticity of any point, say P_1, we draw the tangent to the curve through that point. Our formula then applies: Elasticity is equal to $\frac{AP_1}{BP_1}$. With a curve, however, elasticity is *not* applicable for any considerable distance either way from a price point as it is on a straight line. The elasticity at price P_1 is applicable *only as long as the curve and the tangent actually coincide.* Since, by definition, a tangent "touches" a curve at only one point, and any change in price causes us to move along the curve rather than the tangent, it follows that the relationship E equals 1.25 (that is, a 1 per cent decline in price will result in a 1.25 per cent increase in amount purchased) is applicable only for infinitesimally small changes in price. As soon as we move any distance along the curve, we must draw a new tangent and determine a new elasticity. Figure 3 shows the same type of computation for a curve which is of uniform elasticity equal to unity. On numerical scale paper, such a curve must be a rectangular hyperbola.

This whole explanation shows the difficulties encountered by our apparent unwillingness to use logarithmic scales. On double log paper any curve of constant elasticity will appear as a straight line, and the slope of the line will be equal to the elasticity at all points. For demand curves which are curvilinear when plotted on logarithmic scales, the slope of the tangent to any curve at any point will be the elasticity at that point.

Property No. 3. This property may be derived directly from the definition given for Property No. 2. Let us call dq a small change in Q. Then "the proportional change of the abscissa" is $\frac{dq}{Q}$. Then call dp a small change in P, which makes $\frac{dp}{P}$ the proportional change in the ordinate. Thus our formula for elasticity becomes:

$$E = \frac{dq}{Q} \div \frac{dp}{P}.$$

Performing the division, we have,

$$E = -\frac{P}{Q}\frac{dq}{dp}.$$

The minus sign is introduced arbitrarily into the equation in order to give a positive result (dp must be negative if price is falling), because it is more convenient in economics to think of the elasticity of a falling curve as a positive number. Elasticity, then, regardless of the price and quantity units chosen, depends upon both the position of the price and quantity point $\left(\frac{P}{Q}\right)$ and the rate of change $\left(-\frac{dq}{dp}\right)$. The formula given may be written:

$$E = -\frac{d\,(\log q)}{d\,(\log p)}.$$

This constitutes a generalized proof for the statements made previously about plotting the demand curve on double log paper and reading elasticities directly from the slopes of the tangents.

It must still be remembered that our concepts of elasticity

will apply only to the extent to which our estimate of the demand curve is correct. However, if we use proper methods, there will be no mistake in the *computation* of elasticity, and the only source of error will be in our estimates of the shape and position of the demand curve itself. Businessmen and tax experts must have at least a rough concept of elasticity (whether or not they use the word elasticity) when they attempt to decide whether a higher or lower price or tax rate would yield more revenue.

CHAPTER VI

Demand as Seen by the Seller[1]

IN PREVIOUS chapters we have considered demand for a product in general. In the present chapter we shall devote our attention to the demand for his product which faces the individual seller. In order to do this, we shall have to distinguish between demand under pure competition and demand under monopolistic competition (product differentiation).

Conditions of Pure Competition

Two conditions are requisite for pure competition to exist: (1) *Buyers must be completely indifferent as to which seller they purchase from, as long as different sellers' prices are the same.* Or, to state the proposition in other words, *a lower price is the only element which will lead buyers to prefer one dealer to another under pure competition.* (2) *The amount which each individual seller can offer for sale must constitute so small a proportion of the total supply that he, acting alone, is powerless to affect the price by varying the amount which he offers.* For instance, millions of bushels of wheat are produced and sold every year, and the individual farmer, even though he ordinarily produced as much as 10,000 bushels a year, could not raise the price of wheat by one sixteenth of a

---

[1] This entire chapter is an adaptation of Professor Edward Chamberlin's *The Theory of Monopolistic Competition*, Harvard University Press, 1935. See particularly Chs. IV and V. The terms "pure competition," "monopolistic competition," and "product differentiation" are his.

cent a bushel by cutting his production in half or even by
ceasing production entirely. Nor could he lower the price
one sixteenth of a cent if he alone doubled or tripled his production. (On the other hand, if *all* farmers acting together
should increase or decrease their production by as little as five
per cent, the price of wheat would be materially affected.)

It follows from these two propositions that *under pure competition, the demand for the product of the individual seller*

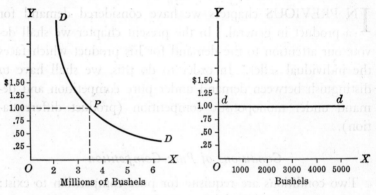

FIG. 1.—MARKET DEMAND FOR WHEAT   FIG. 2.—DEMAND FOR PRODUCT FACING
    UNDER PURE COMPETITION.   INDIVIDUAL SELLER UNDER PURE
                                                    COMPETITION.

Diagram 1.—Demand Under Pure Competition.

will be perfectly elastic at the prevailing market price. (Graphically, the demand curve for his product will be a horizontal
straight line). Under pure competition, if the individual seller
raised his price by the slightest amount over that prevailing in
the market, he would do no business at all. On the other
hand, there is no inducement for him to lower his price below
that of the market, since he can dispose of his entire holdings
at the market price. We may illustrate this by a diagram.

In Diagram 1, *DD* (Figure 1) represents the market demand
for wheat, and *P* is the point on the curve where price happens
to be established at the moment. In Figure 2, *dd* is the de-

mand curve which confronts the individual producer at the price in the market. It is really what we would find if we put a magnifying glass over point *P*. The scale in Figure 1 is drawn in millions of bushels. A change in amount of a few hundred or even a few thousand bushels will not be sufficient to cause a movement along the demand curve *DD* away from point *P*. In other words, although any one individual seller is able to vary his production, he is powerless to affect the price to himself. Acting alone, he need not be hindered from increasing his production for fear of "spoiling the market."

Conditions of Monopolistic Competition

We have been talking in the preceding chapter as though shirts, cigarettes, and butter were homogeneous commodities any unit of which was a perfect substitute for any other unit. Obviously this is not the case. If, for instance, I have been convinced by advertising (whether true or not) that Arrow shirts are of better quality or style than other makes, then my demand for Arrow shirts will be different from my demand for shirts in general. For all practical purposes, under these conditions, Arrow shirts are a commodity by themselves, and other makes are imperfect substitutes for them in my mind. At the same price, I will buy Arrow shirts rather than the other brands. I might be induced to buy other brands, but only at a lower price that would compensate me for the difference (real or imaginary) between Arrow shirts and the others.

If we carry the analysis a step further, we find that even a single brand does not constitute a separate homogeneous commodity for the purpose of drawing a demand curve. Even though two stores are both selling Arrow shirts, when we take into account the other services rendered in connection with the sale, we set up the conditions of a separate individual demand for each store's product. One store may be more conveniently located than the other, in which case I would trade there rather than in another store even though Arrow shirts were selling for the same price in both places. I might even be willing to pay $2.00 for a shirt in the first store although I know that by going to the less convenient shop I could get the same thing for $1.95. One store may give credit and delivery service and another may not; one store may be cleaner, better lighted and ventilated than another. It may be that one store has the reputation of being a "cheap joint" and I do not like to be seen trading there.

Time utility may also be a factor. For instance, if I run out of my favorite brand of cigarettes at 10 o'clock in the evening, I know that if I wait until morning I can buy two packages for 25c at the chain store. Nevertheless, rather than wait, I will pay 16c for a package at the newsstand. Even a difference in the personality of the salespeople may induce me to prefer to buy the same brand of a good at one store rather than another.

The buyer purchases not merely the article itself, but also the services that go with it. To the extent that the preceding conditions prevail, different stores are really selling products that, though physically identical, are different in the minds of the buyers.

Product differentiation may therefore be defined as any situation which induces a buyer to be willing to pay more for a good bought from one seller rather than from another, or as any consideration which causes one dealer to be preferred to another as a seller of a good even though the price is the same with both sellers.

Demand for Product of Individual Firm Under Monopolistic Competition

We saw above that under pure competition the demand for an individual seller's product is perfectly elastic. On the other hand, when product differentiation exists, the demand curve facing the individual seller will be less than perfectly elastic. Because the product has been differentiated from other products in the mind of the buyer, the seller of a differentiated product will not lose all of his business if he raises his price above that charged by other sellers of closely competing substitutes; nor will he be able to take all the business away from the other sellers by dropping his price below theirs.[2]

When we remember that utility is nothing more than an idea which exists in the mind of the buyer, we can readily see the connection between product differentiation and the demand curve for the product which is sold by an individual seller. For instance, certain people are willing to pay a cent or two more for print butter than for the same butter sold from a tub. Others are willing to pay still another cent more for the print butter if it is cut into quarter-pound pieces and the pieces are wrapped separately. In other words, the marginal utility of butter to them has been increased by special packaging. Wrapping in cellophane may increase the utility of some articles that people do not like to buy after handling by others. The reader can supply hundreds of illustrations of this principle from his own experience.

Product Differentiation by Advertising

As we stated above, advertising is an extremely important factor in differentiating a product and building up an individual demand curve for the product of an individual seller. Some advertising (usually by trade associations) is not of this

---

[2] We should not lose sight of the fact, however, that under both pure competition and product differentiation the demand curve for the individual seller will be more elastic than the demand curve for the industry in general. Under pure competition, the individual seller's demand curve is perfectly elastic. But even under monopolistic competition, the seller of a differentiated product will lose some business to the sellers of closely competing substitutes as he raises his price above theirs. For example, if the price of Fords rises but other cars do not, people need not cease buying cars but may buy other makes; demand for Fords becomes more elastic than demand for cars in general.

type, but is designed to influence the demand curve for the product in general. For instance, the sellers of builders' supplies may get together and urge us to "Build a home first," or associated apple growers may confront us with "National Apple Week," and so on. Most advertising, however, is designed to urge us to buy a particular brand or to buy from a particular seller. We are urged to buy "Congoleum" instead of linoleum, "Celotex" instead of insulating lumber, and so on. To the extent that advertisers succeed in their object of making us ask for products by their brand names, the tendency is to establish monopoly conditions in the market for their products. If we get into the habit of asking for a particular brand, other brands of the same product tend in our minds to become imperfect substitutes for our favorite brand. The seller, then, will have a monopoly of this class of people, even to the extent of sometimes being able to maintain the price of his own brand while the prices of other brands are falling, or to raise his price while others are unchanged, which he would not be able to do under perfect competition.

Similar conditions apply to the clientele of the individual store. To the extent that the store, by services of various kinds, can build up its "good will" so that people become accustomed to go there to trade rather than "shop around," it tends to have at least a partial monopoly of its customers' business. This monopoly may allow it to charge prices which are somewhat higher than its competitors' prices for the same goods, or to sell more goods at the same prices than other stores do.

Demand Curve for Differentiated Product

When product differentiation is achieved, the demand curve for the product of the individual seller will no longer be perfectly elastic at the market price. The seller is now attempting to appeal to a special group of buyers in the market rather than to buyers in general. Some of the buyers will place a high value on the additional "service" that is rendered, so that they will be willing to pay a price for the differentiated product which will be considerably higher than they would have been willing to pay for the undifferentiated product. Others will not value the additional service so highly and so will be willing to trade with this dealer only at prices which are slightly higher than those which they would have to pay elsewhere. Still others will attach no value at all to the service and so will trade with this particular dealer only at prices which are the same as others are charging. Finally, some people may dislike the special service and so would trade with this particular dealer only at prices lower than those prevailing for the un-differentiated product (for instance, packaging tea in "tea balls" may discourage its sale to some people who imagine that the muslin bag imparts a disagreeable taste to the tea, although many others consider tea balls a great convenience).

For the purpose of achieving simplicity in illustrating graphically the effect of product differentiation upon the individual seller's demand curve, we shall have to make an assumption that is contrary to what we ordinarily find in practice, namely, that only one dealer differentiates his product, and further, that he differentiates it only in respect to one particular "service."

In Diagram 2, *OA* represents under pure competition the market price of the undifferentiated product. *DD* represents the individual seller's demand curve under the same conditions; *dd* represents the individual seller's demand curve under product differentiation. That part of the curve *dd* which lies above *DD* shows the various amounts of the differentiated product which buyers would purchase from this particular seller at various prices *above* the general market price of the undifferentiated product.

It should be noticed that the relation of the curve *dd* to *DD* is dependent upon the price *OA* of the undifferentiated product. There is no reason why this relation should remain constant if the competitive price changes to a price greater or less than *OA*. For instance, assume that the differentiation factor which gives rise to *dd* is that one particular dealer will deliver while others will not. If the prices of both the undelivered and delivered products should rise, some of the buyers who make up the demand curve *dd* may decide that they no longer are willing to pay the same *price difference* for delivery service that they did before, and instead of buying from this particular dealer, they buy from others who do not deliver and who therefore can charge a lower price. Neither the elasticity of *dd* nor its position relative to *DD* is apt to remain the same when the general market price changes.

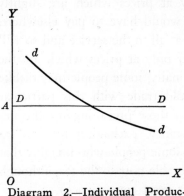

Diagram 2.—Individual Producer's Demand Curves Under Pure and Monopolistic Competition.

There are certain important consequences which follow from the nature of the individual seller's demand curve and which have a definite bearing upon the determination of the price of a product and of the amount offered for sale. Under perfect competition, the individual seller's demand curve being perfectly elastic at the prevailing price, the seller will have no motive to curtail output for fear of the effect on the price he receives.[3] But under monopolistic competition, the demand curve which faces the individual seller is less than perfectly elastic, as we have just discovered. This means that the seller who operates under these conditions must take account of the effect upon himself which his own actions will have upon the

---

[3] The conditions which will then determine his output are discussed in the chapters on supply.

price.   In other words, he has a monopoly of the market *within the limits of the individual demand curve which faces him*. Such a monopolist may do either one of two things: he may decide how much of the product he wishes to sell and then throw this amount on the market for what it will bring, in which case the demand will determine the price (this is the method used in sales at auction), or he may place a definite price upon his product, in which case the amount taken will depend upon the demand for the product at that price (this is the more usual method).   Whichever method he uses, as long as the demand curve which faces him is less than perfectly elastic, he is faced with the fact that a larger amount of his product can be sold only at a lower price per unit.

Average Revenue; Marginal Revenue

An explanation of these alternatives confronting the seller is provided by the very useful economic concept of marginal revenue.   What we have previously called a demand curve might also be called an *average revenue curve,* for it shows the average price per unit at which various amounts of the good can be sold.   The marginal revenue curve is derived from the average revenue curve. *Marginal revenue is the net amount added to total revenue by each successive unit that is added to the number offered for sale.*   To find marginal revenue, we must do two things: first, take the price (or average revenue) at which an additional unit offered will sell; second, from this price we must deduct the loss of average revenue on all previous units, occasioned by the fact that adding this last unit to the amount offered for sale will force all of the units to sell at a lower price than that which the dealer could obtain if he sold the smaller quantity (that is, by offering a larger amount for sale, he will be forced to a lower point on the demand or average revenue curve at which the larger amount can be sold).   When this loss is deducted from the price received for the additional unit, the result will be the *net addition* to total revenue occasioned by offering this one more unit for sale, or in other words, it will be the marginal revenue.

A numerical illustration will make the principle clearer. Suppose the demand curve (average revenue curve) to be such that 40 units of a product sell for $80.00 apiece, and that 41 units sell for $79.00 apiece. The amount received for the 41st unit is $79.00. To sell it, however, we must take $79.00 instead of $80.00 apiece for the other 40 units, a loss of $40.00. The marginal revenue of the 41st unit will be $79.00 minus $40.00, or $39.00. This $39.00 will be the *net addition* to total revenue occasioned by trying to sell 41 units instead of 40. We might state the same proposition as follows:

41 units..........Average Revenue $79.00..........Total Revenue $3,239.00
40 units..........Average Revenue 80.00..........Total Revenue 3,200.00

Difference (Marginal Revenue) $ 39.00

Diagram 3, which follows, shows an average revenue (or demand) curve and its corresponding marginal revenue curve.[4] Note that the marginal revenue curve crosses the zero line and becomes negative at 15 units. This is because total revenue is at a maximum when 15 units are sold ($15 \times 7 = 105$). From this point on, the amount received in revenue by selling a larger number of units is more than offset by the loss in average

---

[4] For the mathematically minded reader, the relation between marginal and average revenue curves may be expressed as follows:

Average Revenue = Selling Price (y) = A Function of the Quantity
    Sold (x)
Total Revenue = Selling Price times the Quantity Sold = $F(xy)$
Marginal Revenue = Rate of change in Total Revenue

$$= \frac{d}{dx}(xy)$$

$$= y + x\left(\frac{dy}{dx}\right)$$

See also Robinson, Joan, *Economics of Imperfect Competition*, pp. 34 ff., The Macmillan Co., London, 1934, a geometrical statement of the relations between marginal and average curves.

revenue on all previous units. In other words, marginal revenue becomes a minus quantity.

Relationship of Average and Marginal Revenue

The reason for the divergence of the average and marginal revenue curves should be noted. As long as average revenue remains constant with an increasing output, marginal revenue and average revenue will coincide. Since under this set of conditions the price (average revenue) is not falling, the addition

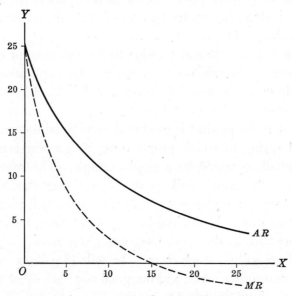

Diagram 3.—Average and Marginal Revenue.

to total revenue is represented by the average revenue received from selling each additional unit, because nothing need be deducted for loss on the previous units. (This condition prevails when demand for the product is perfectly elastic, as in the case of the demand for the product of the individual seller under pure competition.)

However, when average revenue is declining, marginal revenue *will always lie below* average revenue. This is because marginal revenue is the amount of *net change* in total revenue, whereas average revenue is *total* revenue divided by number of units, so that the effect of this change is "divided out" among the units.

To state the proposition differently, average revenue takes into account the decline in price alone. Marginal revenue takes into account not only the decline in price itself but also the loss in revenue on all previous units when successive units are sold at a lower price. Consequently, whenever average revenue is declining, marginal revenue will always be smaller than average revenue.

We shall have repeated occasion to use this concept of marginal revenue in subsequent chapters. An application of it may help to fix the principle in our minds. In order to avoid the question of cost (which will be taken up later), let us assume that the product is produced entirely without cost. A mineral spring to which people come to get water in their own containers would be a good example. The monopolist who owns this spring will try to obtain the greatest possible income from selling the water. At what price will his income be the greatest? If the conditions of demand for mineral water are such as shown in Diagram 3, our answer would be at $7.00 per gallon, at which price he sells 15 gallons. At this output, marginal revenue and marginal cost [5] are equal (in this special case both are equal to zero).

Before leaving the subject of demand, there are certain very important qualifications which we must bear in mind. In the first place, the various points on a demand curve are *alternative* and are *not successive*. For instance, in Diagram 3 the

---

[5] Marginal cost is defined as the additional cost necessary to produce one more unit of the product (see page 83). Since, in the special case above, we have assumed production entirely without cost, marginal cost would also be zero at every output shown in the diagram.

seller has the option of selling *either* 15 gallons at $7.00 or 20 gallons at $5.00. If the seller goes ahead and sells 15 gallons at $7.00 it does not follow that he could turn around and sell 20 gallons at $5.00, nor even that he could sell an additional 5 gallons at $5.00. After the 15 gallons have been sold we would have an entirely new set of conditions of demand for which a new curve would have to be constructed.

To take another illustration, let us suppose you walk into my clothing store prepared to buy either four shirts at $2.00 apiece or six shirts at $1.25. If I sell you the four shirts at $2.00, it does not mean that I could then sell you two or even one at $1.25. The buying of the four at $2.00 has used up $8.00 of your clothing allowance, which may be all that you care to spend for shirts. Even were I to drop my price to $1.00, you might regret that you did not wait for the bargain, but you would not necessarily buy any more shirts for the time being.

Another important consideration is the time, or length of period, for which the demand schedule or curve is drawn. To be strictly accurate, a demand curve cannot apply to any period longer than that in which the conditions of demand remain unchanged. In the Chicago wheat pit, for instance, the demand for wheat futures is the same only for an instant of time, since every item of market news and crop reports that comes in over the wires alters the conditions of demand in the minds of the buyers. For many commodities, however, we find it convenient to speak of the demand per day, per week, per month, or per year. While this is convenient, we should not lose sight of the fact that the longer the period, the more apt is the demand curve to be subject to inaccuracies due to changes in the conditions of demand.

True Demand and Estimated Demand

Under imperfect competition, there are really two kinds of demand curves which merit our attention. The first is the true demand curve that actually represents the conditions in the minds of the buyers. Once the price is actually set, it is this curve which will determine the amount purchased by the buyers. (This is the kind of demand curve we have been speaking about in this and in the preceding chapter.)

The second kind of demand curve is the one that represents the idea or estimate of demand which exists in the mind of the seller. It is this idea or estimate which will influence the seller in determining the price he will place on his product. For instance, the true demand for a certain kind of shoes might be such that, if the manufacturer should drop his price 25c a pair, he would sell 10,000 additional pairs and find his total net profit greater than at his present output. But if he *believed* that by dropping the price 25c the buyers would take only 2,000 additional pairs (selling this additional amount would not compensate for the loss of 25c a pair on his present output), he would not lower his price.

This difference between *true* demand and the seller's *estimate* of demand is well illustrated by the experience of certain public utility companies. In some instances they have fought vigorously against rate reductions ordered by Public Service Commissions, only to find after the lower rates were in effect that their net profits were actually increased by the greatly increased sales at the lower rates. If they had known in advance what the true demand curve was, they would have lowered their rates voluntarily and saved themselves the expense of litigation in fighting the rate reductions.

Two Definitions of Commodity

Up to this point we have been using the term *commodity* without defining it. This has been done purposely, because our definition of a commodity is dependent upon the conditions of competition which prevail in the market. For instance, if the good is subject to product differentiation, we may consider the combination of physical product and the services that go with it as constituting a "commodity" in the mind of the buyer. Under these circumstances, the commodity would be the physical product as packaged, advertised, serviced, and sold by the individual dealer. In other words, the article as sold by an individual seller would be a commodity, while the same or a similar article sold by a competitor would be a substitute for the commodity. If we insist on absolute homogeneity of all units in the mind of the buyer as the test of what constitutes a commodity, we should have to adhere to this definition.

However, it must be obvious that certain commodities under the above definition will be much better substitutes for one another than less similar commodities. For instance, the same brand of corn flakes as sold by different stores in a community, or different brands of corn flakes as sold by the same store, would all be better substitutes for one another than would any brand of rolled oats sold by any store. For this reason there will be conditions of demand and supply that will have great importance in determining the general average price of corn flakes in the community, regardless of the fact that prices charged by the different dealers for different brands may differ slightly. When we are thinking of these general forces of demand and supply, we will find it convenient to think of corn flakes in general as being a commodity. It is in this sense that the term *commodity* is ordinarily used in common speech. To define a commodity in this sense, we should have to say that it was a group of products surrounded by a gap in the chain of possible substitutes.[6]

---

[6] Robinson, Joan, *Economics of Imperfect Competition,* p. 4, The Macmillan Co., London, 1934.

The following table will illustrate both definitions:

Commodity by Second Definition	*Commodity by first definition*	"X" Corn Flakes as sold by Brown's Corner Grocery.
	Close substitutes	"X" Corn Flakes as sold by other dealers in community. Other brands of corn flakes sold by Brown's Corner Grocery. Other brands of corn flakes sold by other dealers in community.

Gap

Less close substitutes	Other kinds of dry cereals (Shredded Wheat, Puffed Rice, Rice Crispies, and so forth). (a) Sold by Brown. (b) Sold by other dealers.
Distant substitutes	Various kinds of cooked cereals (Rolled Oats, Wheatena, and so forth). (a) Sold by Brown. (b) Sold by other dealers.
More distant substitutes	Other foodstuffs (eggs, meat, vegetables, and so forth).
Still more distant substitutes	Other uses for the consumer's money (clothing, movies, gasoline, and so forth).
Most distant substitutes	Investment and savings.

Unfortunately, the gap in the substitutes for some commodities will not be so clearly marked as it is in the above case. However, the principle will usually still apply. When we speak of the demand for the product of an individual seller under imperfect competition, it is the first definition of commodity or product that we have in mind. Conversely, when we speak of the general market demand for a commodity, it is the second definition of commodity with which we are concerned.

This brings us to the definition of a market. A *market* for a commodity may be defined as the area in which buyers and sellers of the commodity are in communication with one another, and an area in which exchanges take place. There need not be any specific market place in which exchanges are carried on, although these market places do exist for many commodities. The area which will comprise the market varies from one commodity to another. For some commodities such as wheat, rubber, and the principal metals, the market is world-wide. For some other commodities there are local markets that are more or less independent of one another. If we are thinking of our first definition of commodity, the market for the individual seller will be limited to the number of buyers who can be induced to trade with him by the prices that he charges or the services that he renders. If perfect competition exists, the price of a commodity cannot differ between different parts of the market for any length of time by more than the costs of transportation, if buyers and sellers have full knowledge of market conditions.

Classification of Monopolistic and Competitive Situations [7]

Now that we have the concept of product differentiation in mind, it might be appropriate to define and classify the different monopolistic and competitive situations which may exist:

1. *Monopoly* is a situation in which there are no close substitutes for the product of a single firm; or, we might say that the monopolist competes with other firms *for the consumer's*

---

[7] This section is partly an adaptation from and partly a disagreement with the article by Fritz Machlup, "Monopoly and Competition: A Classification," *American Economic Review*, Vol. XXVII, No. 3, September, 1937.

dollar only, and that the substitute products offered by other firms or industries are such poor or remote substitutes for the monopolist's product that he formulates his price policy without considering any one of them individually as a competitor.

2. *Duopoly* is a situation in which there are only two firms producing either a standardized product or two products which are only slightly differentiated. (Complete or perfect product differentiation would force us to classify the firms as two separate monopolies, rather than as a duopoly.)

3. *Oligopoly* is a situation in which there are so few sellers that each of them is conscious of the results upon price of the supply which he individually places upon the market. There are several important sub-types:[8]

(a) Oligopoly with standardized products (may be called pure oligopoly).

(b) Oligopoly with differentiated products (a special case under monopolistic competition).

(c) Price leadership is a situation in which one or more large firms base their price and output policies upon the assumption that these policies will directly affect their own returns. Alongside these "leaders," there will be a large number of small firms which might be competitive in the absence of the large firms but which either "follow the leader" in setting their prices or at least wait until the leaders' prices are announced and then use these prices as a point of departure in setting their own prices. Price leadership may exist accompanied by either standardized or differentiated products.

4. Competition with differentiated products (monopolistic competition).

---

[8] See Hoffman, A. C., Monograph No. 35, pp. 15–58, *Large Scale Organization in the Food Industries,* Temporary National Economic Committee, 76th Congress, 3rd Session, for a number of examples of actual cases of various kinds of oligopoly and price leadership. The reader will find that most of these cases are borderline cases which might fall in one classification or the other. The effort to classify them, nevertheless, will well repay the reader's time in attaining a more exact knowledge of what is implied in each concept.

5. Competition with standardized products (pure competition).

The reader should be very careful to distinguish between *pure* and *perfect* competition. *Perfect competition,* as defined by various writers, includes the following:

1. A perfect market; perfect knowledge by both buyers and sellers, and perfect freedom of movement of the commodity and/or of buyers and sellers between different parts of the market.

2. Perfectly elastic supply of the factors of production. (All units of all factors do not have to be perfectly fluid or mobile. It is sufficient if a certain part of the supply of each factor is able to move in order to achieve the assumed result; that is, that the prices of equal factors will be equal in different uses.)

There are four possible ways in which competition of various types may be combined. Competition may be:

1. *Perfect but monopolistic;* perfect as defined above, but accompanied by product differentiation.

2. *Pure but imperfect;* standardized product sold in an imperfect market or produced under conditions of less than perfectly elastic supply of factors to individual firms or to the industry.

3. *Monopolistic and imperfect;* product differentiation plus an imperfect market and/or imperfections in the supply of factors of production.

4. *Pure and perfect;* standardized product, plus perfect competition as defined above.

The above classifications have been inserted here as a convenient reference for the reader. The definitions are not exhaustive, but rather consist of a skeleton upon which we shall attempt to hang more meat in subsequent discussion. Even so, we must recognize that many of the competitive or monopolistic situations which we encounter in actual life are borderline cases, and the classification in which the industry is placed depends upon the judgment of the observer.

CHAPTER VII

Supply of Goods and Market Price

IN THE preceding chapters we have been trying to answer the question, "Why are people *willing* to pay the prices that they do pay for goods?" In this and the chapters immediately following we shall be more concerned with the question, "Why do buyers *have* to pay those prices?" To answer this question, we must examine the motives of the sellers and find out what governs the prices that they charge.

Motives of Sellers

As a first assumption, we shall take it for granted that all sellers are trying to obtain the greatest possible amount of net profits, or if profits appear impossible of attainment, that they will attempt to minimize their losses. With only some few minor exceptions, it is this motive that animates all sellers. In this respect the monopolist is not different from the competitive seller. The mere fact that the monopolist may charge higher prices than those that would be charged by competitive dealers is no evidence of a difference in motives. It is evidence only of a difference in opportunity. The competitors would charge just as high prices as the monopolist does if they were able. Only competition among themselves prevents competing sellers from charging such prices. Indeed, whenever the circumstances seem to warrant it, we find people who were formerly competitors attempting to combine among themselves in various forms of "trade agreements" to nullify the effects of

competition.   We shall assume, then, that the motive of max-
imizing profits or minimizing losses is the underlying motive
that influences all sellers.   In order to indicate what price policies sellers will try to follow, our task will be to show what conditions will govern the point of maximum profits or minimum
losses.

Periods of Supply

There are three different periods of time for which the conditions of supply must be considered separately.   The first
period, called *market supply,* relates to the sale of goods already produced and in existence.*   The second period is related to the production and sale of goods by means of plant
and equipment already in existence and is called the *short-run*
period.   The length of this second period varies considerably from one industry to another.   The third period, usually
called the *long-run* period by economists, takes into account the
manufacture of new plant and equipment either to replace
existing plant and equipment or to add to present plant capacity.
It also takes into account the length of time necessary for old
plants to wear out, when contraction of output is desired.

We shall consider first the conditions of supply in the first
period, usually called *instantaneous* or *market* supply.   For
goods which are already produced, there is no absolute minimum price below which all sellers would refuse to sell.   It is
true, of course, that the seller would like to recover what the
goods cost him.   Indeed, he would like to obtain as much
above that cost as possible.   But as we have seen, it is the conditions of demand that determine the amount of a good which
will be taken from the market at various prices.   If the conditions of demand are such that buyers will not take, at the price
the seller would like to charge, the full amount of which he
would like to dispose, the seller has no choice but to lower his
price or fail to sell all that he would like to sell.   With a given

---

* Specialized goods such as automobiles, however, will lose value more rapidly
than standardized goods.

demand, the eagerness of the seller to dispose of all or part of his goods is then the only factor that will govern the price that he will charge in the market for the goods he has on hand.

Sellers' Reservation Prices

If goods which are not sold now, at this instant, could never be sold in the future, the prices which sellers would be willing to take would be extremely low. With most goods, however, there is usually a possibility of waiting until later in the day or until some future day and disposing of them at the prices which then prevail. Consequently every seller will have a *reservation price*[1] for his goods. Rather than sell below this reservation price, he will be willing to wait and to take a chance on selling his remaining stock of goods at future prices. There are certain general principles governing the upper limit of these reservation prices that we shall now proceed to explain.

Usually, the more perishable the commodity, the lower will be the reservation price. If the reader will visit one of the large produce markets on a Saturday night, he will find the dealers in strawberries and other perishable commodities offering them for extremely low prices rather than have them spoil over the week end. The principle of greatest gain or least loss nevertheless operates here also. For instance, if a dealer has 100 quarts of strawberries left, and in the two hours during which the market is to remain open he estimates that he could sell either the entire 100 quarts at 5c a quart, or 60 quarts at 10c, he will choose the latter course. Even though 40 quarts would spoil and have to be thrown out, he would be better off receiving $6.00 for the 60 quarts than if he received $5.00 for the entire 100 sold at 5c each.[2]

With goods that are less perishable, one of the most impor-

---

[1] As far as I am able to determine, this term originated with Professor H. J. Davenport, although other authors have used the term *reserve prices,* perhaps with priority.

[2] This is another example of a conflict between individual and community economic welfare.

tant elements in determining the reservation price is the seller's estimate of what he thinks the future price will be. Goods which are held over from the present will have to compete with a new supply of goods on the market in the future period. Consequently if the seller knows or believes that costs of production for his product are falling, he will tend to place his reservation price lower than would otherwise be the case, since his goods, if held for the future, would have to compete with others produced at lower cost. The reverse situation would be true in the case of anticipated rising costs. Similarly, if he believes that demand will decrease in the future, his reservation price will be low; if he believes that demand will increase, his reservation price will be high.

Another closely related factor is the anticipated length of time the goods will have to be held before they can be sold at the estimated future price. The carrying charges will determine the advisability of waiting for higher prices in the future or of selling at present prices. For instance, suppose I hold a stock of wheat, the present price of which is 95c per bushel. I am sure that three months from now wheat will sell for $1.00; however, it will cost me 3c per bushel per month in interest and warehouse charges to hold the wheat. I would be better off selling now, because, even though I could obtain 5c a bushel more three months from now, it would cost me 9c a bushel to hold the wheat till then. If it is anticipated that the future price will be lower, the carrying charges are an added incentive to lower the present reservation price.

Still another factor influencing reservation price will be the seller's need for cash. If the banks are pressing him to repay loans, or if he has other bills which must be met, he will be more eager to turn his stock of goods on hand into cash. Consequently he will have lower reservation prices for the stock than would otherwise be the case.

The length of time it will take for a new supply to reach the market will also have a bearing on reservation prices. If, for instance, there is an extreme scarcity of a certain agricultural crop, sellers may feel free to hold out for high prices until threatened by the approach of a new harvest. On the other hand, if there is a temporary scarcity in a manufactured article that can be quickly reproduced, dealers would do well to dispose of their stocks quickly while the high prices continue.

Effect of Monopolistic Competition on Reservation Prices

Product differentiation may act as a partial deterrent to both extremely high and extremely low reservation prices. For instance, during times of high prices that appear to be only temporary (for example, in a town surrounded by a flood), dealers may hesitate to exact the last possible nickel from their customers for fear of losing good will. On the other hand, when prices in general are falling, the seller of a differentiated product may not drop his reservation prices as rapidly or as far as he would if pure competition existed. He will recognize that many of his customers are *held to him by considerations other than price*. Furthermore, if the products of his competitors are also differentiated, he will not be able to attract so many buyers to himself by a small cut in his price as would be the case under pure competition.

The more perfect the degree of monopoly in a commodity (that is, the fewer and poorer close substitutes there are), the stronger will be the tendency for the monopolist to keep his reservation price high. If there are no adequate substitutes for his product, those people who are deterred from buying by a high price will spend their money for entirely different kinds of commodities. Under these circumstances, if the want for the good persists, the monopolist can rely on being able to dispose of his stock of goods eventually; the only effect of a high price will be to slow down the rate at which he can dispose of his stock. On the other hand, if there are fairly close substitutes for a commodity and the seller charges a high price, buyers may turn to the substitutes to satisfy their want. In this case the seller may run the risk of a permanent loss of business, and he may be threatened with the possibility of having to accept a much lower price for his stock later on.

Different Reservation Prices for Parts of Stock

Another element must be taken into consideration in connection with reservation prices; the reservation price for a part of the seller's stock on hand may differ from that for the entire amount. For instance, the dealer who is hard pressed for cash might be willing to sacrifice a part of his stock at a very low price; but once his most pressing needs are met, he would prefer to hold on to the balance in hopes of a better market. Also, a seller who believes that the price will be higher in the future may not be willing to take a chance on that belief with his entire stock. He will therefore sell a part of his stock for what it will bring at present and hold on to the remainder. (This is a common practice with certain wheat farmers.) The amount of storage capacity which a seller has may be a factor in such a decision; he might be willing to sell at a low price the excess amount which he could not conveniently store, but it would require a higher price to make him part immediately with that amount for which he has available storage capacity.

A different reservation price for part of a stock may also be due to the seller's own demand for the product for his own use. Thus, if a seller has need for his own product, it may take a higher price to induce him to part with all of his stock than the price at which he might be willing to sell that part of the stock which constituted a surplus over his own needs. The price which will be required to induce him to part with that portion of the stock which he could use himself will depend upon the relative intensity of his desire for his own product as compared to the intensity of his desire for the various other products which he might purchase with the money received from selling his own product.

While past cost should have no effect in determining reservation prices, nevertheless it does influence some dealers. They have paid too high a price for goods in the past and are reluctant to admit that they have made a mistake, or that they have been poor price forecasters. Such individuals very often keep a stock of goods on hand for a considerable length of time, refusing to sell for a price below cost. Quite often the result of this obstinacy is that they take a greater loss in the end. Either the price drops further and they take a greater loss, or, even if the price remains constant, they take a loss in interest and storage charges for the length of time that they hold on to the goods. Knowledge of when it is best to take a small loss in order to avoid a greater loss is one of the most important attributes of successful dealers.

Supply Defined

With the principles underlying these reservation prices in mind, we are prepared to analyze the conditions of instantaneous or market supply of goods. We shall consider first the case of pure competition. We may define *supply* as *a schedule of the amounts of a good that would be offered for sale at all possible prices at any one instant of time,* or during any one period of time (for example, a day, week, and so on, in which the conditions of supply remain the same).

Considering the factors mentioned above, we can easily see that most sellers are apt to have different reservation prices. Of those sellers who believe that the future price will decline, some will be more pessimistic than others and consequently will have lower reservation prices. Of those sellers who believe the future price will rise, some will be more optimistic than others and will have higher reservation prices. Certain sellers will be hard pressed for cash; others will not. Some will have ample storage capacity; others will not. Hence, starting with the lowest reservation price which any dealer is willing to accept, each possible price above it will satisfy more dealers who are willing to offer part or all of their goods for sale. This brings us to a statement of *the first law of supply* which is: *under the same conditions of supply, the amount which is offered for sale will vary directly with the price.* The higher the price, the greater will be the amount of a good offered for sale. Once the entire stock in existence is offered for sale, however, it is obvious that still higher prices will be able to bring forth no more goods to be offered for sale. From this point on the supply curve would be perfectly inelastic, and the remainder of the curve would be represented graphically by a vertical straight line.[3]

We are now prepared to draw up a demand schedule and a supply schedule for the same product to show the action of competition in determining a market price:

ASSUMED DEMAND AND SUPPLY FOR WHOLESALE MARKET
92 SCORE BUTTER AT CHICAGO JUNE 19, 19—

Demand Schedule: Amount that Would be Purchased (Pounds)	Prices (Cents per Pound)	Supply Schedule: Amount that Would be Offered (Pounds)
300	31¾	3,400
500	31½	3,250
700	31¼	3,100
900	31	2,900
1,150	30¾	2,750
1,400	30½	2,500
1,700	30¼	2,250
2,000	30	2,000
2,350	29¾	1,750
2,750	29½	1,350
3,250	29¼	1,000
3,750	29	500

[3] The extreme upper limits of such a curve might even turn backwards toward the Y axis and become negatively elastic. For example, a farm wife selling butter or eggs might find that at an extremely high price for her product she could obtain the other goods that she needs without sacrificing so much butter and so many eggs from her own table. Thus a very high price might cause her to offer for sale a smaller rather than a greater amount of butter or eggs.

Market Price Determination

The above schedules show the amounts that buyers would be willing to purchase and the amounts that sellers would be willing to offer for sale at the various prices listed in the second column of the table. From these schedules we can readily see that the market price for butter will be 30c, since at that price the market will be *cleared*: that is, at a price of 30c the amount offered for sale will be *equal* to the amount purchased. Two thousand pounds will be exchanged, and there will be left no unsatisfied buyers or sellers willing to do business at 30c.

That no other price, under perfect competition would be possible with these particular demand and supply schedules may be easily demonstrated. The proof of this is very simple: assume, for a moment, a price of 31½c; at this price, buyers would be willing to take only 500 pounds, while sellers would be willing to offer 3,250 pounds for sale. All of these sellers, rather than lose a sale, would then cut their price down to their minimum reservation price as indicated in the supply schedule. Although buyers would be willing to pay 31½c per pound for 500 pounds of butter if they had to, they would, of course, be delighted to obtain this amount at a lower price. Consequently, when they find a number of sellers competing for their order and willing to cut prices to get it, they will hold off in an effort to obtain the lowest possible price for the amount that they wish to buy. On the other hand, each cut in the prices by the sellers will attract more buyers into the market who are willing to purchase more. At the same time, with each cut in price, some of the amount previously offered for sale is withdrawn from the market as the price falls below the reservation price of any of the sellers. This process would continue until the price of 30c is reached. At this price there is no further inducement for sellers to cut prices, since they can sell all that they wish to sell (2,000 pounds) at that price.

An analogous proof can be advanced to show that no price

below 30c would be a possible market price under the given conditions of demand and supply. Assume a price of 29c. At this price sellers would be willing to offer only 500 pounds for sale; but buyers would be willing to purchase 3,750 pounds. The buyers, rather than go unsatisfied, will start to make offers in excess of 29c. While some sellers have reservation prices so low that they would be willing to sell 500 pounds at 29c per pound, they will be delighted to get more if they can; they therefore hold out for the highest offer when they find buyers bidding against each other for their goods. Each increase in price offered, however, now attracts more sellers into the market as their reservation prices are reached. At the same time, each increase in price causes some buyers to withdraw from the market as the price goes above the amount they are willing to pay. This continues until the price of 30c is reached. At this price there is no further inducement for buyers to bid higher for the product, since they can buy all that they wish (2,000 pounds) at that price. Thus we have shown that, under the given conditions, the price can be neither higher nor lower than 30c. Proof can also be shown by a diagram.

In Diagram 1, $D'D'$ is the demand curve, SS is the supply curve, and PM represents market price. At this price the amount purchased is AP and the amount offered for sale is also AP. Amount purchased equals amount offered for sale, and the market is cleared. Market price is an *equilibrium* price.

At any higher price (represented by RN), amount purchased will be BR and the amount offered for sale will be BC. The amount offered for sale is in excess of the amount that will be purchased, and the tendency will be for a lower price to be established. RN is not an equilibrium price.

At any price lower than PM (represented by TU), the amount that would be purchased is represented by DT and the amount that would be offered for sale by *DE*. The amount that would be purchased is in excess of the amount that would be offered for sale, and the tendency is for a higher price to be established. *TU* is not an equilibrium price.

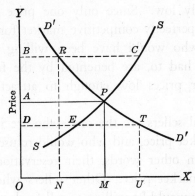

Diagram 1.—Assumed Demand and Supply Curves for Wholesale Market 92 Score Butter at Chicago 9:00 A.M. June 19, 1936.

Marginal Buyers and Marginal Sellers

Note that there are two general forces at work in establishing market prices. *Competition among buyers tends to force prices up; competition among sellers tends to force prices down.* The important individuals in establishing the exact market price are the *marginal buyers* and the *marginal sellers*.[4]

---

[4] Since each buyer has his own demand schedule, any or all buyers may be marginal buyers with respect to a small part of their purchases. That is, they will continue to buy more up to the point where the marginal utility of the good is just equal to the marginal utility of the money they must part with to obtain the last units. Or, under indifference curve analysis, they will buy up to the point where the marginal rate of substitution of the commodity for money equals the price ratio. If the price rises, they will buy fewer units. These units are then marginal units in respect to the price, and are as important in determining price as the units purchased by those buyers who would leave the market entirely if the price rose.

On the sellers' side the same thing may be true. If some sellers have a different reservation price for a part of their stock, the units that they would refuse to sell at a price lower than the market price are marginal units as well as those units offered by sellers who would withdraw completely from the market if the price should fall.

The marginal buyers at any given price are those who are just induced to buy at that price and who would refrain from buying if the price were the least bit higher. In order to include the marginal buyers in the market and to sell to them, the sellers must compete with one another to make the price sufficiently low. Since only one price can prevail at one time in a perfectly competitive market for a commodity, other buyers who would have been willing to pay higher prices, if they had to, are benefited by the fact that sellers must put their prices low enough to attract the marginal buyer.

The marginal sellers are the ones who are just induced to sell at the market price, and who would refuse to sell at any lower price. In other words, their reservation price is just equal to the market price. Other sellers whose reservation prices are lower would be willing to sell for less, but, since the buyers must offer a price sufficiently high to attract the marginal sellers into the market, the other sellers (sometimes called the *intramarginal* sellers) are enabled to obtain the same price for themselves.

For the true market price to be established immediately, there must be a perfect market. We have already defined pure competition as a condition in which there is no product differentiation and in which there is a sufficiently large number of buyers and sellers so that none of them individually can dominate the market.

The requirements of a perfect market are that all buyers and all sellers be perfectly acquainted with all the conditions both of demand and of supply. Obviously such a perfect market has never existed and never will. The primary markets for certain agricultural products and minerals do at times show a remarkable degree of close approximation to the conditions of a perfect market. Most markets, and more especially retail markets, are characterized by a large and varying degree of ignorance of market conditions on the part of both buyers and sellers.

In the absence of perfect market conditions, the true market price will not be attained immediately. In actual practice there will be a few scattered sales at prices either above or below the true market price until, by a process of trial and error, the buyers and sellers discover the true market price at which the bulk of the exchanges will take place.

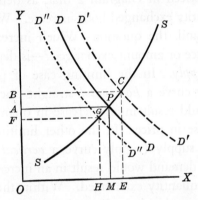

Diagram 2.—Changes in Demand.

Changes in Demand and Market Price

We must now consider the effect of changes in demand upon price. We shall assume, for the moment, that the supply schedule remains absolutely unchanged while demand is changing.[5]

In Diagram 2, DD is the demand curve, SS is the supply curve, PM is the market price, and OM (equal to AP) is the amount sold, as in Diagram 1 two pages back.

---

[5] This condition is possible under pure competition but *not* under a perfect market. Perfect knowledge by both buyers and sellers must assume that sellers would *instantaneously* revise their reservation prices to take account of the change in demand. Thus we could not have a change in demand without at least some change in supply. Since demand and supply are thus not independent of one another, we have to reserve this question for general equilibrium analysis.

Now let us assume that demand increases. The new demand curve is *D'D'*, CE is the new market price (higher than *PM*), and *OE* (equal to *BC*) is the new amount purchased (greater than *OM*).

Or, assume that demand decreases. The demand curve may then be represented by *D"D"*; *GH* will be the new market price (lower than *PM*), and *OH* (equal to *FG*) will be the new amount purchased (less than *OM*).

It will be noticed in Diagram 2 that, as demand increases, price and quantity exchanged both increase. With a given increase in demand, the question—Which increases in greater proportion: price or amount exchanged?—is dependent on the *elasticity of supply*. In the limiting case of perfectly elastic supply (supply curve a *horizontal* straight line) any increase in demand would result in an increase in quantity exchanged with no increase in price. In the other limiting case of perfectly inelastic supply (supply curve a *vertical* straight line) any increase in demand would result in an increased price with no increase in quantity exchanged. Within these two limits, we are now prepared to formulate a proposition concerning one of the influences of demand and supply on market price: *Other conditions remaining unchanged, an increase in demand has a tendency to increase both price and quantity exchanged, and a decrease in demand has a tendency to decrease both price and quantity exchanged. With a given change in demand, the more elastic the supply, the less will be the proportionate change in price and the greater the proportionate change in quantity exchanged. The less elastic the supply, the greater will be the proportionate change in price and the less the proportionate change in the quantity exchanged.* (The same change in demand with different elasticities of supply is shown in Diagram 3.

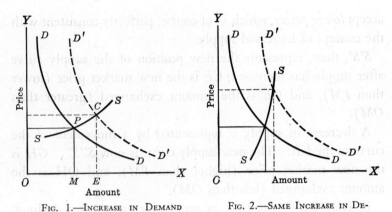

FIG. 1.—INCREASE IN DEMAND
WITH ELASTIC SUPPLY.

FIG. 2.—SAME INCREASE IN DE-
MAND WITH INELASTIC SUPPLY.

Diagram 3.—Changes in Demand with Elastic and Inelastic Supply.

Changes in Supply and Market Price

We now turn to the effect of changes in supply upon price. We shall assume in this case that the demand schedule remains absolutely unchanged while supply is changing.[6]

In Diagram 4, *DD* represents the demand curve, *SS* the supply curve, *PM* the market price, and *OM* the amount exchanged, as in the other diagrams.

An increase in supply will be represented by a movement of the supply curve to the right to the new position represented by *S'S'*. Note well that an increase in supply is shown by a shift of the supply curve to the *right* on the diagram, and a decrease in supply by a shift to the *left*. A movement to the right represents an increase in supply because it shows that at the *same prices* represented on the old supply curve, *greater* amounts will now be offered for sale. The mere fact that parts of the curve *S'S'* lie below the curve *SS* should not confuse the reader into calling the movement from *SS* to *S'S'* a decrease in supply. The reason why *S'S'* lies below *SS* is that it indicates that for the *same amounts* dealers are now willing to

---

[6] The same limitation to pure competition as was stated in the previous note applies here.

accept *lower prices,* which is, of course, perfectly consistent with the concept of increased supply.

S'S', then, represents the new position of the supply curve after supply has increased, *CE* is the new market price (lower than *PM*), and *OE* is the amount exchanged (greater than *OM*).

A decrease in supply is represented by a movement of the curve to the left. The new supply curve is now *S"S".* *GH* is the new market price (higher than *PM*), and *OH* is the amount exchanged (less than *OM*).

In Diagram 4 note that, as supply increases, price declines, while amount exchanged increases. With a given increase in

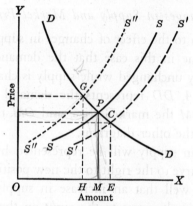

Diagram 4.—Changes in Supply.

supply, the proportionate decline in price and the proportionate increase in amount exchanged will depend on the elasticity of demand. In the limiting case of perfectly elastic demand (demand curve a *horizontal* straight line), any increase in supply will bring no decline in price, but only an increase in amount exchanged. In the other limiting case of perfectly inelastic demand (demand curve a *vertical* straight line), any increase in supply will result in a decline in price but no change in the amount purchased. Within these two limits we are now prepared to formulate a second proposition concerning the influence of supply and demand on market price: *Other conditions remaining unchanged, an increase in supply will have a tendency to decrease price, and to increase quantity exchanged; a decrease in supply will have a tendency to increase price, and to decrease quantity exchanged. With a given change in supply, the more elastic the demand, the less will be the proportionate change in price and the greater the proportionate change in the amount exchanged. The less elastic the demand, the greater will be the proportionate change in price and the less will be the proportionate change in the amount exchanged.*

Market Price When Demand and Supply Both Change

The principles we have developed above may be applied to cases where demand and supply are both changing. Combining them, we arrive at a further set of principles:

1. *When both demand and supply are changing in the same direction, the tendency will be for each to offset the effect of the other on price and to intensify the effect on quantity exchanged.* Thus a decrease in supply tends to raise price and to decrease quantity exchanged. A decrease in demand tends

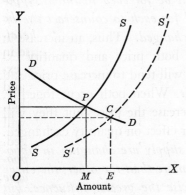 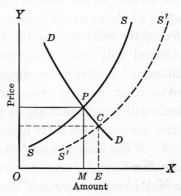

FIG. 1.—INCREASE IN SUPPLY WITH ELASTIC DEMAND.   FIG. 2.—SAME INCREASE IN SUPPLY WITH INELASTIC DEMAND.

Diagram 5.—Changes in Supply with Elastic and Inelastic Demand.

to lower price and to decrease quantity exchanged. When both occur together, they tend to cancel each other in their effect on price, but both will be contributing to effect a decline in quantity exchanged.

2. *When both demand and supply are changing in the same direction but one changes more than the other, the curve which changes more will exercise the greater influence, but its effect on price will be less and its effect on quantity exchanged will be greater than it would be if the other curve had remained unchanged.* Thus an increase in demand would tend to increase both price and quantity exchanged. An increase in supply would tend to decrease price and to increase quantity exchanged. If the supply increases by more than the demand, the effect of the change in supply will overbalance the change of demand and price will fall, but it will not fall by as great an amount as it would if supply increased alone. The effect of the increase in demand upon quantity exchanged will reinforce the effect of the increase in supply upon quantity, and the quantity exchanged will be greater than if supply had increased alone.

3. *When both demand and supply are changing in opposite directions, the tendency will be for each to intensify the effect of the other on price and for each to counteract the effect of the other on quantity exchanged.* Thus, an increase in demand will tend to increase both price and quantity exchanged. A decrease in supply will tend to increase price and to decrease quantity exchanged. When both occur together, both will be contributing to increase the price, but they will tend to cancel each other in their effect on quantity exchanged.

4. *When both demand and supply are changing in opposite directions, but one changes more than the other, the curve which changes more will exercise the greater influence, but its effect on price will be greater and its effect on quantity will*

be less than would be the case if the other curve had remained unchanged. Thus, a decrease in demand would tend to decrease both price and quantity exchanged. An increase in supply would tend to decrease price and to increase quantity exchanged. If the increase in supply is greater than the decrease in demand, price will fall by a greater amount than if supply had increased alone. The change in supply being greater, the tendency of the increase in supply to increase the quantity exchanged will overbalance the tendency of the decrease in demand to decrease quantity exchanged, and quantity exchanged will increase, but it will not increase by as great an amount as it would have if supply had increased alone.

We have not mentioned the effects of the elasticity of the curve that changes, because no simple general rules can be drawn to cover the situation. When demand increases or decreases, parts of the new demand curve may be more elastic and parts of it less elastic than the corresponding parts of the old demand curve. For instance, advertising may not only increase the demand for a commodity—it may decrease the elasticity of part of the curve as well; that is, the advertisement may not only convince new buyers that they should buy the product, but it may also convince the old buyers that the product is so good that they should not give up buying the same amount even at much higher prices.

We have listed in the following table several possible changes that may take place in supply and demand and the subclassifications of different elasticity where applicable. It will be a useful exercise for the reader to try to apply the rules we have given in this chapter to these cases and answer the questions, "What will happen to price?" and "What will happen to quantity exchange?" in each case. Or, the reader may draw the diagrams representing some of the cases and find the answers to the questions from the diagrams.

POSSIBLE CHANGES IN SUPPLY AND DEMAND

1. Demand increases, no change in supply.
    (a) Supply elastic.
    (b) Supply inelastic.
2. Demand decreases, no change in supply.
    (a) Supply elastic.
    (b) Supply inelastic.
3. Supply increases, no change in demand.
    (a) Demand elastic.
    (b) Demand inelastic.
4. Supply decreases, no change in demand.
    (a) Demand elastic.
    (b) Demand inelastic.
5. Demand and supply both increase equally.
6. Demand and supply both decrease equally.
7. Demand and supply both increase but demand increases more than supply.
8. Demand and supply both increase but supply increases more than demand.
9. Demand and supply both decrease but demand decreases more than supply.
10. Demand and supply both decrease but supply decreases more than demand.
11. Demand decreases but supply increases equally.
12. Demand increases but supply decreases more.
13. Demand increases but supply decreases less.
14. Demand increases but supply decreases equally.
15. Demand decreases but supply increases more.
16. Demand decreases but supply increases less.

CHAPTER VIII
Various Forms of Competition and Market Price

W E SHALL reserve a full discussion of imperfect competition for consideration in connection with cost of production, but it will be advisable now to point out some of the peculiarities of a market in which product differentiation exists.

Market Price Under Pure Competition

In a purely competitive market,[1] buyers will have no preferences between sellers except as to prices charged. Any seller who chooses to cut his price below that of the others could attract all of the buyers to himself. However, even if his reservation price should be below the market price, he will have no inducement to drop his own price below that of the market since it is one of the conditions of pure competition that any one individual seller can dispose of his entire stock without depressing the market price. As we have seen in the last chapter, sellers take advantage of the competition between buyers to secure the highest price that they can; buyers take advantage of the competition between sellers to secure the lowest price that they can. Movements in the supply curve will occur only as all, or a great number, of sellers alter their reservation prices;

---

[1] Chamberlin, E., *The Theory of Monopolistic Competition*, pp. 16 ff., Harvard University Press, 1934.

movements in the demand curve will take place only as all, or a great number, of buyers change their minds as to the amounts they would be willing to take at various prices. Inelasticity of demand will be an important factor in causing market price to fall rapidly only as a large number of sellers increase the amounts which they offer for sale. As far as any individual seller *acting alone* is concerned, he may take it for granted that demand is perfectly elastic for all that he cares to offer for sale *at the existing market price*. In short, under pure competition, any seller who puts his reservation price above the market price will sell nothing at all; on the other hand, since his product is identical with that of the marginal sellers, there is no need for him to accept a lower price than all other sellers are willing to take.

Market Price Under Monopolistic Competition [2]

In the market for a commodity that is subject to product differentiation, a very different situation exists. Competition is no longer purely on a price basis. Buyers are now buying a combination of the physical product and the "services" which go with it (location of store, packaging, trade-mark, personality of salespeople, and so on). If we take an assumed market price for the standardized product as a point of departure for the purpose of measurement, we find that different buyers are willing to pay various prices above the assumed base, depending on the estimate that they have of the value of the services of the dealer selling the differentiated product. Furthermore, as between two differentiated products (that are very close but imperfect substitutes for each other) some buyers will prefer the product sold by dealer A to that of dealer B if both are

---

[2] Note that while we have paid some attention to the differentiation based on persuasive selling, most of the conclusions of this chapter would still be valid for a perfect *market* with differentiated products. Even with perfect knowledge on the part of buyers, they may still have "a scale of preferences" between differentiated products.

offered at the same price; others who consider A's product much better than that of B will be willing to buy it even at a higher price. The amount of difference which these buyers will be willing to pay in order to buy from A rather than from B will vary from one buyer to another, depending on their individual estimates of the superiority of A as a dealer. At the same time there will be a different group of buyers who consider B's product to be superior to that of A. Some of these will buy from B rather than from A if both A and B are charging the same price, and others will be willing to pay various higher prices in order to trade with B rather than with A. Still another group of buyers may be entirely indifferent as to A and B. Whichever dealer is selling at the lower price will get their business; and if both dealers are selling at the same price, it will be a matter of chance with which dealer they trade. It should be noted that these differences between the two products need not be real differences subject to any sort of exact measurement. All that is necessary for them to affect the demand curve is that they create a preference in the mind of a buyer, whether such preference is logical or not.

Let us take a specific example. Which is the better motor car, Ford or Chevrolet, and exactly how much more is the better one worth in terms of dollars and cents? If the reader will go to the Ford dealer, the latter will gladly supply him with a long list of features in which the Ford is alleged to be superior; and if he will go to the Chevrolet dealer, he will be supplied with a similarly long list of features in which the Chevrolet is said to excel. Even two automotive engineers might be in disagreement as to the relative mechanical merits of the two cars, since it is not only a question of the merits of each feature in itself (six cylinders versus eight cylinders; different springs; oil and gas consumption, and so on), but there is also a question as to the importance to be attached to each feature in making a final comparison between the cars as a whole. Even if the two engineers were in agreement as to the relative merits of the two cars, they might find it a difficult task to decide what the difference was worth in dollars and cents. In influencing the demand for cars, however, it is not the absolute truth or falsity of the dealers' claims that is important so much as the way in which these claims *impress the minds of the different buyers.* Even if the mechanical merits of each feature could be objectively established, the different features would still be of different importance in the minds of various buyers. For instance, a man who plans to drive only 5,000 miles a year will not attach as great importance to low gasoline consumption as a man who will drive 50,000 miles; but he might attach much greater importance to the ability of the motor to start readily after long idleness in cold weather. When it comes to features of design and appearance, the preference for one car over the other will be entirely a matter of individual taste. Tall, thin men will be concerned about leg room; short, fat men will want wide seats. Features of appearance that may be considered beautiful by one buyer may appear cheap and ugly to another. Enough has been said to indicate that there will be one group of buyers who consider Fords better than Chevrolets and who would buy Fords if they had to pay more for them. The actual differences which buyers in the group would be willing to pay for a Ford, rather than buy a Chevrolet, will vary with the mental estimate of each individual as to the superiority of the Ford. There will be another group of buyers who will prefer Chevrolets, and different individuals in this group will be willing to pay various higher prices for a Chevrolet than for a Ford.

Buyers can be induced to leave one of these groups and to buy the car that they do not prefer only as the difference in price between the two cars is greater than the difference in value between the two which exists in the mind of the buyer. This, then, constitutes an important difference between price-making by individual sellers under product differentiation and under pure competition. For, as we have said, under pure competition any seller who offers a lower price than his rivals will attract all the buyers to himself. Under pure competition the demand curve for the product of the individual seller is perfectly elastic at the market price. Under product differentiation the demand curve for the product of the individual *will be less than perfectly elastic at any price*. This will have an important bearing on the reservation prices which sellers will charge.

Under pure competition, we saw that each seller set his reservation price and then was able to obtain as much above this as the market was willing to pay, the actual market price being fixed at the reservation prices of the marginal sellers. Under product differentiation, the reservation price becomes the actual price at which the goods are sold.[3] That is, the seller sets a price on his product, then the buyers decide how much they will buy at that price. Instead of being able to sell all or as much of his product as he wishes at the existing market price (as would have been the case under pure competition), the seller is now faced with the fact that the price which he sets will determine the amount that he individually can sell. The seller of a differentiated product is really a monopolist in the determination of his own price; but the existence of a very close substitute for his product exerts a very sharp limitation on the amount which he can sell at any given price he decides to set.

If two differentiated products are close substitutes for each other, we can draw up a complete demand schedule for one of them only if we assume that the price of the other remains fixed and will not change during the period for which the demand schedule is constructed. Thus, if we assume a price of

----

[3] The reservation price is also likely to be higher than under pure competition, since under monopolistic competition the seller will take declining marginal revenue into account.

$700.00 for the Chevrolet Tudor Sedan, we might draw up a schedule of the number of Ford Tudor Sedans which could be sold at various prices ranging from $800.00 down to $500.00 (assuming, of course, that we can read the buyers' minds). As the price of the Ford is set lower, each price from $800.00 on down will attract more buyers away from Chevrolet, since the difference in price between the two cars acts to overbalance the difference in estimate of value which exists in the individual buyers' minds. As the price of the Ford drops, not only will more buyers be attracted away from Chevrolet, but a new source of demand will appear. That is, there will be some buyers who would not have bought either car at the previous higher price who now begin to feel that at various lower prices they can afford to buy a car. If we were attempting to draw a demand schedule for Chevrolets, we should have to reverse the above process and assume a fixed price for the Ford.

Now let us assume that Mr. Henry Ford has given you the job of determining the best possible price at which he can dispose of all or a part of the cars he happens to have on hand; let us say that you are trying to get rid of the remaining cars of this year's model before the new model comes out. Disregarding the cost of production, you are to decide at what price the number of cars sold times the price per car will yield the greatest gross income. Let us see what your problem would be.

Determination of Market Price of a Differentiated Product

First, to make the problem as easy as possible, we will assume as we did above that the price of Chevrolet will stay fixed at $700.00 and that you are able to read the buyers' minds and to draw up the true demand schedule based on that assumption. Now then, starting at $800.00, each possible price $5.00 lower that you might set will attract more buyers away from Chevrolet, plus new ones, and enable you to sell more Fords.

On the other hand, each $5.00 decline in price will mean a loss of $5.00 per car on all the Fords that buyers would have bought anyway at the next higher price. What will be the best price to set? You would solve this problem by finding the price at which marginal revenue was equal to zero (see pages 85 and 86)—that is, the price at which the gain in revenue occasioned by selling more cars would be just exactly balanced by the loss in revenue occasioned by accepting a lower price on the other cars which could have been sold at the next higher price. If we were able to take our assumptions for granted, the problem would be relatively easy.

In actual practice you would not dare to make these assumptions.[4] If the price which you set according to the above principles should happen to be one that would draw a large number of buyers away from Chevrolet, there is no reason why you should expect the Chevrolet manufacturer to keep his price at $700.00 and stand idly by while you take customers away from him. He would most likely retaliate by cutting his own price in order to retain these customers. In this event you might find yourself selling no more cars, or only a very few more, at a lower price, than you could have sold at a higher price, and the loss in revenue on the cars which you do sell will be a dead loss uncompensated for by any gain in volume of sales. The only factor that might deter Chevrolet from making such a cut would be the fear that you might fight back by cutting your price still further, and the distaste which the Chevrolet Company might have for engaging in a costly "price war."

There may be, however, a price that you might hit upon, which, although it would take some business away from Chevrolet, would not take away enough to make it worth their

---

[4] Particularly because this is a situation of duopoly as well as product differentiation.

while to cut their price to meet yours. That is, if the price which you happen to set should take away from them only one or two thousand buyers, they might be willing to lose these buyers rather than cut their price $10.00 per car if they believe that they can still sell 100,000 Chevrolets at the old figure of $700.00.

The achievement of such a price might be much more feasible in the field of low-priced cars than would appear at first sight. For the purpose of simplicity, we have been tacitly assuming above that there was merely a two-sided competition between these two cars. But actually, of course, Plymouth, Dodge, DeSoto, Pontiac, and others will be competing at various price differences. Consequently, if the increased business which you do at a certain low price is drawn somewhat equally from all of them, the loss to any one firm might be so negligible that they would not care to retaliate by cutting their prices. On the other hand, should you appear to be able to sell a very great number of cars at a low price, you have no assurance that one or all of them will not try to imitate you and thus cut into your volume of sales.

Now, if you wish to keep your job with Mr. Ford very long, there is another factor which you must take into consideration. We have been assuming that you are trying to dispose of as many of the remaining cars at the best possible price that you can before the new model comes on the market. But you cannot afford to neglect the fact that the price you set on the remaining cars may have a very important influence on next year's market for Fords. If, by setting a low price on this year's cars, you can sell more of them to people who would not otherwise have bought Fords at all, this may be all right. But if this low price merely induces some persons to buy Fords now who would otherwise have waited and bought the new model next year at presumably a higher price, the gain will not be nearly so great. It might prove to be the case that you would have been better off selling fewer of the present models at a higher price and thus not decrease next year's business.

Another factor enters in this same connection. If you make a regular practice of drastic price cuts at the year's end, a large number of buyers may decide that it is to their advantage to wait for these low prices, and you will not sell very many cars at all at the full new car price. This is an example of negative time preference in buying. See the chapter on interest.

Finally, we must remove one other assumption. We assumed at the start that you were able to draw an accurate demand schedule, provided the prices of other cars remained fixed. Of course, this will not be the case. You can assume with reasonable certainty that you will sell more cars at a lower price than at a higher price, but exactly how many more you can discover only by experience. Furthermore, the experience of one year will be only the roughest and most inaccurate guide as to what would happen another year. If you lower your price, only to find that your sales are not so great as you anticipated, it will not ordinarily be possible to restore your price and still sell the same amount that you could have sold had you held to the higher price in the first place. The points on a demand curve are alternative, not successive. You will be still less able to raise your price again if a competitor has cut his price to meet your reduction.

Peculiarities of Market Price of Differentiated Products

What may we conclude from all this discussion? First, that the elasticity of demand for a differentiated product is less than the elasticity for the individual seller under pure competition, because the various differentiated products are not perfect substitutes for one another. Second, that if there are only a few sellers, each will have to take into account the effect of his price policy on his competitors as well as the possibility of retaliation. Third, that the seller of a differentiated product must pay attention to the long-run effect of a temporary market price policy, while a purely competitive seller need not do so. Finally, that once a price has been established for a differentiated product which appears to yield a volume of sales that is at all satisfactory, the seller will be extremely reluctant to change such a price, since he does not know accurately what his sales would be at a different price, nor what retaliation might be expected from competitors.

The regular practice of department stores and other retail stores in holding "bargain sales" at cut-rate prices is no exception to the above rules, but rather a recognition of them. It will be noticed that the most extreme slashes in price are on clothing and other articles with a very important style factor; that is, goods which, if not sold this season, are not likely to be sold at all. Moreover, the extreme reluctance of many women to be seen in "last year's styles" is a reasonable assurance that the bargain sale this year will not materially injure next year's business. The statement that the store has "overbought" an article is often an ambiguous one. It is true, of course, that they bought more than they could sell at the original price which they placed on the article; but the real error may not have been in *buying* too much, but in *placing too high a price* on the article at the beginning so that they now have so much left on their hands that they are forced to "sacrifice" it to make room for other goods.

Usually stores are very careful to indicate in their advertising the reason for the "sale." This is done not only in an effort to convince the buyer that these actually are "bargains" but also to acquaint her with the fact that she need not expect to find these same low prices after the "sale" is over. It is thus hoped that sales resistance to higher prices on "regular-priced merchandise" will be overcome.

The practice of many grocery and other retail stores that handle a wide variety of goods of cutting prices on certain

standard articles as "price leaders" should not be confused
with ordinary price policy. It is the hope of the storekeeper
that these price leaders will attract people into the store who
will also buy other goods on which the price is not cut. Properly speaking, the use of price leaders is a form of advertising
and not a price policy. With some exceptions, competitors
usually do not try to compete on articles used as price leaders,
but they cut prices on different commodities as price leaders of
their own.

CHAPTER IX

Temporary or Short-Run Equilibrium of the Firm or Industry

IT WILL be remembered that in Chapter VII we identified the short-run period with plant and equipment already produced and in existence. We found that in the instantaneous or market supply period, cost of production was either ignored or, if considered, was considered in terms of anticipated future cost.

In the present chapter we are taking into consideration the possibility of increases or decreases in output to be achieved within the limits of plant and equipment already in existence. It is obvious that, where the individual seller is free to change his output (and such action will have an effect on his costs), he will consider costs in connection with the supply that he offers for sale.

Our first principle is: *each seller, if not deterred by other considerations, will endeavor to adjust his output to that point at which total revenue will exceed total costs by the greatest possible amount, or at which losses are smallest.* In other words, we are saying that each seller will try to obtain the greatest possible net returns. The "other considerations" in the qualifying phrase might be fear of government interference if too high a price is charged, or fear of attracting new competitors into the field. However, when the seller does take these other considerations into account, he is merely deciding

126

that a lower price may yield a greater return in the long run than a higher price which yields a greater net return for a short time but brings about the consequences of government regulation or increased competition. If we bear this in mind, we may safely drop the qualifying phrase.

Notice that there is no difference in *motive* here between the purely competitive seller and the monopolist; both attempt to gain maximum profits. (We shall find that, under certain circumstances of pure competition, the *attempt* of each seller to obtain maximum profits actually *results* in zero profits or a loss for all, but this is due to a difference in *circumstances* and not to a difference in *motive* between monopolists and competitors.)

Our second principle follows naturally from the first: *the individual firm will be in equilibrium with respect to output at the point of maximum net returns.* If a given firm should discover that by either expanding or contracting its output it could make a larger return, the firm would be motivated to expand or contract as the case might require. Equilibrium will exist only at that point where there is no motive to expand or contract, that is, at the point of maximum net profits (which might be zero or a minimum loss, as indicated above).

For our next two principles we must turn our attention to the industry as a whole. We may define an industry as a group of firms producing a homogeneous commodity or a group of commodities that are close substitutes for each other. *If entry to and egress from an industry are unimpeded, a rate of profit above that which is being made in other industries having similar risks will tend to attract new firms to enter the industry; conversely a rate of profit below that which is being made in other industries will encourage firms to leave it.*

Combining the above principles, we arrive at the test for equilibrium in an industry. *An industry will be in equilibrium when there is no motive for the number of firms to be increased or decreased and no motive for the existing firms to expand or to contract their total output.*[1]

Opportunity Cost

Now, let us assume that we know the demand curve for the product of a particular firm. If we are able to discover the laws which govern production costs for various amounts of output, we shall be able to determine the point of maximum net returns. Before we go further, we must define what we mean by cost of production. *The cost of production of any unit of a commodity is the value of the factors of production used in producing that unit. The value of these factors of production is measured by the best alternative use to which they might have been put had this particular unit of the commodity not been produced.*[2]

The working of this principle can be easily seen in the case of a self-sufficing farmer who is producing in order to consume the products himself. If he uses a certain piece of land and a certain amount of labor in growing corn which might otherwise have been used to grow tomatoes, the cost to him of the number of bushels of corn that he harvests is the number of bushels of tomatoes that he might have obtained, assuming that raising tomatoes would have been the best alternative use for the amount of land and labor needed to grow the corn. This is also the only sense in which we can speak of a *social cost* of production, and would be the principle on which a communist society would have to allocate its resources. Thus, if the rulers of Russia decide to use a certain amount of labor and materials in making airplane motors which might

---

[1] There is always a motive for each firm to desire to see the *other* firms reduce output or leave the business, but whether this motive results in attempted action depends upon other conditions which are discussed elsewhere.

[2] See Henderson, H. D., *Supply and Demand*, p. 94, Harcourt, Brace & Co., New York, 1922.

otherwise have been used in making tractor motors, the cost of the airplane motors to the Russian people will be the number of tractor motors that they might have had. Whether the welfare of the Russian people will be greater with more airplanes and less tractors is a question to which it is not easy to find the answer, and we will not try to do so here.

What we are interested in immediately is the influence of costs in regulating output in an economy based on money and exchange. In such a society it is the money costs of production to which we must pay attention. *The money costs of production of a unit of any commodity is the amount of money necessary to induce the factors of production to be devoted to this particular task rather than to seek employment elsewhere.* These costs have been called, very properly, *opportunity costs.* They are the money which the factors of production must be capable of earning in one firm or one industry in order to induce their continued use in that firm or industry rather than to transfer to another firm or industry. Thus, if I am an automobile manufacturer and wish to make 100 more cars a day, I must pay the necessary number of mechanics a sufficient wage to induce them to work for me rather than for the airplane factory across the street. The fact that both the airplane factory and I may be paying the same wages should not confuse the reader, because, if I were not hiring these men, they would be competing for jobs with the men now employed by the airplane factory, and the airplane factory would then be able to hire these men and the men they now employ at a lower rate of wages than they are now paying. If the demand for automobiles should increase again while the demand for airplanes remained unchanged, I would be able to offer a still higher wage to attract more men away from the airplane factory. The airplane factory would then have to raise wages to meet my increase in order to keep any men at all. The airplane manufacturer will not be able to hire so many men as before, however, since, with a higher cost, if he charges higher prices for airplanes, he will not be able to sell so many.

This principle of opportunity costs applies to all factors of production and to all kinds of businesses. Thus, if I wish to set up a shoe store in a certain corner building, I must pay the owner a sufficient rent to induce him to lease it to me rather than to someone else who might be eager to start a grocery store or a haberdashery in the same location. Similarly, if I wish to borrow money to buy a stock of shoes for the store, I will have to pay a rate of interest which will be sufficient to induce the bank to loan the money to me rather than to someone else.

Opportunity costs are not always cash expenditures. For example, if I am managing my own business and wish to fig- ure my costs properly, I must charge as one of the costs of doing business the wages I might have obtained working as a hired manager for someone else. It is true that I do not have to pay out any money to anyone else because of this cost; but if, on that account, I do not consider it a cost, I am only de- ceiving myself. Let us suppose I am running a corner grocery for myself, but I could, if I wished, have a job as manager of a chain store at $2,000.00 a year. At the end of a year's busi- ness, after deducting from my receipts all costs except my wages of management, I find $1,500.00 left over which I might be tempted to call a profit. Actually, I have had a net loss of $500.00 in doing business for myself rather than working for the chain store. In terms of the illustration, in running my own business I have sacrificed the opportunity of making $2,000.00 working for someone else. This same way of figur- ing must be applied to all costs.[3]   If I am using my own money

---

[3] Except in filing income tax returns, where you must be prepared to abide by arbitrary rules or to fight a court action against the Treasury Department. Where the result will yield more tax reserve, the Treasury Department often recognizes opportunity cost. For example, they count as income the rental value of your home if you own it and live in it yourself.

in my own business, I must figure as a cost the interest I might have received if I had loaned it to someone else or invested it in stocks or bonds.   Similarly, if I own my own store building, I must figure as a cost the rent which I might have received if I had leased it out to someone else.

For the present part of our discussion of costs we must make a very important assumption.   We shall assume that no new inventions or innovations[4] take place.   Thus, for the moment, we are not concerned with what might happen to costs should a new, more efficient machine or process be discovered.   Nor are we now interested in tracing the historical movement of costs in the past as improvements have been made in the productive process.   What we are trying to do is to isolate the effects of changes in output of a firm or an industry, as the case may be.   The question we are asking is: What costs will be associated with different amounts of output, using methods of production which are already known?   Any change in method that occurs will be only such change as is occasioned by a different amount of output.   For example, picks and shovels are known and in existence, and so are steamshovels. Whether it will cost less to use one or the other will depend largely upon the size and the number of holes we wish to dig.

Fixed and Variable Costs

In the short run there are two main types of costs, *fixed costs* and *variable costs*.   Fixed costs are those which remain constant as a *total* over a considerable range of output.   Some fixed costs are fixed for years (for example, interest charges on bond and mortgage indebtedness; depreciation through obsolescence); others are fixed over months (salaries of superintendents and foremen); still others are fixed for at least parts of the plant (heating and lighting and so on).   These costs are often

---

[4] See Schumpeter, J. A., *The Theory of Economic Development*, pp. 66 ff., Harvard University Press, 1934.

called *overhead costs* by businessmen. It will be obvious that these costs will remain fixed only over certain ranges of output. For instance, if we wished to expand output by a large amount, it would be necessary to hire more foremen, and hence the total item for wages for foremen would not remain absolutely constant. However, as long as the same number of foremen are hired, their total wages will remain fixed regardless of increases or decreases in the number of units produced by the firm.

Variable costs are those which vary directly as a *total* with the number of units produced. Common examples of variable costs are the cost of raw materials and of the labor used directly in the manufacture of a product.

While we have said that fixed costs will remain constant *as a total* over a large range of output, *average fixed costs* per unit of product will decrease steadily with each increase in the number of units produced with the same fixed costs.[5] Thus, if with a certain fixed cost we produce 10 units of a commodity, 1/10 of the total fixed cost will have to be assigned to each unit produced; whereas, if with the same fixed cost we produce 100 units, each unit would then have to bear only 1/100 of the overhead cost. If fixed costs were the only costs to consider, and if it were possible to produce an infinite amount of the product with the same sized plant and investment, average costs per unit of product would always be lower whenever the volume of output increased.

The Law of Nonproportional Outputs

But there is the matter of variable costs to consider. Here we encounter the *law of nonproportional outputs*[6] which is

---

[5] See *Production Organization* by Black, John D., and Black, A. G., Henry Holt & Co., New York, 1929, for a more thorough discussion of least cost combinations. The article, "On the Law of Variable Proportions," by Cassels, John M., in *Explorations In Economics,* McGraw-Hill Book Co., New York, 1936, is also recommended.

[6] This law is more usually called the *Law of diminishing returns*. The change of terminology is used to avoid the confusion which the beginning student usually has with the terms *diminishing returns, diminishing utility,* and *maximum net returns.*

stated: *if one or more factors of production are held constant and one or more other factors are allowed to vary in amount, the total output will not vary in continuous proportion to the amount of variable factors employed.* This law might also be stated as follows: If one or more factors of production are held constant, and one or more other factors are allowed to vary in amount, the output per unit of variable factor will not continue to remain constant, but will increase, reach a maximum, and then decrease.

An example may help to illustrate how this law works. Let us suppose that we have a small factory for making brass ashtrays, that the factory is equipped with five stamping machines, and that we wish to find the best number of men to use with these machines. If we started out experimentally, adding one man at a time, the results might be as follows:

INPUTS		Daily Output of Ashtrays	Marginal Physical Product per Man Day	Daily Output per Machine	Output per Man Day	
Machines	Man Days					
5	1	91	91	18.2	91	
5	2	200	109	40.0	100	
5	3	324	124	64.8	108	Range of increasing proportional output per man
5	4	460	136	92.0	115	
5	5	605	145	121.0	121	
5	6	756	151	151.2	126	
5	7	910	154	182.0	130	
5	8	1064	154	212.8	133	
5	9	1215	151	243.0	135	
5	10	1360	145	272.0	136	
5	11	1496	136	299.2	136	
5	12	1620	124	324.0	135	Range of decreasing proportional output per man
5	13	1729	109	324.5	133	
5	14	1820	91	364.0	130	
5	15	1890	70	378.0	126	
5	16	1936	46	387.2	121	
5	17	1955	19	391.0	115	
5	18	1944	−11	388.8	108	Absolute decline of output
5	19	1900	−44	380.0	100	

The term *nonproportional* has also the advantage of referring to the entire output curve and not merely to the diminishing part of it. It also has reference to the cause of varying output, namely, the use of factors of production in other than optimum proportion.

In the preceding table, the point between which the 10th and 11th man is added gives the greatest output per man. This point would be called *the point of maximum efficiency of labor,* assuming that the number of machines remains fixed at five. Whatever the wages may be, this point will represent the lowest labor cost per unit of output if wages are the same for each man hired.

While the output per man falls steadily after the addition of the 11th man, the output per machine increases up to the point at which the 17th man is added. This point is the point of maximum efficiency of machines. From this point on we could obtain a greater product only by adding *both* more men and more machines. As long as the number of machines is held at five, this point will give us the lowest machine cost per unit of output.

Least Cost Combinations

Which point will give us the least total cost of both men and machines per unit of output? Is it the point of maximum efficiency of men, or the point of maximum efficiency of machines, or is it some point between the two? We *cannot* answer this question unless we know both the wages of the men and the number of dollars per day that it costs to run each machine. For example, let us assume that wages are $3.00 per man per day, and that it costs $8.00 per day to run each machine (depreciation, interest charges, and so forth). The physical output of ashtrays associated with each combination of machine and man days is taken from the previous table. The costs for the part of the table in which we are interested would then be:

Number of Machines	Number of Man Days	Total Machine Cost	Total Labor Cost	Output of Ashtrays	Machine Cost per Unit of Output	Labor Cost per Unit of Output	Cost of Both per Unit of Output
5.....	10	$40	$30	1360	.0294	.0221	$0.0515
5.....	11	40	33	1496	.0267	.0221	0.0488

Number of Machines	Number of Man Days	Total Machine Cost	Total Labor Cost	Output of Ashtrays	Machine Cost per Unit of Output	Labor Cost per Unit of Output	Cost of Both per Unit of Output
5.....	12	40	36	1620	.0247	.0222	0.0469
5.....	13	40	39	1729	.0231	.0226	0.0457
5.....	14	40	42	1820	.0220	.0231	0.0451
5.....	15	40	45	1890	.0212	.0238	0.0450*
5.....	16	40	48	1936	.0207	.0248	0.0455
5.....	17	40	51	1955	.0205	.0260	0.0465

* Least cost combination.

We find that the least cost combination, under these circumstances, is that of five machines and fifteen men, the total man and machine cost per ashtray being $0.0450. Now let us see what happens if the machine cost per day is kept at $8.00 while the wages per man rise to $4.00 per day:

Number of Machines	Number of Man Days	Total Machine Cost	Total Labor Cost	Output	Machine Cost per Unit of Output	Labor Cost per Unit of Output	Machine and Labor Cost per Unit of Output
5.....	10	$40	$40	1360	.0294	.0294	$0.0588
5.....	11	40	44	1496	.0267	.0294	0.0561
5.....	12	40	48	1620	.0247	.0296	0.0543
5.....	13	40	52	1729	.0231	.0301	0.0532
5.....	14	40	56	1820	.0220	.0308	0.0528*
5.....	15	40	60	1890	.0212	.0317	0.0529
5.....	16	40	64	1936	.0207	.0331	0.0538
5.....	17	40	68	1955	.0205	.0348	0.0553

* Least cost combination.

We now find that with machine costs of $8.00 each per day and labor cost of $4.00 per man per day, the least cost combination is that of five machines and fourteen men. We can thus say that the rise in the price of labor has decreased the ratio of men to machines, or that it has increased the ratio of machines to men, in the least cost combination.

On the other hand, an increase in the cost of machines, say to $15.00 or $20.00 each per day, would result in a least cost combination of more men per machine if the wages remained unchanged. The rate at which one factor of production will be substituted for another in response to a change in their relative prices is called the *elasticity of substitution of the factors*.

It should be noted that we could just as well have conducted our experiment by holding the number of men constant at a certain figure and varying the number of machines. (A further application will be found in a later chapter.)

Notice that so far we have been considering only two of the cost elements involved—men and machines. To make a thorough cost experiment, we should have to try varying the number of both men and machines (in their least cost proportion) while keeping the size of the building constant; we might vary the number of foremen used with a fixed number of men and machines; or we might vary the horsepower of the motors used on the machines, and so on. If we wished to expand output by any great amount, we should have to consider the effect upon costs of varying the size of the building as well as the other elements.

Whether a given cost element will be considered as a fixed cost or as a variable cost depends upon the amount of change in output which is under consideration. Thus, for a very small increase in output it might be desirable to hire one or two more men rather than to purchase another machine. For a somewhat larger output, it might give lower costs to increase the number of both men and machines without increasing the size of the factory building. For a still larger output, lowest costs might be achieved only by increasing the size of the factory as well.

Adjustment of Output to Selling Price

However, before going into the question of varying the size of the factory, let us see how output is adjusted to selling price with a given set of cost conditions and a fixed size of plant. We can see this best by means of an example and a diagram. Let us suppose that you have a small factory for making lamps and that your costs are given by the table that appears on the following page.

In the table, column 1 represents various possible amounts
of output. Column 2 represents total fixed costs per day (assuming $9,600.00 annual fixed charges and 300 working days
in the year). Total fixed cost will remain unchanged as long
as we keep the same investment and overhead expense (as it

DAILY COST SCHEDULE FOR SMALL FACTORY

(1)	(2)	(3)	(4)	(5)	(6)	(7)	(8)
Output: No. of Units	Total Fixed Costs	Average Fixed Costs	Total Variable Costs	Average Variable Costs	Total of All Costs	Average Total Unit Cost	Marginal Cost
1	$32.00	$32.00	$ 7.20	$ 7.20	$39.20	$39.20	....
2	32.00	16.00	12.90	6.45	44.90	22.45	$ 5.70
3	32.00	10.67	17.40	5.80	49.40	16.47	4.50
4	32.00	8.00	21.00	5.25	53.00	13.25	3.60
5	32.00	6.40	24.00	4.80	56.00	11.20	3.00
6	32.00	5.33	26.70	4.45	58.70	9.78	2.70
7	32.00	4.57	29.40	4.20	61.40	8.77	2.70
8	32.00	4.00	32.40	4.05	64.40	8.05	3.00
9	32.00	3.55	36.00	4.00	68.00	7.55	3.60
10	32.00	3.20	40.50	4.05	72.50	7.25	4.50
11	32.00	2.90	46.20	4.20	78.20	7.10	5.70
12	32.00	2.67	53.40	4.45	85.40	7.12	7.20
13	32.00	2.46	62.40	4.80	94.40	7.26	9.00
14	32.00	2.28	73.50	5.25	105.50	7.53	11.10
15	32.00	2.13	87.00	5.80	119.00	7.93	13.50
16	32.00	2.00	103.20	6.45	135.20	8.45	16.20
17	32.00	1.88	122.40	7.20	154.40	9.08	19.20
18	32.00	1.78	144.90	8.05	176.90	9.83	22.50
19	32.00	1.68	171.00	9.00	203.00	10.68	26.10
20	32.00	1.60	201.00	10.05	233.00	11.65	30.00

is assumed that we do). Column 3 is derived by dividing
the items in column 2 by the items in column 1. It will be
noticed that if we could continue to increase output with the
same fixed cost, the items in column 3 would be constantly
decreasing, approaching but never quite reaching zero. Column 4 shows the amount of variable costs (labor, materials,
and so on) which we estimate or have found by experience
would be associated with each possible amount of output.

Column 5 is the result of column 4 divided by column 1, show-ing the variable cost per single lamp at each output. Column 6 represents column 2 plus column 4, showing the total of costs (fixed plus variable) of the entire amount produced at each output. Column 7 may be found either by dividing col-umn 6 by column 1, or by adding column 3 and column 5. It shows the total cost per lamp at each output. Column 8 is obtained by moving down column 6, stopping at each item,

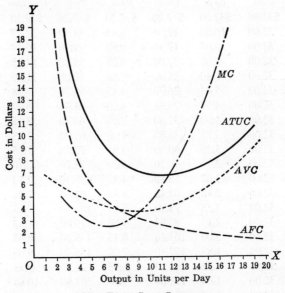

The Four Cost Curves.

and subtracting the preceding item from it. *Marginal cost* (column 8) *is the addition to total cost* made necessary by producing the *last additional unit* at each output. Marginal cost may also be found from the table by moving down column 4, stopping at each item, and subtracting the preceding item from it. This shows that marginal cost is dependent on *total variable cost* alone and *not* on fixed cost, so long as total fixed costs remain unchanged.

The diagram is drawn from the figures in the table. In the diagram, *AFC,* the broken line, is average fixed costs; *AVC,* the dotted line, is average variable costs; *ATUC,* the solid line, is average total unit costs.

MC, the dash-dot line, is marginal cost. At each output, *MC* shows the amount of increase in total cost which is necessary to produce the last unit of output.

As long as marginal cost lies below average variable cost, average variable cost will continue to decline, and marginal cost will intersect average variable cost either at its lowest point or between the lowest cost unit and the next higher unit. If the units are finite, the intersection will be one half-unit to the right of the low point of the average curve.

As soon as marginal cost crosses average variable cost, average variable cost will start to rise. Marginal cost will always rise more rapidly than average variable cost, since marginal cost represents the additional cost necessary to produce the last unit, whereas in average variable cost this addition is divided among all the units. The same relations exist between marginal cost and average total unit cost; that is, marginal cost will intersect both curves at approximately their lowest points.[7]

If the table and the diagram represent the cost conditions of your lamp factory, what will be the best output for you to produce? The unthinking reader will look at the

---

[7] If the units are chosen sufficiently small, the marginal curve and the average curves must intersect at exactly the lowest points on the two average curves. By calculus:

Let x = output, y = average variable cost, and K = total fixed cost.

Total variable cost = $F(xy)$.

(1) Marginal cost = $\dfrac{d}{dx}(xy)$

$= y + x\,\dfrac{dy}{dx}$, and marginal cost = average cost

when $x\,\dfrac{dy}{dx} = 0$; that is, when average cost is at minimum.

schedule or curve of average total unit costs and say immediately, "eleven units, at which output the cost will be $7.10, the point of lowest total unit cost." However, we must remember that we are not interested in the greatest profit, or least loss, per unit of product. What we are interested in is making the greatest possible amount of *total* net profit, or the least amount of *total* net loss on the output we produce. Therefore we cannot say what the best output would be until we also know the price at which each amount of output can be sold.

To take the simplest case first, let us assume that the lamp market is a purely competitive one. Under these circumstances, the demand for lamps made in this factory will be perfectly elastic, and marginal revenue and average revenue will coincide; that is, you may take it for granted that any amount between zero and the greatest possible output can be sold without causing the price to fall. Hence, for each additional unit, you get the same price and total revenue increases always by the price received for the additional unit—that is, marginal revenue is equal to price. Assuming, then, that changes in your output alone will not change the price, let us see what your output will be at various market prices.

In the first place, unless price is *at least equal* to average *variable* costs at some output, *no production will take place under pure competition in the short run except through the desire to*

Total of all costs $= F(xy) + K$

Marginal cost $= \dfrac{d}{dx} [F(xy) + K]$

$\qquad\qquad = \dfrac{d}{dx} (xy)$ which is the same as (1) above.

If $\dfrac{K}{x}$, average fixed cost, is added to y, then marginal cost will intersect

the curve $y + \dfrac{K}{x}$, average total unit cost, at its lowest point also.

maintain a force of key employees, and if there is a future prospect of higher prices or lower costs. In our example, if the price were $3.60 and nine units were produced, the total costs would be $68.00 and the total revenue ($3.60 times 9) would be $32.40, leaving a total net loss of $35.60. At any other output, if the price is $3.60, the loss will be greater than $35.60. However, if the business is shut down completely, the loss would be only the fixed charges of $32.00 per day. Of course, as we showed in the last chapter, if there were some lamps on hand already completed, it might be advisable to take what you could get for them. But if they were only partly completed, the price would have to be above the additional cost necessary to complete them in order to induce you to finish their production. (This is the unfortunate situation in which farmers sometimes find themselves when the price of fruit will not cover even the cost of picking, and the fruit is allowed to rot on the trees.)

Now let us be a little less gloomy and assume a price of $4.50. What will be the best output at that price? Our governing principle is: *At any price above minimum average variable cost, the output at which marginal revenue is equal to marginal cost will be the point of least total net loss.* Since we have assumed perfectly elastic demand, marginal revenue is the same as price, $4.50. Looking down column 8 of our table, we find a marginal cost of $4.50 at the output of 10 units. At this output, total revenue at a price of $4.50 would be $45.00; looking down column 6, we find total cost would be $72.50, leaving a net loss of $27.50. This is the point of least loss, if the price is $4.50. At any other output the loss would be greater. Would you shut down? No, because, if we assume that you could save none of your fixed costs by shutting down completely, then you would be better off producing ten units at this price than by shutting down. Your total revenue covers all your variable costs and leaves $4.50 over to go to fixed costs.

While you might continue to produce for some time at a price of $4.50 under these cost conditions, this is not for you a long-run equilibrium price; this is not a price which will encourage you to continue in business indefinitely, producing the same amount. As your plant and machinery wear out, you will not be encouraged to buy new machines to replace them, but will rather invest your money somewhere else where it promises to earn at least a normal rate of interest. Unless something happens to raise the price (for instance, if a number of your competitors quit the business and so decrease supply; or demand increases), or unless something happens to lower costs, you will either leave the business voluntarily or, in the long run, be forced out through bankruptcy. That is why we say that this is not a long-run equilibrium price. *Hope* that the price might rise or that your costs will fall might encourage you to stay in business, operating at a loss, for a longer period of time than you would consider justified were you certain that present prices and costs would continue.

Now let us be really optimistic and assume some price above the cost of production, say, $9.00. What will be the optimum output at this price? Our guiding principle here is: *At any price above average total unit costs, the output at which marginal revenue is equal to marginal cost will be the point of maximum net profits.* The reason for this should be clearly understood: At any output less than this point, the addition to total revenue (marginal revenue) of a larger output would be greater than the addition to total cost (marginal cost) occasioned by the larger output; consequently, total net profits could be increased by expanding output. On the other hand, at any output beyond this point, marginal cost (the addition to total cost) of producing the last unit will be greater than marginal revenue (the addition to total revenue) occasioned by producing and selling the last unit; total net profits could then be increased by contracting output. Reading down column 8, we find that a marginal revenue of $9.00 would be equal to marginal cost at the output of 13 units. At this output, total revenue is $117.00 and total cost is $94.40, leaving a total net profit of $22.60. No other output would yield a greater net profit. The reader should note that this is true in spite of the fact that price would still be above cost at an output of 14 units. At 14 units, total revenue, with price $9.00, would be $126.00, and total cost would be $105.50, leaving a net profit of only $20.50. If we assume that *no other sized plant* would have lower costs, this *individual firm* at a price of $9.00 would be in equilibrium at an output of 13 units.

While we have just said that the *individual firm* would be in equilibrium under these cost conditions and at this price and output, $9.00 would not be an equilibrium price for the *industry* if there were no obstacle to the entrance of new firms (one of the conditions of perfect competition). If any new firm that might start up would encounter the same cost conditions, a price of $9.00 which yielded a clear net profit of $22.60 per day, or $6,780.00 per year after all charges for interest and wages of management had been allowed, would be bound to attract new competitors into the industry. If the conditions of demand remained unchanged (one of the assumptions of long-run equilibrium), the greatly increased amount of product thrown on the market would force the price down. Where, then, will equilibrium for the industry be reached? *If there are no factors of production which are scarce in the industry or firm, and all firms have the same cost conditions, the industry will be in equilibrium at the point where price is equal to the minimum average total unit costs of each firm.* Any higher price would tend to encourage new firms to enter the industry; any lower price would tend to force some of the existing firms to leave it. (For the short run, the immediate effect of a price above minimum average total unit cost would be to cause existing firms to expand their output to the point where marginal revenue was equal to marginal cost; but such a price would yield abnormal profit to every firm in the industry, and an inducement is immediately set up for new firms to enter. Under pure competition, such a price could exist only for the length of time necessary for the existence of the profits to be recognized by others together with the length of time necessary to put a new firm into productive operation.)

So far we have been assuming, for simplicity, that the existing firms in an industry were all of optimum size. To bring our theory of costs closer to reality, we must now remove that assumption. In attempting to expand output with the same plant and equipment, we found that the chief source of increasing average variable costs was due to the influence of nonproportional returns, caused by attempting to apply more labor to a fixed amount of plant. Our lowest average total unit cost ($7.10) with this plant was at the output of eleven units. At this point, average variable cost was $4.20; average fixed cost $2.90. If the plant is not already at optimum size, we might find, for instance, that an addition to plant and equipment might make it possible to double this output at the same variable cost with an addition to total fixed costs of, let us say, only $12.00 per day. This would make average fixed costs ($44.00 ÷ 22) equal to $2.00, average variable cost equal to $4.20, and average total unit cost of $6.20. We could not say that this was a minimum cost for the larger plant unless we drew up the entire new cost schedule for the new cost conditions. However, we can clearly see that what we called equilibrium points for the individual firm above are equilibrium points only on the assumption that the firm is already at optimum size. Otherwise all that they show is what would be optimum outputs for the plant at its present size at various prices, and do not take account of the fact that it might be possible to achieve lower cost with a plant of a different size.

CHAPTER X

Long-Run Partial Equilibrium Under Pure Competition

WE DEFINE the long run as the *time necessary to achieve equilibrium within an industry*. We can be slightly more definite if we say that it is the time necessary to construct new plant and equipment; or, for plant and equipment to be disinvested (that is, to wear out and not be replaced). It is assumed that there is no change in production techniques and no new inventions. Under these conditions the supply and cost curves for an industry or firm will be identical if pure competition prevails.

The Planning Curve

Now, when a new firm is considering entering an industry, it is, of course, not burdened with any fixed plant or equipment, nor is it committed to a plant of any particular size. It is free to make its decision on the basis of what it considers will be the optimum size of plant. The cost curve that would confront such a firm before it starts has properly been called a *planning curve*.[1] Let us try to construct such a planning curve. The only element which might now truly be considered a fixed cost regardless of different possible plant sizes will be the wages of management necessary to induce the owner or

---

[1] Professor Schumpeter uses this term in classroom presentation. I am **not aware** that it has appeared in print elsewhere.

owners to go into the business at all on any scale, that is, their "opportunity" costs. Interest charges, maintenance costs, and the like will *become* fixed charges *after* the size of plant is decided upon and the plant is in operation. However, as long as the question is what size plant is to be adopted, the estimated amount of these charges will vary with each size of plant under

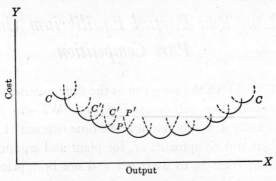

Diagram 1.—A Planning Curve.

consideration. The planning curves correspond to the ATUC curve on page 138, one curve for each possible size of plant. Such a curve would look like Diagram 1.

In Diagram 1, the small dotted curves such as $C'C'$ represent the cost conditions of each possible size of plant. The solid wavy curve CC represents the planning curve and shows the average total unit cost for each output with the size of plant best suited to that amount of output. The reason why this curve is wavy rather than smooth lies in the indivisibility of certain factors of production.[2] For example, we cannot add one half or one quarter of a machine to a plant. A machine which is capable of adding 1,000 units a year to total output might cost $500.00, meaning an addition to interest charges of $25.00 (at 5 per cent) and maintenance costs of, say, $20.00, adding a total of $45.00 to annual costs. If, then, at some one

---

[2] Sometimes called "lumpiness" of factors.

output it is desired to increase production by one more unit per year, to do so by adding a machine would mean a machine cost for that unit of $45.00. If we wished to increase output by 500 units, adding a machine to do so would mean a machine cost of only 9c per unit on the added units. Obviously, if only a small addition to output is desired, it will be better to work a smaller plant beyond its optimum capacity rather than enlarge the plant. Thus, in the diagram, although point P is on a rising part of the cost curve for one sized plant, to shift to a larger plant in order to produce only one or two more units would jump average costs up to point P' on the next cost curve. The point where it would just pay to shift to a larger plant is the point where one small curve intersects the next, that is, the point where average total unit cost of the smaller plant is just equal to that of the next larger plant. For the purposes of subsequent diagrams, however, we shall draw the planning curve CC as a smooth line, assuming that we are interested only in such large changes in output as to make the best use of the added facilities.

Decreasing and Increasing Costs

The reasons for the declining slope of CC are the *economies of large-scale production*. First, there is the fuller utilization of indivisible factors (in this case, the owner's services of management).[3] In addition, there are possibilities of better division of labor. For example, in a small factory, workers would all grind their own tools, wasting time whenever they went to the emery wheel. In a larger factory it would pay to hire one man to do nothing but grind tools while the others remain steadily at their machines. Specialization of workers increases efficiency, but becomes feasible only as output is large enough to employ workers full time at each task. The use of certain

---

[3] External economies may become internal whenever the firm is large enough.

kinds of machinery is also often feasible only with a large output. For instance, a conveyor system costing $200.00 per week to operate may be capable of replacing 20 laborers at $25.00 per week (a labor cost of $500.00). The machine cost of a fully utilized conveyor is then only two fifths of the labor cost for the same kind of work. But for a small factory which uses only four men at this kind of work at a labor cost of $100.00, it would not pay to install a conveyor. The same principle applies to hired executives of particular efficiency. It would not be good business to hire Alfred Sloane at his present salary to manage a small retail shop, but it might be advisable to pay this much or more to hire him to run the purchasing activities of a large-scale firm. Another economy of large-scale production might be the possibility of a lower price for raw materials when bought in carload lots. While decreases in cost of this sort are very great as between the smaller sized plants and the next larger ones, the fall in costs will not continue at the same rate as the plants become larger and larger.

If we continue to retain the assumption *that there are no scarce factors of production,* that is, that the factors of production are in perfectly elastic supply to the individual firm, the only factor that would operate to cause the cost curve to rise eventually as a larger sized plant is adopted would be the *diseconomies of large-scale management.* As the plant becomes larger and larger, the central managing authority is less and less able to give its attention to details. If any pretense of efficiency is to be maintained under these circumstances, more and more authority must be delegated to subordinate managers and foremen. But there are limits to which such authority can be delegated with success. If left entirely to itself, one department might increase its own efficiency at the expense of other departments and consequently at the expense of the general efficiency of the plant. If disputes are to be avoided, the central authority must exercise at least a coördinating function. However, each time a subordinate official must consult the central authority, he wastes time which he might have spent on his routine work; and there is, of course, a limit to the number of such questions that the central authority can handle. The usual solution to this problem is to set up rules for the guidance of subordinate officials. But the more specific the rules, the less they will fit the different situations which may arise and the more occasions there will be to consult the management. The more general the rules, the more probable will be failure in coördination, and the more dependence must be placed on the judgment of the subordinate officials. The point at which this influence toward increasing costs will tend to overcome other tendencies to decreasing costs will be different for different industries.

Conditions of Equilibrium Under Pure Competition

Under pure competition, so long as any individual firm is of less than optimum size, there will be no point of equilibrium for the industry. Any firm of less than optimum size can lower its costs by increasing its output. It will be able to sell a greater output by cutting its price just under competitors' prices, and thus, under pure competition, selling all of the product it wishes at the expense of the other firms. The other firms, in order to meet this competition, must lower their price, and in order to do so will expand their output to achieve lower costs. If the demand is not sufficient to take the full output of all the existing firms at their optimum size, some of the firms will be forced out of business, the business being divided up among the few firms that remain. The persistence of decreasing costs for the individual firm over a wide range of output is thus one of the forces tending toward oligopoly [4] or monopoly when the demand is not large enough to retain a large number of firms in competition at optimum output.

[4] See the chapter on "General Equilibrium under Monopolistic Competition."

If there are no scarce factors of production and no impediments to the entry of new firms, the industry will not be in equilibrium while existing firms are greater than optimum size. Even though all the existing firms might be content to continue at a price which was equal to marginal cost of the larger output, thus making a profit from the difference between price and average cost, new firms would be free to start plants of the optimum size and undersell the existing firms, forcing the existing firms to take a loss until they can contract their plants to the optimum size. If we draw up a long-run supply curve for the industry under these conditions, it will appear as follows:

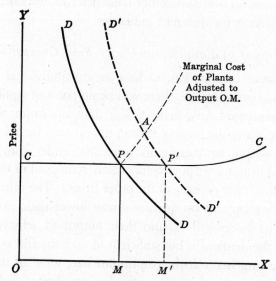

Diagram 2.—Increase in Demand Under Constant Costs.

In Diagram 2, *DD* is the demand or average revenue curve. *CC* is cost of production for the industry and is identical with long-run supply price. *PM* represents the equilibrium price, and *OM* the equilibrium output. A considerable portion of *CC* continues horizontal, representing the addition to the industry of more and more firms each producing at its optimum output and at minimum average total unit cost. The reason why the curve starts to turn upward after a while is that, although each firm is operating under identical cost conditions, as more and more firms are added to the industry, all would have to pay a higher price for raw materials or for labor so as to attract these factors away from other industries of increasing importance.*

Although *PM* is a long-run normal equilibrium price, there is no reason to expect market price to be equal to it at any given moment. The equilibrium price is the price that market price will reach if the same conditions of cost and the same conditions of demand persist long enough. Thus, in the diagram, if demand increased (*DD* would then shift to the right to *D'D'*), the increased demand would first be met by an expansion of output by existing plants until the higher marginal cost of the increased output equalled the higher price. Temporary market price might be at point *A,* but the tendency would be for new competing firms entering the industry to drive it down to the new equilibrium price of *P'M'* at the new equilibrium output of *OM'*. A permanent decrease in demand would first force all firms to sell below average total unit cost at the point of least loss until some were forced out of business and the new long-run price was approximated.

So far we have been assuming as a condition of constant cost that there were no scarce factors of production; that is, that the factors of production were in perfectly elastic supply to the industry. We must now remove that assumption. Obviously, the first units of factors to enter an industry will be those whose opportunity costs to the industry are lowest. Those owner-managers whose opportunities of earning wages of management are poorest in other industries will be most attracted to a particular industry. Or it may be those who are best in other industries but who find superior opportunity to exercise

---

* This means, however, that the industry has passed beyond the point of constant costs.

their talents in a new industry. Of laborers of a given grade of efficiency, those will be hired first away from other industries where their services are of least value to their present employers. Capital will be drawn first from other sources where it is earning the least return; the same will be true of land suitable for the type of enterprise in question. If buyers wish more of the product than can be supplied by the units of the factors with the lowest opportunity costs, they will have to pay a price which will be sufficient to attract the units of factors with the next higher opportunity costs into the industry.

But the units of the factors already in use will be able to command a price equal to that of the units with the higher opportunity costs. This difference between what a unit of a factor must be paid to retain it in the industry and the price it is able to get because of the necessity of paying higher prices to attract other units is sometimes called a *rent*. This will be more fully discussed in Chapter XIV.

If this type of rent is not considered as a cost of production,[5] then equilibrium will be reached when the price is equal to marginal cost of the lower-cost firms and to minimum average total unit cost (and to marginal cost) of the highest-cost firms which remain in the industry. These highest-cost firms will be the marginal firms, that is, the ones that are just induced to stay in the industry by the present price. These marginal firms will be the ones to leave the industry first if the price falls.

It should be noticed that these highest-cost firms are not necessarily the least efficient ones. For instance, it may be that

---

[5] It makes no difference in the determination of output whether this type of intra-industrial rent is considered as a cost or not. If the units of the scarce factor with low opportunity costs are owned by the owner of the business, the rent will be a part of the net return which he is trying to maximize, and he will produce up to the point where marginal revenue is equal to marginal cost (not including rent). If others own the units, and he has to pay rent for them, he will produce to the point where marginal revenue is equal to average cost (including rent). Marginal cost (not including rent) and average cost (including rent) are the same, under these conditions.

they have the most efficient managers, and hence managers
most capable of commanding a high wage in other industries
so that they will be the first to leave this industry if it does
not give them a return equal to what they could earn elsewhere.   The same would be true of land.   If the price of corn
drops, that land which will be withdrawn from corn production first will not necessarily be that which is worst suited to
corn production; it may be that which is best suited to
wheat production.

We are now prepared to sum up the conclusions we have
drawn: *Under pure competition, in the long run—*

(1) Price will have to be at least equal to minimum average
total unit cost at the optimum output for any firm which is
to remain in the industry.

(2) There will be no competitive equilibrium for the industry while any firm is producing under conditions of decreasing cost (that is, if any firm is less than optimum size, or,
if at optimum size, is producing less than the minimum average total unit cost output).

(3) There will be no competitive equilibrium if firms are
greater than optimum size, and if free entry to the industry
is possible for other firms under the same cost conditions.

(4) If there are no scarce factors, price will be exactly equal
to minimum average total unit cost, at optimum size, of all
firms in the industry.   Production is then under conditions
of constant cost as more firms are added.

(5) If there are scarce factors, giving rise to higher factor
prices as the industry expands, price will be equal to marginal
cost (not including rent) of the lower-cost firms, and will be
equal to minimum average total unit cost of the highest-cost
firm which it is necessary to attract into the industry to satisfy
the demand for the product.

(6) If rent of scarce factors is considered as a cost, price will

be equal to minimum average total unit cost of all firms. (See the discussion of rent in Chapter XIV.)

Notice that we have at least six "ifs" here. Failure of any one of them to be fulfilled may either prevent equilibrium or destroy pure competition, replacing it by monopolistic competition or oligopoly.

CHAPTER XI

Normal Price Under Monopoly and Monopolistic Competition[1]

I N THE last chapter we assumed, as the criterion of pure
competition, that the demand curve for the product of an
individual firm was perfectly elastic; that is, the individual
seller could take the market price for granted without fear
that expansions in his own individual output alone would
cause the price at which he could sell that output to fall.

Another concept of pure competition is the sale of a standardized product by a large number of small firms.

In modern economic society, however, the industries in
which such a situation exists or is even closely approximated
are fairly few, being confined mostly to the terminal markets
for agricultural products and raw materials. Two simple
tests, while not infallible, will help the reader to determine
whether the market for an industry is purely competitive or
not. In the first place, the prevalence of advertising by individual firms is presumptive evidence of monopolistic competition in the market for a product. If the market were purely
competitive, any firm could sell all that it wished at the existing market price and could take business away from any
and all competitors by the slightest drop in its price, so there
would be no need to advertise. The second test is the units

---

[1] The presentation here is also an adaptation of that in Chamberlin, Edward, *The
Theory of Monopolistic Competition*, Harvard University Press, 1935.

of value in which prices are quoted. Thus, in the grain markets, price changes are quoted in eighths of a cent a bushel, and in cotton and some other commodities quotations are in 100ths of a cent a pound. The natural inference is that buyers are responsive to these small differences in price and that one dealer can take business away from another by varying his price by these small fractions. In less purely competitive markets the different prices charged by different sellers will vary by much wider amounts. Thus, in the prices charged by different retail stores in a city, the differences may amount to several cents on low-priced articles and to several dollars on high-priced articles. The use of a trade-mark or brand name is also usually an evidence of less than pure competition. If the reader will try to apply these tests to the markets for various products with which he is familiar, he will see how few of them are purely competitive.

Equilibrium Output of Monopoly [2]

We must now analyze the conditions of long-run supply price and output under product differentiation. The chief cause of difference from purely competitive conditions lies in the fact that the demand curve for the product of an individual firm will be less than infinitely elastic. This means that marginal revenue and average revenue (price) will no longer be identical. The individual firm will thus have to take into account not only the changes in cost which will be associated with different outputs, but also the changes in price which it will be able to obtain from buyers for various amounts of output. The situation is illustrated in Diagram 1.

In Diagram 1, *ATUC* represents average total unit costs on

---

[2] The monopoly solution is the best applicable to the individual firm under monopolistic competition also when the demand curve can be taken for granted. This solution must be modified with competitive elements when firms are selling differentiated products which happen to be close substitutes.

a planning curve as explained in the previous chapter. *MC* is the marginal cost curve which is marginal to *ATUC*. *AR* is the average revenue or demand curve for the product of a particular individual firm, showing the prices at which various amounts of output can be sold. *MR* is the marginal revenue curve showing the net addition to total revenue occasioned by selling each additional amount of output at the price or average revenue indicated by the corresponding point on *AR*. Point *S* is the point at which marginal revenue and marginal cost are equal (in this case, at the output *OQ*). At this output the average revenue (price) is indicated by *PQ*, and the average cost by *DQ*. Monopoly profits are shown by the area of the rectangle *FPDE*. Total revenue at this output

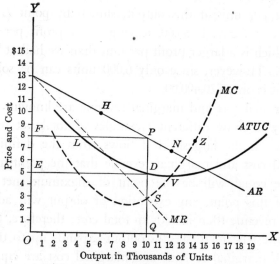

Diagram 1.—Adjustment of Monopolistic Output and Price Under Decreasing Cost.

is shown by the area *FPQO*, and total costs by the area *EDQO*. The area of the rectangle *FPDE* representing monopoly profits is the largest possible one which can be drawn on the diagram under these conditions of cost and of demand. Numerically, as can be seen from the scale, *FPDE* is $30,000.00. Price is $8.00, and cost per unit is $5.00, leaving a profit per unit of $3.00 on 10,000 units.

But point *D* is still on a falling part of our cost curve. Suppose we try to increase profits by moving on to point *V*, the point of minimum average cost. At this point average cost is only $4.80, but this amount can be sold only at the price represented by point *N* on the average revenue curve, that is, at $7.00, leaving a profit per unit of $2.20 on an output of 12,000 units. Total net profit is only $26,400.00.

Suppose that, instead of trying to produce so much, we produce a smaller output which we can sell at a higher price. Let us put the price at $10.00. At this price, as indicated by point *H* on the average revenue curve, 6,000 units can be sold. Our cost per unit at this output, shown by point *L* on the average cost curve, is $6.60, leaving a net profit per unit of $3.40, which is a larger profit per unit than we had at the output *OQ*. However, since only 6,000 units can be sold, *total* net profit is only $20,400.00.

If marginal cost and marginal revenue are known, it is not necessary to draw different rectangles of total net profits to see which is the largest. It follows from the definitions of marginal cost and marginal revenue that the point at which they are equal will be the point of maximum net profits. Short of this point, any expansion of output will add more to total revenue than it adds to total cost; therefore, total net profits must be increasing as output expands up to the point at which marginal revenue and marginal cost are equal. Beyond this point, further expansion of output would continually be adding more to total cost than to total revenue, so that total net profits would be decreasing.

Some differences should here be noted between this monopoly firm and a purely competitive firm which might happen to have the same size and type of cost curve. For a firm in pure competition, the individual demand curve *AR* for its product will be a horizontal straight line, and *MR* will coincide with it. Thus, at a price of $8.00, *AR* and *MR* would lie along *FP* and extend to point *Z*, which would be the best output for this firm if it could depend on the price remaining at $8.00 as it expanded output. However, in the absence of monopoly conditions, the profits to be made at this point will draw other firms into the industry until competition forces the price down to the point where the horizontal individual demand curve (*AR* and *MR*) is tangent to *ATUC* at the point *V*, that is, at the point where price is just equal to minimum average cost of each competitive firm.

Although we said in the last chapter that there is no equilibrium for purely competitive firms when the individual firm

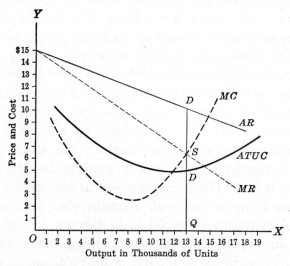

Diagram 2.—Monopolistic Output and Price Under Increasing Cost.

is still operating under conditions of decreasing cost, point *P* is a point of *monopoly* equilibrium as long as the revenue curves and the cost curves remain the same as they are in the diagram.

Diagram 2 illustrates monopoly output under conditions of increasing cost for the firm. The cost curves are the same as in Diagram 1, but in this case demand is sufficient to cause the monopolist to produce beyond the point of minimum average cost. Here again, the output which yields maximum net returns is the one at which marginal revenue and marginal cost are equal, as indicated by point S. Although average cost would be lowered and price would be increased by contracting output to 12,000 units, the loss in revenue from not selling the last 1,000 units would more than offset these gains, and total net returns would be less than at the output of 13,000 units.

Practical Adjustment of Output by a Monopolist

The reader might here object that our analysis is a little too finespun to suit the conditions of the actual world, since the average monopolist is not likely to know the demand curve for his product throughout its length, nor is he apt to be able to draw up a planning curve such as ours and to estimate accurately *in advance* before any plant is built at all what his costs would be in operating plants of each possible size. It is true that probably no monopolist starts in business producing exactly at the point of maximum net returns.

However, when we analyze carefully the actual process which the monopolist goes through, much of the force of this objection is lost. The monopolist who is just starting up in a business is apt to start with a smaller plant than the one that will eventually be found to be the best in size. This may be due in part to the difficulty in raising borrowed capital. It is also better to err on the side of underestimation, since it is easier to add to a plant which is found to be too small than it is to contract without loss a plant which is too large. Once a plant of a certain size is in existence, any monopolist with a good system of cost accounting should be able to estimate fairly closely what the marginal cost would be in expanding his output by adding one or two machines or a few thousand square feet of floor space. Once he is in business, he will discover one point on the demand curve, that is the price at which he can sell his present output. After he has produced and sold this output for a while, he should be in a position to make at least a shrewd guess as to the price at which he could sell the slightly larger output that could be made with a small addition to the existing plant. Thus, by a series of small adjustments through a process of trial and error, he would find what he considers to be the point of maximum net returns. The longer the conditions of cost and of demand remain the same, the closer will the monopolist tend to approximate the true point of maximum net returns. There is always the possibility, however, that through ignorance the monopolist will discontinue these experiments and stop short of the point of maximum net returns, being satisfied so long as he is operating at a profit. Under these circumstances, *both the monopolist and the general public would be the losers:* the monopolist, because he would be making less than the greatest possible profit; and the public, because it would obtain fewer goods at higher prices than it could, had the monopolist been awake to his own self-interest. On the other hand, if his price is set low through ignorance, the public gains at the expense of the monopolist.

In this dynamic world of ours, however, there is the additional difficulty of forecasting changes in demand and changes in cost conditions. Not even subsequent experience will prove which were the better businessmen, the Interstate Commerce Commission which ordered railroad passenger fares cut to 2c a mile, or the managers of the railroads who opposed the cut. Other conditions may change so as to render the results of the experiment inconclusive. This reiterates our contention in Chapter VI that the important factor in pricing policy is the seller's idea of what the demand curve is. The true demand when discovered by experience is merely a guide to better estimation in the future.

Perfect Monopolies

So far in this chapter our analysis applies to what might be termed "perfect" monopolies, that is, the control by a single firm of a product for which there are no close substitutes. The necessary condition for such a perfect monopoly is the ability to prevent competing firms (offering close substitutes) from entering the industry. This might be made possible by the ownership of all sources of raw material by a single firm, by the control of basic and indispensable patents either on the product itself or on the process of manufacture, by a monopoly charter granted by a government, or by other means. The degree of approximation to perfection of the monopoly will then depend upon the absence or existence of other products which are capable of satisfying the same want. Thus the control of the water system of a large city is practically a perfect monopoly. On the other hand, a monopoly of aluminum faces close competition from other metals in many uses, although in those uses in which aluminum is either indispensable or infinitely superior to other metals the monopoly approaches perfection. The only influences which might alter the demand curve facing a perfect monopoly would be those of changes in tastes and incomes of the population. It follows from the definition of perfection that no competing firms may be able to affect the demand curve of the monopoly. If we are considering competition for the consumers' dollar, there are *no* perfect monopolies.

Duopoly and Oligopoly

Logically the next classification to that of perfect monopoly is that of *pure duopoly:* a situation in which there are only two sellers, each selling a product identical with that of his competitor (no product differentiation) and with no agreement, either tacit or expressed, between the two sellers as to price or amount of output.   Unable to find an example of such a situation in the actual world, Cournot, one of the first economists to treat this problem, invented the imaginary example of two people each with a mineral spring located within a few feet of the other, the two selling the same mineral water in competition with each other and without a price agreement. Under these circumstances, either seller, by cutting his price below that of the other, could take away all of his competitor's business, provided the second seller did not also lower his price.

An extension of the problem of pure duopoly is that of *pure oligopoly:* a situation in which there are a few sellers, selling a completely standardized product, each of them producing a large enough proportion of the total output so that changes in the price or output of any single seller will have an appreciable effect upon the prices that can be obtained and the outputs that can be sold by the competitors.

Many solutions of the problems of pure oligopoly have been attempted by economists, particularly by the mathematical economists.   However, since the solutions are so dependent upon the assumptions that are made, and since so many different assumptions are possible, we will not burden the beginning student with a consideration of them here.[3]

Elements of Product Differentiation

We must now examine the situation under product differentiation.   This has been called a form of "monopolistic competition," a situation where there may be many sellers, but with differentiated products so that competition is no longer on a purely price basis.   By combining services with a product, the different sellers have succeeded in differentiating the prod-

---

[3] The student who is interested in the problem might consult Chamberlin, Edward, *The Theory of Monopolistic Competition*, Ch. III, Harvard University Press, 1935.

uct in the minds of buyers and so have within limits a monopoly in selling their product, although the products of all sellers are fairly close substitutes for one another and would all fall within our second definition of a commodity as previously defined. Under these conditions the determination of equilibrium output for the individual firm, and the point of maximum net returns, would be exactly the same as in the above analysis, *so long as the demand curve for the product of the individual seller remained unchanged*. However, we must now face the fact that the entrance into the industry of new firms producing close substitutes may shift the demand curves for the products of the dealers already in the industry.

Successful product differentiation may act as a deterrent to the entry of new firms into an industry insofar as they may be afraid that they will be unable to take business away from the other firms, or that they will have to incur heavy advertising costs in order to do so. It is not, however, as absolute a bar to the entry of new firms as is the control of raw materials or basic patents. If some of the existing firms in the industry are making large enough profits so that the prospect of making similar profits is enough to offset the risks and expense of entering the industry, new firms will enter.

New firms which enter such an industry will naturally first attempt to attract to themselves those customers who can be most easily enticed away from the other dealers. Depending upon the circumstances of the case, this may involve either the closest possible duplication of the services offered by an older dealer or the offering of different services which might be calculated to be of superior attraction to a certain part of the older dealer's clientele. Take, for instance, the matter of location of a store. If the present dealer's store is most conveniently located for the vast majority of his customers, a new competing store will do well to locate as close to the old store as possible. On the other hand, if the old store is conveniently located for some buyers but inconvenient to a large number of others, the new store might do well to locate in a place which would be more convenient to the latter group. The same principle applies to all other types of services. Competition with an existing restaurant might be made most effective under some circumstances by opening another restaurant of the same type, under other circumstances by opening a cafeteria. If the present restaurant has beautiful waitresses and this appeals to all customers, the new restaurant might do well to hire a "Follies" chorus to wait on the tables; but if a considerable part of the present restaurant's trade is made up of married men accompanied by jealous wives, the new one might attract more trade by hiring homely women. This is enough by way of illustration. The important point to notice is that the new competitors will have the power to take away a part of the demand for the product of the older firm and so cause the older firm's demand curve to shift to the left.

Diagram 3 on page 167 shows some of the possibilities of this situation. In Figure 1 we have the revenue and cost curves of the individual firm before a competitor enters the field. These curves are drawn on the same principles as in the earlier diagram. (*ATUC* is average total unit cost, *MC* is marginal cost, *AR* is average revenue, and *MR* is marginal revenue; point *S* shows the point at which marginal revenue and marginal cost are equal, giving the output *OQ* at which net returns are at a maximum; *PQ* is the price at which the output *OQ* can be sold; *DQ* is the average cost of this output; and *FPDE* is the monopoly profit.)

Results of Monopolistic Competition

Figure 2 shows the situation after a new competitor has entered the field duplicating the old firm's services as far as possible. If the personality of the dealer or his salespeople is

one of the factors which induce buyers to trade with him, perfect duplication is of course impossible, so there will be some
few buyers at least who will prefer the old dealer if he sells
at the same price as the new one, and some buyers will even
be willing to pay a slightly higher price to the old dealer.
What can be closely duplicated are the business methods of
the old dealer and many of the services which he renders
(credit, delivery service, location of store, packaging, and so
on).   Now insofar as these methods and services were the sole
factors which attracted certain customers to the old dealer,
and to the extent that these factors are exactly duplicated by
the new firm, this group of customers will have no preference
between dealers and will trade with whichever dealer offers
the lower price.   Another group of buyers may still prefer
the old dealer to the new, but they will no longer be willing
to pay the same price difference for the privilege of trading
with him that they did before the new competitor started business.   This might well be the situation where there was at first
only one grocer in a village and the choice lay between trading
with him and driving into the city to buy.   He could then
charge much higher prices than the city stores and still find
customers.   A new grocery then starts up in the same village.
The choice is now between two stores of comparatively equal
convenience of location.   Even though people prefer the old
grocer to the new, they will not be willing to pay the same
price differences to trade with him as before when the only
alternative was to go to the city.

   The net result of all this is to shift the old firm's demand
curve to the left and to make it more elastic.   We see in Figure 2 that if the old dealer should try to charge the same price
as he formerly did (shown by point H), he could sell so little
that his costs would be much higher than his selling price.
On the other hand, if he tried to sell his old output (shown
by OA in Figure 2), he could do so only at the price GA,

which yields him no profit. At his best output, as shown by
OQ in Figure 2, his costs are now higher, his selling price is
lower, and his profits are much less than before the new competitor entered the field.

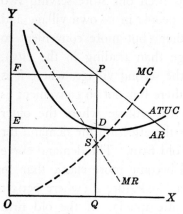

FIG. 1.—INDIVIDUAL FIRM'S DEMAND
AND COST CURVES.

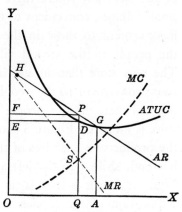

FIG. 2.—SAME FIRM AFTER A COM-
PETITOR HAS DUPLICATED ITS SERV-
ICES (DUOPOLY WITH SLIGHT PROD-
UCT DIFFERENTIATION).

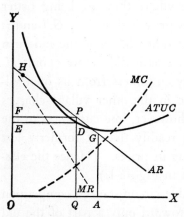

FIG. 3.—SAME FIRM AFTER A COM-
PETITOR HAS OFFERED SERVICES CON-
SIDERED BETTER BY A PART OF THE
OLD FIRM'S CUSTOMERS (DUOPOLY
WITH IMPORTANT PRODUCT DIFFEREN-
TIATION).

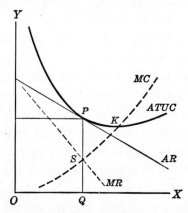

FIG. 4.—POSSIBLE FINAL RESULT OF
MONOPOLISTIC COMPETITION.

Diagram 3.—Some Results of Monopolistic Competition.

We now turn to another possible situation in which the new competitor, instead of duplicating the services of the old firm, attempts to take away a part of the old firm's customers by offering very superior services to a part of them. This might be the situation where there has been one store serving two small villages, convenient to the people in its own village and inconvenient to those in the other (but more convenient to the people in the second village than trading in the city). The new store then locates in the second village, where it is more convenient to the people there but not so convenient as the old store to the people in the village where the older store is located. Figure 3 shows the effect on the demand for the products and services of the old firm. The demand curve has both shifted to the left and become more elastic than in Figure 1, but it is less elastic than in Figure 2 (where perfect duplication of the service was attempted). If the old firm now tried to sell the same output (shown by OA in Figure 3), it would have to drop its price low enough to attract customers from the second village where they are being better served by the new store. Such a price is shown by GA and is extremely unprofitable. On the other hand, if the old firm attempts to charge the same price as it did before (point H, Figure 3), it will not lose many customers from its own village even though the new store in the other village charges a slightly lower price. It will, however, lose customers to the store in the other village more readily than it formerly lost its customers to the city by raising its prices. (Hence the elasticity in Figure 3 is greater than in Figure 1.)

Under quite possibly conceivable circumstances, competition by a new firm that is directed toward only a part of the old firm's customers may cause the old firm to charge a higher price to its remaining trade than it did before the new competitor entered the field. This will be the case when the old firm's original trade consists of two classes of customers, the demand of one class being very inelastic, and that of the other being very elastic. If a competitor then enters and, by offering low prices and different service, takes away the customers whose demand is elastic, the price at the point of maximum net returns which the old firm will charge the remaining customers (whose demand is inelastic) will be higher than it was before. For instance, an independent grocery might be serving two classes of people: a wealthy group who will buy what they want without much attention to price but who insist on charge accounts and delivery service and on being able to order by telephone, plus a poorer group who have no telephones and who, although they may appreciate the charge and delivery service, are primarily influenced by price in the amount they buy, and hence would carry their groceries and pay cash if they could get them cheaper. In order to get a volume of business by selling to the latter group the grocer must keep his prices low; thus his point of maximum net return is at a fairly low price. A chain store starts up (doing a cash-and-carry business and selling at a very low price) and takes away the poorer customers. The independent grocer then finds that it would not pay to drop his prices low enough to compete with the chain store for the business of the poor group. However, he also finds that his remaining customers are so insistent on having telephone, charge, and delivery service that they will not leave him or curtail their purchases even if he raises his prices somewhat, so he specializes in being an "exclusive" store. But even at the high prices, his total net profit will not be so great as it was before the chain store started competing with him. Otherwise he would have set his price higher in the first place and would not have tried to appeal to the lower-income group. The business of the lower-income group was well worth having when there was no competition for it, but it would not pay to drop prices to try to get it back.

There is, of course, no reason why the new competition which enters the field should be confined to either of the two types we have been discussing. It may (and does) happen in the actual business world that first one firm will compete by duplicating the services offered by an existing firm, and then a third firm takes business away from both of the first two by offering superior service to a certain class of buyers. Or it may happen that the first competitor starts by offering superior service to a certain group, and if each firm is still making a profit by catering to a group of customers, two or more new competitors will try to compete by duplication of services within each group. In the illustration we gave above, if both the chain store and the independent store were making profits, a new chain store might start to compete for the cash-and-carry business, and a new independent store to compete for the telephone-charge-and-delivery business.

If the existence of any profit whatever is sufficient to attract new competitors into an industry, the final result of monopolistic competition is shown by Figure 4. Here we find that *PQ* represents both the average revenue and the average cost of the output *OQ;* in other words, selling price is just equal to average cost, and the area representing monopoly profits has disappeared. While there are no monopoly profits at point *P, OQ* still represents the best possible output for the firm under these conditions, since any other output could be produced only at a loss. (It should be remembered that interest and wages of management have been included in costs.) If monopolistic competition is carried to its logical conclusion, Figure 4 will be typical of each firm that remains in the industry. It is not necessary that each firm sell at the same price nor that each have identical cost curves. What will happen will be that each firm's average revenue curve will be tangent to its own average cost curve at only one point. If average revenue were less than average cost at every output, the firm could not operate except at a loss and would eventually be forced out of the industry. If average revenue is above average costs at any output, the net monopoly profit resulting would attract competition if a new firm could duplicate the old firm's facilities at the same or lower cost. Even if a new firm encounters higher costs, these would not be a positive bar to its entry provided that it estimates that total revenue would be equal to or above total cost at some possible output.

While we have devoted most of our attention to the effects of monopolistic competition upon the demand curve of the individual firm, it should not be ignored that such competition may also have its effect on the cost curve. In Figures 2, 3, and 4 of Diagram 3, the higher average cost of the decreased output is occasioned only by the inroads of competitors on the business of the firm. If the existing firm has been paying the factors of production the full value of their services, this is the only change in costs that will take place. However, if the old firm has been making a profit by exploiting the factors (paying them less than their value to the firm), a new competitor may raise the entire cost curve of the old firm by forcing it to pay the full value of the factors. Thus, if customers are attracted to a store, not by the personality of the owner but by the personality of his hired sales-people, a new competitor may force the owner to pay the salespeople their full value by attempting to hire them away from him; or individual salesmen may start in the business for themselves if the employer is not paying them what they are worth. Similarly, if the owner of the business has been paying less than the full rental value for the location which he occupies, as soon as his lease expires competition will force him to pay the full value. If we are trying to represent a true long-run equilibrium situation, we must draw our cost curves on the assumption that the factors are paid their full value. This is the assumption which underlies the figures in Diagram

3; we must not ignore the fact that such an assumption has been made.

In actual practice, the final solution shown in Figure 4 of Diagram 3 is most closely approximated in certain retail trades where the first cost of setting up a new firm is small. For example, the comparative ease with which a barber can start in business for himself is sufficient to prevent the average master barber from earning any more than he could as a hired journeyman if all his costs are properly figured. The same is true of a great many small manufacturing and retail trades, such as the grocery business, shoe repairing, garage business, and so forth. The fact that certain men of superior managerial or technical ability are making large earnings in these trades should not deceive the reader into believing that they are making large profits. Most of what is commonly called a "profit" in these cases is really a wage of management; it is the comparative scarcity of these men of superior ability which enables them to make such earnings.

Even after all costs have been properly figured, there will be found some people who are receiving a true net monopoly profit in these trades. However, a careful examination will always disclose that this is only a temporary situation. The firms which are first to enter a new industry, the firms which first enter a new location, and the firms which first adopt a new way of appealing to buyers in general or to a particular class of buyers, usually have an opportunity to make a profit before competition catches up with them. This will be more fully discussed in the chapter on profits. It is sufficient for us to note here that such profits are purely temporary whenever a new firm can duplicate the services of an old firm at anywhere near the same cost.

Different Results of Pure and Monopolistic Competition

Certain differences between monopolistic competition and pure competition in their ultimate results should now be observed. Let us refer to Figure 4 in Diagram 3. Under pure competition, if new firms which enter the industry have the same costs as the old firms, long-run competitive price would be at point *K,* the point of minimum average costs for each firm, and each firm would be operating at its lowest cost output. On the other hand, under product differentiation the existence of less than infinitely elastic demand curves for the products of the individual firm forces each firm to operate at less than its competitive optimum output and at higher costs.

For instance, it has been estimated that if the average gasoline station could double its sales, it could afford to cut the price 2c a gallon, still making the same return as it does at present. However, under monopolistic competition as it exists in the industry no dealer can permanently double his sales by a 2c cut. If a single dealer does drop his price by 2c, some of his competitors who are more conveniently located to their own customers might be able to retain most of their own business by only cutting their price 1c; if they cut 2c, they would retain all of their business. Thus, while "price wars" occasionally do occur in the retail gasoline business, we find them "deprecated by the industry as a benefit to nobody." Consequently there are too many gas stations, none of them operating at a profit and all of them operating at less than capacity; and the public pays a much higher price than it would have to pay if it had no preference as between dealers, thus allowing pure competition to prevail and service to be given by fewer stations operating at capacity and selling at minimum average cost. The public is of course better served by a wide distribution of gas stations. The ability to buy within a short distance of wherever one runs out of gasoline is a privilege perhaps worth paying for. But certainly we are not much better served by having four stations at one crossroads or six to eight in one block. The fact that most of us are unable to test gasoline and are therefore forced to buy by brand instead of on a strict price and quality basis also helps to complicate the situation. As Professor Chamberlin has so well demonstrated, many of the so-called "wastes of competition" are really wastes not of pure competition but of monopolistic competition.

CHAPTER XII

Selling Costs[1]

IN THE previous chapters we have largely ignored the question of selling costs and have concentrated our attention upon costs of production. As long as we were concerned with the analysis of pure competition, this was sufficient, because when competition is pure there are no selling costs. There may be costs of transportation and handling; but if competition is pure, it will be a matter of indifference whether these are paid by the seller and included in the delivered price or whether they are paid by the buyer and the price is quoted f.o.b. In one sense, these may be regarded as increasing costs of production, as an increasing output must travel a greater distance to find its market. Insofar as there are differences in these costs due to the location of different firms, such differences will tend to be offset by differences in rent and will be discussed in the chapter on rent.[2]

Selling costs may be defined as the costs necessary to *persuade* a buyer to buy one product rather than another, or to buy from one seller rather than another. If all buyers knew exactly what they wanted and could not be changed in their estimations of the satisfactions derived from different commodities—if they were able to detect all differences in quality

---

[1] *Cf.* Chamberlin, Edward, "Selling Costs and the Theory of Value" (Ch. 8), *The Theory of Monopolistic Competition,* Harvard University Press, 1935.

[2] See, however, a divergent view expressed by John Ise, "The Monopoly Element in Rent," *American Economic Review,* February, 1940, pp. 33 ff.

—such selling costs would never be incurred by any dealer. "Salesmanship," whether in direct selling or by means of advertising, consists of the art of persuasion. Sales managers are fond of using the term "order taker" as a term of reproach for their less aggressive salesmen. In other words, all these men do is take orders for what the buyers want. The true salesman in the language of all of the craft is the man who "makes the customers want what the firm has to sell." If competition were pure and perfect, there would be no need for "salesmen" or sales managers, and one or at most a very few "order takers" could handle all the orders for an extremely large firm.

On the other hand, whenever the buyer's knowledge is less than perfect, whenever he lacks objective standards by which to judge the quality of goods, whenever his choice between dealers may be influenced by considerations other than price and quality, and whenever he is undecided and open to persuasion as to which product he will buy or from which dealer to buy, then selling cost may be necessary to sell any output at all and will most certainly be encountered as the attempt is made to expand output. Even where no active "persuasion" is intended, some selling effort will be necessary to acquaint the buyer with the mere fact of the existence of a new product. In this modern world where so many dealers are clamoring for the buyer's attention, it may be necessary to exert some selling effort merely to remind him of the fact that an old product is still in existence. If buyers cannot or do not keep themselves acquainted with the prices which are being charged by all sellers, it may be necessary even to advertise a price cut in order to secure increased business from cutting price.

The previous paragraph dealt with types of selling costs which are associated with an *imperfect market*. Presumably, in the long run if no new products, or new advertisements, or new kinds of sales efforts were introduced, or, more briefly, if we could assume *perfect* knowledge on the part of the buyers, these sales efforts would lose their force and would disappear.

More important, however, are certain types of product differentiation which would persist even with perfect knowledge of the market. A differentiated product which is actually superior in a technological sense may require selling costs in order to acquaint the public with it simply because it is differentiated, and not standardized so that lower prices may induce greater volume. Sometimes advertising may create product differentiation. Sometimes, on the other hand, product differentiation may create the need for selling costs.

Influence of Selling Costs on Demand Curve

In terms of our previous analysis, the purpose of all advertising and selling efforts is to influence the demand curve for the product of an individual seller or a group of sellers. The aim of any dealer who incurs selling costs is to sell a greater output at any given price than he could have sold without incurring these costs. Any successful selling effort will shift some part of the demand curve for the firm's product to a location lying to the right of where it would have been without such effort. This is the result either of inducing the same buyers to take more of a product at any given price or of inducing additional buyers to take the product at prices they would not have paid before the sales effort was made.

Depending upon circumstances, the new demand curve that is the result of advertising and selling effort may be more or less elastic, or parts of it may be more or less elastic, than the old demand curve that existed before the selling effort was made. In general, if the effect of the effort is to convince buyers (rightly or wrongly) that the product sold by a particular firm is much superior to its close substitutes, the tendency will be for the upper segments of the new demand curve to be less elastic than the old; that is, the firm will not lose proportionately so much business to its rivals by raising its price as it would have under the previous conditions of demand. On the other hand, if there is a large group of people who feel that they cannot afford to buy the product at all except at low prices, but who become convinced of the superiority of this firm's product, the elasticity of the lower part of the new demand curve may be greater than that of the old. The buying habits of additional buyers who are attracted by a given sales effort will also influence the elasticity of the new demand curve. If they are people who will vary the amount of a product they purchase in response to a change in price, the new demand curve will tend to be more elastic than the old. If they are not very responsive to price changes in the amount they purchase, the new demand curve will tend to be less elastic than the old one.

Influence of Selling Costs on Determination of Output

The individual firm under monopolistic competition has a choice of means by which to sell a larger output. It may lower its price; it may improve the quality of its product; it may increase its selling efforts; or it may do all three. We shall not deal here with changes in quality but solely with selling costs. In the preceding chapter we were concerned primarily with changes in output occasioned by changes in price, and we found the principles governing the point of maximum net returns for the firm. When we have to consider selling costs as well, the problem becomes much more complicated. Even if we knew the amount of selling costs which would be required to sell each possible output at each possible price, we could not represent them by a single curve on a two-dimensional diagram as we did with costs of production. This is because selling cost is one of three interdependent variables: output, price, and selling cost. At any one price, a higher total selling cost will be required to sell a larger output at the same price. At any one output, a higher total selling cost will be required to sell the same output at a higher price.

The formula that confronts the firm that is trying to determine the most profitable output is as follows:

(Price) $\times$ *(Output)* — *(Production Cost + Selling Cost) = Net Returns.*

We will assume that we know the total cost of production of each possible output. Output may be increased by lowering the price (thus reaching another point on the same demand curve), or it may be increased by increasing selling costs (thus creating a new demand curve), or by a combination of cutting price and increasing selling costs (creating a new demand curve and selecting a new price point on the new demand curve). The problem is: Which of these alternatives will make net returns the largest possible amount?

One way of solving this problem is to regard the selling costs which will create a certain demand curve as a fixed cost to be associated with that particular demand curve. It will then be necessary to draw up a separate diagram for each possible selling cost and the demand curve it creates.

In Diagram 1, *PC* represents average cost of production for each output. *ATUC* is average total unit cost, *including sell-*

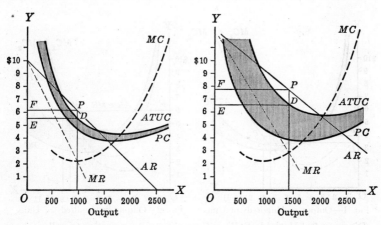

Fig. 1.—Selling Cost $1,000 to Create New Demand.

Fig. 2.—Selling Cost $4,000 to Create New Demand.

Diagram 1.—Fixed Selling Costs.

ing cost. Selling cost per unit of product at each output is shown by the vertical height of the shaded area, a unit cost which becomes smaller as output is increased, because of the spreading of this fixed cost. *MC* is marginal cost, *AR* is average revenue or demand, and *MR* is marginal revenue. The area *FPDE* indicates maximum net returns under each set of demand and cost conditions.

It should be noted that while the profits shown by Figure 2 are greater than those in Figure 1, they are not necessarily the greatest profits that could possibly be achieved. It might be that greater profits could be made with a selling expenditure either greater or less than $4,000.00. The only way in which we could find the point of greatest profits would be to draw every diagram for every different selling cost.

It will be seen in Figure 2 that, although profits are greater than in Figure 1, selling costs are greater than profits and nearly as great as costs of production. This is by no means an unusual situation in the actual business world of today. Many products whose sole value, or the greater part of whose value, is the illusion created in the minds of the public by advertising would show a similar set of cost conditions. For instance, it

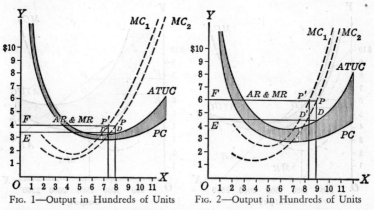

Fɪɢ. 1—Output in Hundreds of Units   Fɪɢ. 2—Output in Hundreds of Units

Diagram 2.—Variable Selling Cost assumed necessary to sell each output at given prices.

is very doubtful if the ingredients and the preparation of most patent medicines cost as much per bottle as it does to advertise and sell them.

Another way to attempt to solve the problem of the most profitable combination of price and selling cost is to consider the price as being fixed and the selling cost as a variable cost necessary to sell an increasing output at the same price.

In Diagram 2, the symbols are the same as in Diagram 1, except that, since price is to be held constant, average revenue and marginal revenue coincide and become a horizontal straight line. *AR* no longer represents a demand curve, as in the earlier diagrams; it now is made up of a number of points on *different* demand curves, each new demand curve being created by the selling costs necessary to sell more goods; also MC_2 includes variable selling costs while MC_1 does not.

Here again we cannot be certain that Figure 2 shows the point of greatest profits. If at a higher price the selling costs would not increase very much more, such a price might yield more profits. On the other hand, it might be that at a price of $3.50 selling costs would be so low for a very large output that this would yield the greatest profits; or the best price may be somewhere between $4.00 and $6.00. We cannot tell until we draw a diagram for each possible price.

These diagrams illustrate how increasing selling costs can turn decreasing costs of production into increasing average total costs long before the point of minimum cost of production is reached.

The reader should not become too enthusiastic about this type of analysis but should remember that three very important assumptions are involved:

1. That we know the costs of production to be associated with each output in which we are interested.

2. That we must know or be able to estimate closely the

nature of the demand curve to be associated with changes in price with selling costs unchanged.

3. That we must be able to estimate the results to be achieved with each kind and amount of expenditure on selling costs.

A reasonably accurate guess may often be made in connection with assumptions 1 and 2, but assumption 3 requires a higher order of prophecy, as will be found from the following discussion.

Peculiarities of Selling Costs

While costs of production present many difficulties of calculation, intelligent effort will usually yield a result that is within a reasonable range of probable error, and experience will usually help to lessen such range of error. Not so with selling costs, since here the effort is to appeal to the mind of the buyer. A given sum spent in one way may yield results out of all proportion to the cost; spent in another way, it may bring no sales at all or even do harm to the business. The field of selling and advertising costs is a splendid example of the old adage that "all generalities are wrong including this one."

One reason for this lies in the fact that the success of many advertising or selling schemes consists in the appeal of uniqueness or novelty. The first chain stores to paint their fronts red attracted a considerable volume of trade by it, but now that so many have done so, an agreeable shade of some other color is not only a relief to the eye but is also a superior means of identification.

On the other hand, many trade practices that start out by giving a unique advantage to the first firms which employ them end by being necessary practices that all competing firms must adopt if they hope to remain in business. The first gas stations to buy an air compressor and put up a sign announc-

ing "free air" reaped a harvest in the good old days when mo-
torists took their exercise pushing a hand pump. Today the
possession of such a compressor confers no peculiar advantage
to any station, yet every one must have one for fear of losing
business if it did not. The same is rapidly becoming true
of the practice of gas station attendants of washing the customer's windshield when he stops for gas. The economics of
such "free services" should be clearly understood. When only
a few firms are giving them, so that they attract a large volume
of business to a particular firm, the firm can very well afford
to give them without advancing the regular price of the product. But when all firms are giving them, they tend to become one of the common costs of doing business and may be
passed on to the consumer in the price of the product. This
is one of the ways in which monopolistic competition through
added "free" services may tend to raise rather than lower the
price of the product.

If all customers appreciate these services sufficiently to pay
what they cost, the solution may be satisfactory to everyone.
However, since the services are usually not charged for separately but are simply included in the price of the product,
many people who do not care for the services at all, or who
do not care for them enough to pay what they cost, may be
paying for them in all ignorance of the fact that they are
doing so. Thus, anyone who goes into a charge-and-deliver
store and buys for cash and carries his own parcel home is
helping to pay for the charge-and-delivery service available to
other customers, even though he makes no use of it himself.
When there is a sufficient number of customers who do not
care about such services, a new competitor may make a successful bid for their trade by not giving the services and not
charging for them. When this happens, the unit cost of the
old firm will go up to the extent that all the remaining customers insist on receiving the services, but the cost of giving

the service can no longer be "averaged out" over so large a number of customers as before.

One difficulty that confronts us in the analysis of selling costs is the extreme disproportionality between advertising costs and volume of sales. Not only is it impossible to predict with any fair degree of accuracy what volume of sales will result from any particular sum spent on advertising, but it is also often impossible to determine the extent to which any particular increase in sales has been due to any particular advertising expenditure which has been made in the past.[3]

Another difficulty is that the selling costs that any one firm will encounter may be influenced by the actions of its competitors. If the possible market for any one firm is largely confined to taking business away from its competitors within the same industry, then the expenditure of a greater selling effort by any one firm may make it necessary for other firms to increase their selling expenditure merely to retain the same volume of sales that they had before. This sort of competition eliminates the profits of the various firms, not by causing them to cut their prices to the benefit of the customer, but by causing them to increase their costs to the benefit of nobody but the advertising agencies and salesmen. If the results of selling effort were always in direct proportion to its cost, so that when one firm spent more on selling costs and took business away from another firm, the second firm could always get the business back by making a similar expenditure, then no firm would start such a competition, since to do so would be merely to invoke retaliation. But, the peculiarities of the mind of the buying public being such as they are, there is always the possibility that a small expenditure for advertising and selling—if done in a very clever way—may yield at least temporary results out of all proportion to its cost. Fur-

---

[3] Some firms have attempted recently to obtain answers to these questions, with some degree of success.

thermore, customers may become so firmly attached to the firm which first increases its selling effort that the other firms from whom the business was drawn might have to spend a much greater sum to recapture it than the first firm spent to get it away from them. Consequently there is always a temptation to start this sort of competition.

The problem is further complicated by another of the peculiarities of advertising. Where there is a large potential market to be drawn upon by attracting customers away from entirely different industries, the advertising by any one firm may bring trade not only to itself but also to other firms in the industry. For example, a Chevrolet advertisement may be the factor that arouses a desire in the mind of a buyer to buy a new car rather than take a trip to Brazil; but after making the rounds of the dealers to find out what they will allow on his old car, he may end by buying an entirely different make, such as a Plymouth or Ford. Thus Chevrolet advertising will have sold a car for Plymouth or Ford. That this is not at all an unusual result may be deduced from the proceedings of many a trade-association meeting. It is not at all unusual at such meetings for the large advertisers to stand up and berate their competitors for not spending their fair share to make the public "fountain-pen conscious" or "window-sash conscious." Among industries we are thus confronted with what has been called "competition for the consumer's dollar."

We must now observe certain peculiarities of this inter-industrial competition in selling effort. In the first place, if only one industry puts on an intensive advertising and selling campaign, the additional business thus obtained may happen to draw from such a great number of other industries and from such a still greater number of individual firms that the amount of business lost by any one firm or industry may be so negligible that it will not bother to try to get the business back. Of course, as more and more industries tend to do the same thing, the increase in business which any of them can gain from a given amount of advertising will tend to diminish. At the same time the losses suffered by the firms and industries that have not previously advertised will begin to approach such serious proportions that they too will be motivated to increase their selling efforts, either to try to recapture their lost business or to retain what business they still have. Sooner or later, the increased selling efforts of all industries and firms will tend to nullify or at least to detract considerably from the benefits gained by the firms which first started the competition. However, the full effects of this retaliation may be so long delayed that the interim gains which they have made will have exceeded the increased selling costs.

The same thing may be true even when the gain of one industry that increases selling effort is largely at the expense of another single industry. It is seldom indeed that retaliation will be immediate and direct. For example, the automobile industry may increase its advertising and draw most of its business from people who would otherwise have taken trips to Brazil. If the steamship companies increase their sales efforts in turn, instead of having any immediate effect on the automobile industry most of the steamship tickets may be sold to people who would otherwise have bought an electric refrigerator. Refrigerators may then recover at the expense of radios; and so on. It may thus be a considerable length of time before the automobile industry, which started the process, begins to feel the effects of retaliation either in loss of business or in increased costs of maintaining the same volume of business. And even if it eventually does feel the effect, it may not be conscious of the cause.

The tacit assumption that underlies the preceding discussion is that there are a large number of buyers ready to change their purchases from one product to another or from one firm to another under the influence of advertising and selling efforts on the part of the various firms and industries. However, we must not ignore the fact that among the customers of any firm or any industry there will be extreme variations in the degree of such willingness to change the direction of their purchases. We are here concerned with two conflicting psychological tendencies: the desire for novelty or improvement and the force of habit. The strength of these two tendencies will differ widely from one individual to another. We are all familiar with individuals who buy the same products from the same stores in an almost unvaried routine; we are also familiar with other individuals who are never satisfied and who are always changing both the products they buy and the firms from which they buy them. These psychological forces will also differ in the same individual with respect to different products and different firms. All of us have at least some few products with which we are so well satisfied or which we consider so necessary to our well-being that it would require a tremendous amount of inducement to make us cease purchasing them and buy something else. This applies to the products themselves, to brands of products, and to the firms with which we trade. On the other hand there are usually some commodities in respect to which we are just on the margin of doubt as to whether we shall buy that particular commodity or another.

Good Will

This brings us to the most important source of permanent or quasi-permanent gains from advertising and selling effort; that is, what is known to the trade as "repeat orders." When people are just on the margin of doubt as to whether to continue buying the same commodity or trading with the same firm, a comparatively small expenditure of well-directed advertising or selling effort may induce them to start buying a different commodity or to start trading with a different firm.

Once they have made the change, some of these buyers may become so well satisfied with the new commodity or the new firm that either they refuse to change again at all, or that the necessary effort to induce them to change again would be so costly that no other firm could gain enough from these customers' trade to cover the costs of inducing them to buy. Once a firm's clientele is made up of a majority of this type of customers, it can retain the same volume of business with relatively negligible selling costs. This condition is what is known as the "good will" of a business.

The value of such a good will can often reach fantastic amounts in the case of products which are sold nationally or internationally under a certain trade-mark or brand name. Consider, for instance, the value of such names as "Wrigley's Spearmint," "Smith Brothers Cough Drops," "Frigidaire," "Chesterfields," and so on. The name "Wrigley's Spearmint" is undoubtedly worth many times the value of the plant and equipment with which the chewing gum is made. I might start to manufacture a chewing gum identical in chicle and flavor content with "Spearmint"; but if I spent 100 times or even 1,000 times the amount which the Wrigley Company is now spending on advertising, it is still a doubtful question whether I would be able to attain a volume of sales equal to theirs. I should certainly hesitate to risk my own money in such a venture, and I doubt very much whether I could find a banker foolish enough or optimistic enough to lend me the money.

The existence of good will, coupled with the heavy expenses which a new firm would have to incur to enter the competition, will often prove to be such a deterrent to the entrance of new firms into an industry that the successful older firms may attain a degree of monopoly power with respect to their own customers which may be nearly perfect over a long period of time.

Difficulty of Allocating Advertising Cost

Advertising that falls into the hands of customers who would have bought from the firm anyway without such advertising is sheer waste. Why, then, do successful, established firms continue to advertise to the extent that they do? In the first place, the firm may have no way of knowing how much of its business is made up of repeat business and how much is made up of a constant succession of new customers who buy only once. A small retail business, or any business in which selling is conducted by direct personal contact, may easily recognize which customers are "regular." Thus, the "family tailors" and "family bootmakers" of London may be entirely justified in their scorn of advertising, since they lose none of their present business by not advertising, and the additional volume of trade to be gained by advertising might not be worth what it costs. On the other hand, the seller of a nationally advertised product may have no way of ascertaining the identity of his customers so that he can distinguish new business from old. Under these circumstances it may sometimes be the case that the manufacturer could increase his net profits by curtailing his advertising, but that he is not aware of the fact.

With some products, particularly high priced "durable" goods, a single sale to each customer may be sufficient to make a given expenditure on advertising profitable. With low-priced perishable goods, the net return per single sale may be so small that advertising which only induces customers to buy once may be conducted at a net loss. However, the manufacturer will have no way of knowing ahead of time what proportion of the new business secured by advertising will come from single-time buyers and how much will come from repeat customers.

This brings us to another great difficulty in the analysis of advertising cost. It will usually be impossible to determine whether a given expenditure on advertising should be treated as a "fixed cost" or as a "variable cost." To the extent that a certain advertisement attracts repeat customers to the firm, it should be considered as a fixed cost; that is, the advertisement will not have to be repeated for these same customers, and the more that they buy over a period of years, the smaller will be the cost per sale of this particular advertisement. In other words, the annual output of the firm is increased by an expenditure which has to be made but once. To the extent that advertising attracts only single-time buyers, it must be regarded as a variable cost; it will be necessary continually to repeat the expenditure to try to maintain the same volume of business. Under these circumstances, the full cost of the advertisement should be assessed against the sales which result from it today, this week, or this month. We have seen from the previous discussion how difficult it is to determine whether advertising attracts repeat customers or single-time buyers. Even a department store which advertises a "sale" to last only one day may thereby attract some customers who will become permanent customers, so that some unknown part of the advertising cost of the sale should be considered a fixed cost and the rest a variable cost.

Price Cutting versus Increased Selling Costs

We may now consider for a moment some of the merits of price cutting *versus* increasing selling costs. We shall not have space here to exhaust the subject, but some of the salient points may be given attention. Such a question may be considered both from the point of view of the individual businessman and from that of society.

The individual businessman is of course interested in trying to make the greatest possible net profits or the least amount of loss. As we have seen, it is not always easy for him to determine whether cutting prices or increasing selling costs will yield him the best results. When such a doubt exists, he may prefer to advertise rather than cut prices, since if advertising does not pay he may discontinue it, losing only the cost of the advertising; whereas, if he cuts prices, he may find (if the results are not to his satisfaction) that it is difficult or impossible to raise them again and still retain the old volume of sales he had before the cut.

There is another objection to price cutting from the businessman's point of view. The increased business obtained by a price cut may happen to come largely at the expense of other firms in the same industry, in which case retaliation may be immediate and drastic. On the other hand, the increased buying created by advertising may happen to come largely at the expense of other industries. There is also the possibility, as we have seen, that the advertising by one firm may bring some business to a competitor in the same industry. In the case of increased advertising, the effects of retaliation by other firms or other industries may be so long delayed that temporary profits are possible; and, in any event, cause and effect may not be clearly apparent to the businessman himself. Thus we have the rather curious statement by trade associations that price cutting is an "unethical" form of competition, while using advertising to overpraise one's own product to the point of downright lying is apparently entirely "ethical."

Then, too, from the point of view of the businessman, business that is secured by a price cut may be lost to a competitor who cuts prices still further or offers better quality for the same price; but building a complete delusion in the mind of the buyer through advertising may secure business for the firm which cannot be taken away by a competitor's price cut and sometimes not even by a competitor's advertising. Only in the event that a firm is selling a product whose merits will be obvious to a buyer when he uses it can the firm feel confident that a price cut will bring it a large number of permanent new customers.

Now let us consider the question from the viewpoint of society. First, any advertising which does not influence buyers is a sheer economic waste. This will be a waste from the point of view of the businessman also; but while the businessman would regard a loss through bad advertising and a loss through an unwise price cut with equal horror, the buying public would gain from the price cut.

Some advertising may actually increase the satisfaction which a buyer derives from a product. Thus, if an advertiser succeeds in convincing me that the cheap car which I drive is just about as good as a $7,000.00 car, and if I stay convinced *all the while I own the car*, the satisfaction I derive from owning the car is greatly enhanced and my sense of well-being has been increased by the ad. Against such a merit of advertising must be set the fact that it may make me aware of the merits of articles I cannot afford to buy and dissatisfied with those that I can buy. The advertisements for beautiful sailing yachts may thus be a source of disutility to me.

Something may even be said for the much-abused patent medicine ad. Insofar as people take these medicines for imaginary illnesses, the advertisement may constitute the principal part of the cure. The statement in the testimonial, "It did wonders for Mrs. Blue and will do wonders for you," may be as efficacious as the work of any faith healer. Against this, of course, must be set the fact that such advertisements very often prevent people from going to a physician for real illnesses which a physician alone may be able to cure.

Advertising may also claim that it makes us acquainted with more and different kinds of products and with more and different firms, and thus is an aid to the buyer in making wise choices. Whoever makes this claim, however, must actually show that consumers' choices are wiser as a result of advertising. Such a claim can only be made for truthful advertising, and even then, if advertising raises the cost of goods to the consumer, it must be shown that he is better off with fewer goods well chosen than he would be with a greater number of unadvertised but cheaper goods.

This brings us to the much-discussed question of whether advertising raises or lowers the price of a commodity. If a commodity is being produced under decreasing costs of production, and advertising is capable of expanding the market in such a way that the point of maximum net returns for the manufacturer will be at a lower price than it was before, then the price of the product as a result of advertising may be lower than it would have been without, *provided* the manufacturer is sufficiently aware of the nature of the demand curve to realize that a greater profit could be secured at a lower price. This may be true of a great many industries as long as we are looking at only one firm at a time. However, when all or a great many firms and industries are competitively clamoring for the buyer's attention, the amount of selling costs which will have to be incurred by each of them to gain a large market may be such that it will prove that increased selling costs will have more than offset the gains in lowered production costs. If such is the case, then the public could have been better served had the competition been on a price basis alone. We have not sufficient data on which to answer this question as regards the sum total of all products. From a casual examination it would appear that advertising has increased the price of some products and lowered that of others. To the extent that advertising succeeds in inducing buyers to select products by particular brand names rather than by comparing the price and quality of *all* products before they buy, it is certainly an inducement to the manufacturers to compete on a basis of increasing selling costs rather than cutting selling prices.

CHAPTER XIII

General Equilibrium Theory Under Perfect Competition

THE concept of general equilibrium varies among different economists.   One concept maintains that general equilibrium is the *static state,* a condition in which all prices are long-run equilibrium prices; each person is spending his income in the manner which yields him the greatest satisfaction; each firm and each industry is in a state of equilibrium with respect both to prices and output; and the supply and demand for factors of production are equated at equilibrium prices.   In short, general equilibrium is a condition in which there is no economic motive for change.   Changes may occur, however, due to changes in crop yields or other natural causes.   The holders of this view do not believe that the static state ever exists.   However, they do view the general movements of the economic system as a series of attempts to attain such an equilibrium condition, or as movements from one static state to another, which is never quite attained because new disturbances to equilibrium occur before full adjustment is ever achieved, or because of economic "friction," which permanently delays the adjustment until a new state of equilibrium is required by new circumstances.

The *circular flow,* Professor Schumpeter's creation,[1] is con-

---

[1] See the chapter on "Business Cycles"; also *The Theory of Economic Development,* Harvard University Press, 1934.

ceived of as a sort of constantly moving equilibrium in which people can take past experience as a guide for future conduct, and rules of thumb apply. The only economic factor which could disturb this situation is "innovation." Professor Schumpeter allows for quantitative changes within the circular flow, but they must be within the range where the old rules of economic conduct hold.

Frank H. Knight would agree partly with Professor Schumpeter. Knight's idea of a state of general equilibrium is that of a situation in which all forecasting is perfect, so that instantaneous adjustment could place the system in equilibrium with anticipated conditions which would actually be fulfilled.

These statements do not represent fully the different theories of general equilibrium prevailing, rather they are brief descriptions of "imaginary states" under which the various theories of general equilibrium might operate perfectly.

Professor Wicksell also assumes that competition is both pure and perfect and that output is produced under conditions of constant cost.[2] In order that there will be no residual income (profits) to be accounted for, he makes the additional assumption that any one of the factors of production, or rather the owner of the factor—the landlord, the laborer, or the capitalist —may also act as manager of the business and hire the other factors. Then in order for the firm and for the industry to be in equilibrium, average total unit cost must be at a minimum, and at this minimum the cost must equal the selling price.

The Production Function

Wicksell then stated his condition of equilibrium as a mathematical equation which we can simplify by stating it in words:

---

[2] Constant cost is achieved by adding to or subtracting from the industry firms operating at minimum cost, which is uniform for all firms.

$$\left.\begin{array}{l}\text{Total receipts from}\\\text{sale of the product}\end{array}\right\}\text{ is equal to }\left\{\begin{array}{l}\text{Total cost}\\\text{of production.}\end{array}\right.$$

$$\left.\begin{array}{l}\text{Total cost of}\\\text{production}\end{array}\right\}\text{ is equal to }\left\{\begin{array}{l}\text{Quantity of factor A times the price of A, plus}\\\text{quantity of factor B times the price of B, plus}\\\text{quantity of factor C times the price of C}\ldots\end{array}\right.$$

and so on for as many factors as are employed in making the product. It also follows from the condition of minimum cost and uniform cost that any increase in the use of all the factors combined will result in the same proportionate increase in the product. Equilibrium among industries will be fulfilled by the condition that all total receipts of all products must be proportional to the amounts of the factors used.[3]

Most people who explain a general equilibrium theory start with the idea that consumers' choices determine relative prices and quantities of goods sold. A careful examination of the above propositions or of actual conditions will convince the reader that every price is related to every other price in the whole economic system either directly or indirectly. Thus we are acting under a system of mutually interrelated prices. We might just as well say that prices depended upon consumers' income, which in turn was derived from the prices and quantities of the factors of production.

We have made a fairly detailed study of partial or temporary equilibrium of the prices of commodities. It may help us to repeat in somewhat simpler language the conditions which tend to regulate the prices of the factors of production.

In one sense there is no need for making a special problem of these prices. They are all determined by supply and demand in the same way as the prices of commodities. However, there are certain peculiarities in both the supply of, and demand for, the factors of production which are different from the supply and demand for commodities, which merit the treatment of

---

[3] Mathematically, we may say that we have a set of simultaneous equations, one for each industry.

the prices of the factors of production as special price problems.

In the first place, the demand for the factors of production is a *derived* demand. The owners of a business are not ordinarily hiring laborers to satisfy their own personal wants. What they are doing is hiring laborers to make goods which will satisfy some want of the public. The demand for labor is thus derived from the demand for goods. If the public's demand for a certain type of goods increases, then the demand for labor by the firm which makes those goods will increase. The same thing is true of the services of management, whether performed by a hired manager or by the owner of a firm. The public does not demand the services of the manager directly. What it demands is the product which the manager's services help to produce.

Another problem that is common to any price analysis will occupy our attention more here than in the previous chapters. This is the problem of mutual interdependence of prices and, in this case, the mutual interdependence of the prices of the various factors of production. We cannot consider the price of any one factor as being uniquely determined, independent of the other factors. This does not mean that the price of any factor is indeterminate or that the problem is insoluble. What it does mean is that our problem is not that of a simple single cause-and-effect relation, but rather one of a resultant of forces.

Conditions of Equilibrium of Prices of the Factors of Production

We may best approach this problem by first attempting to discover the necessary conditions under which the prices of the various factors of production will be in equilibrium. To simplify the problem, we shall start by making certain assumptions which will seldom be fulfilled by the conditions of the actual economic world. When we have discovered the principles involved, we will remove these assumptions one by one (in this and the following chapters) in order to explain what goes on in the actual world when these assumptions are not fulfilled.

We shall assume: (1) that the tastes for the various commodities which the public buys are known and will not change; (2) that there are no new inventions and no improvements in the knowledge of methods of production (this assumption implies that the only changes in productive technique which take place will be changes in the amount of the factors of production used or in the proportion in which they are used); (3) that the units of each factor of production will be homogeneous, so that there is no difference in productive ability between different units of the same factor; (4) that there is perfect competition both on the supply and on the demand side of the markets for the factors of production; (5) that there is perfect mobility of all factors of production.

Under these assumptions, the first condition of equilibrium would be that all units of a factor would have to be paid the same price. Thus, if some laborers offered to work for less than others, any employer could gain by discharging the higher-priced laborers and hiring the cheaper ones, and the labor market would not be in equilibrium. Similarly, if he could borrow money capital at a lower rate of interest than he is now paying, he could gain by borrowing to pay off the old loans, and the capital market would not be in equilibrium.

The second condition of equilibrium is that the prices of the various factors of production must be in proportion to their marginal products. The *marginal product* of a factor of production may be defined as *the net amount added to total revenue by the last unit of the factor employed.*[4] For example, if a firm hires one more worker and his employment

---

[4] Note that this marginal revenue product will be different, depending on whether the firm is operating under conditions of pure or monopolistic competition.

results in an addition to the daily output of the firm of five units of the product, and the sale of these units adds $5.00 to total revenue, then the marginal product of labor is $5.00.

The statement of the second condition of equilibrium then becomes:

$$\frac{\text{Marginal Product of Factor } A}{\text{Price of } A}$$

must equal

$$\frac{\text{Marginal Product of } B}{\text{Price of } B}$$

must equal

$$\frac{\text{Marginal Product of } C}{\text{Price of } C}$$

and so on, for as many factors as there are. If it should so happen that these ratios are not equal, for example, if

$$\frac{\text{Marginal Product of } A}{\text{Price of } A}$$

is greater than

$$\frac{\text{Marginal Product of } B}{\text{Price of } B}$$

then it will pay the firm to use more of factor A and less of factor B, and this will not be a state of equilibrium. A numerical example may help to illustrate this principle. Suppose that the wages of a certain kind of labor are $10.00 per day, and that the marginal product of this kind of labor is $30.00 per day. At the same time, suppose that the machine cost of a certain type of machine is $20.00 per day and that the marginal product of the machine is $40.00 per day. Our ratios would then stand:

$$\textit{Labor} \qquad\qquad \textit{Machines}$$
$$\frac{\text{Marginal Product } \$30.00}{\text{Price } \$10.00} \quad > \quad \frac{\text{Marginal Product } \$40.00}{\text{Price } \$20.00}$$

Under these circumstances, each dollar spent for labor adds $3.00 to total revenue, whereas each dollar spent for machines adds only $2.00 (the marginal product of labor is in the ratio of 3:1 to its price; the marginal product of machines is in the ratio of 2:1 to its price). It would pay us more to add labor rather than to add machines. If the price does not change, we would add more labor alone until the marginal product was driven down to $20.00. The equation would then be:

$$\frac{\text{Labor}}{\text{Marginal Product \$20.00}}{\text{Price \$10.00}} = \frac{\text{Machines}}{\text{Marginal Product \$40.00}}{\text{Price \$20.00}}$$

which satisfies the second condition of equilibrium. All of this is merely another way of saying that a necessary condition of equilibrium is that the firm must be using the *least cost combination* of factors of production. If, at any time, the conditions are such that a firm could gain by employing more labor and less capital,[5] or more capital and less labor, such a firm is not in equilibrium in respect to its demand for the factors of production. This second condition is also known as "the principle of substitution."

The third condition of equilibrium is an extension of the second: In equilibrium, the prices of each of the factors of production must be equal to their marginal products. If the second condition were fulfilled but not the third (for example, if the prices of all the factors are proportional to their marginal products, but the marginal productivity of each factor is greater than its price), then it will pay the firm to vary the amount of all the factors employed. If the marginal product of each factor is greater than its price (as is the case in the numerical equation above), then the addition to total revenue would be

---

[5] Note that money capital is a homogeneous factor, while capital goods are not homogeneous as a class but are only homogeneous within various subgroups (for example, particular kinds of machines or tools). The implication of this will be considered in the chapter on interest.

greater than the addition to total cost if more of each factor were employed. Conversely, if the marginal product of each factor is less than its price, then the subtraction from total revenue would be less than the subtraction from total cost if less of each factor were employed. This third condition is merely another way of saying that the *output* of the firm must be in equilibrium, that is, that the firm is already so adjusted that it could not profit by expanding or contracting its output by employing more or less of all factors of production. Thus, the second condition refers to the *proportion* in which the factors are used; the third condition refers to the *amount* of all of them which is used.

The fourth condition of equilibrium is that all of the units of each factor of production whose supply price is equal to or lower than the prevailing market price of the factor must be employed. Thus, if there are unemployed workmen who desire work and are unable to find it, they may offer their services to the employers at less than the prevailing rate of wages. The employers will then have a motive either to discharge their present working force and hire the workers who will work for less or to insist that the present force work for lower wages. In either event, the previously prevailing rate of wages will not have been an equilibrium rate. Similarly, if loanable funds are unemployed, the owners—rather than receive no interest at all—will loan them at a lower rate of interest, thus forcing down the previously prevailing interest rate. Some people may prefer to spend their money on consumers' goods rather than loan their funds at the lower rate of interest; this will remove some of the supply of loanable funds from the market.

Process by Which Equilibrium Is Attained

We are now equipped with a knowledge of the four conditions of equilibrium for the prices of the factors of production under the five assumptions we have made. A little further analysis will show us that we are also equipped with a knowledge of the process by which this equilibrium is reached.

The first condition—uniform price for all units of a factor—will tend to be fulfilled by the action of competition. Competition among workers will tend to depress wages, and competition among employers to obtain workers will tend to force wages up, until a true market price is established at which demand and supply will be equal. Similarly, competition among lenders on the one side and borrowers on the other side will establish a single market rate of interest. The same holds true for all other factors of production.

Elasticity of Substitution

The second condition—factor prices proportional to marginal products—will tend to be fulfilled by the process of substituting one factor for another whenever their prices happen to be disproportional to their marginal products. Whenever labor is cheaper than capital in proportion to the efficiency of each in production, it will pay employers to use more labor and less capital, and they will tend to adopt productive methods that will take advantage of this situation. Thus, if the rate of wages is very low and the rate of interest is extremely high, contractors for excavating work will tend to use laborers with picks and shovels for all possible jobs; whereas, if wages are high and interest rates low, there will be a great many jobs on which the lowest cost can be achieved by using ditch-digging machines and steam shovels, with fewer laborers.

Note that the fulfillment of the second condition can be attained either by a change in the prices of the factors or by a change in their marginal productivity, or by both. Thus, when labor is cheaper relatively to its efficiency than capital, the attempt of a large number of employers to use more labor results in a competition among them which tends to raise the price of labor. At the start of this process (substitution of labor for capital), employers will first take advantage of this cheap labor situation by putting the added labor to those uses in which its marginal productivity is the highest. In other words, labor will first be substituted for machines in those uses in which the labor cost is much less than the machine cost for doing the same job. As more and more labor is used, it will have to be put to work in jobs where the cost advantage of the labor method over the machine method is less and less. Thus the marginal productivity of labor will be declining relatively to the marginal productivity of capital as the substitution of labor for capital is pushed into those uses where machinery has a greater technical advantage over labor, that is, in those tasks where it requires a greater number of cheap laborers to take the place of a high-priced machine.

But, as less and less capital is being used, its price will tend to decline. At the same time, the high-priced capital will tend to be withdrawn first from those uses in which its marginal productivity is least. Thus, the capital which is retained will be retained in those uses in which its marginal productivity is greatest, and the marginal productivity of the capital which is still used will have increased.

We can thus see that a readjustment to equilibrium conditions when the prices of factors of production are out of proportion to their marginal products is accomplished by a rise in the price of the *underpriced factor* and a *decrease* in its marginal product as successive units are put to less productive uses. Equilibrium may also be attained by a *decline* in the price of the *overpriced factor* and an *increase* in the marginal product of those units of the factor which are retained, since the factor will be withdrawn first from its least productive uses.

The governing principle in all this readjustment is the *elasticity of substitution*. The elasticity of substitution is a measure of the readiness to substitute one factor of production for

another in response to a change in their relative prices.[6] If
the same amount of labor would always be required to make
a unit of a product, regardless of the method of production
employed, the elasticity of substitution of capital for labor would
be zero. If one unit of labor would always yield the same
product as one unit of capital (regardless of the proportions
in which they were used), then the elasticity of substitution of
either factor for the other would be infinite; that is, with the
slightest drop in the price of capital while the price of labor
remained the same, all capital and no labor would be used in
production; and vice versa. Obviously, neither zero nor infinite elasticity of substitution is a possible condition in the
actual world. The extent to which capital will be substituted
for labor, or labor for capital, in any productive process will
depend both on the relative efficiency of the factors and on the
relative change in their prices.

If a state of equilibrium has previously been in existence, it
may be disrupted by a change in the supply of any of the factors
of production (for instance, an increase or decrease in the
supply of capital, resulting in the offering of the same amount
of capital at lower or higher interest rates). The equilibrium
of proportionality between prices and marginal products might
be altered by a change in the productivity of any factor. Such
a change would most likely be occasioned by the invention of
a new machine or by the discovery of a new process (conditions
ruled out by our second assumption, but which we shall have
to consider later). Regardless of its source, the disturbance
will have given rise to a new set of data with which adjustments will have to conform to reëstablish equilibrium under

---

[6] Mathematically, the elasticity of substitution is the proportionate change in the
ratio of the amounts of the factors employed divided by the proportionate change in
the ratio of their prices to which the change in ratio of amounts of factors is due.

$$\frac{\Delta\left(\frac{QA}{QB}\right)}{\frac{QA}{QB}} \div \frac{\Delta\left(\frac{PA}{PB}\right)}{\frac{PA}{PB}} = \text{Elasticity of Substitution, where } P \text{ and } Q \text{ are prices and quantities of factors } A \text{ and } B.$$

the second condition. A new equilibrium will therefore take the place of the old, based upon the new conditions of supply of the factors of production. The prices of the factors may or may not be the same in the new equilibrium as in the old; nor need the marginal products be the same as they were before. It is only necessary that the new prices be proportional to the new marginal products to fulfill the second condition of equilibrium again.

If it should happen that optimum output for a firm should be the same after the disturbance as before, some time might be required for the adjustment to take place, particularly if the new adjustment to the second condition of equilibrium required the substitution of labor for capital. Insofar as a firm's capital is invested in the form of fixed capital goods (such as plant and machinery), it will not be possible immediately to reduce the amount of capital used. If established firms do not make this adjustment, new firms can start up, using the better proportions of labor and capital, and undersell the old firms. In this case, the old firms will have to "write off" a part of their capital investment as a loss. In no event will they replace the same amount of fixed capital as it wears out. If the old firms are able to stand this loss, they will carry on under the same ownership. If not, they will go bankrupt, and whoever buys the business at the bankruptcy sale will only pay such a price for it as is justified by the new conditions.

However, if the new optimum output for a firm is larger than the old, adjustment will be much more rapid. Even where a heavy fixed investment exists, it will be possible to increase the proportion of labor to capital by working longer hours or double shifts. The additional output can and will be produced by methods which use more labor and relatively less capital.[7]

Where the adjustment is in the other direction (requiring

---

[7] An absolute increase in the amount of labor used with a fixed amount (or a smaller proportionate increase in amount) of capital means a substitution of labor for capital.

the use of more capital and less labor), it can be made just as rapidly as the capital goods can be manufactured and the new methods can be installed in the plant.

In any event, the most rapid adjustment to the new conditions will be likely to take place among the new firms which start up. Any new firm will be in a position to take advantage of the new relations between the prices and the productivities of the factors. Furthermore, if it so happens that labor is cheaper relatively to its efficiency than is capital, new firms will be most encouraged to start up in those industries making those products which require the greatest proportionate amount of labor and the least amount of capital; and vice versa.

The third condition of equilibrium—that the price of each factor of production must be equal to its marginal product—will be fulfilled by the combined effect of the profit search of firms and of perfect competition (which we have thus far assumed). If in any industry the factors are being paid in *proportion* to their marginal products, but the prices of each are *less* than the marginal products, this is just another way of saying that the firms could increase their profits by hiring more of the factors, and thus expanding output. Expansion of output, whether by old firms or new, will do two things: it will tend to raise the price of all the factors of production and (since we assume the demand curve for the product does' not change) the increased output will have to be sold for a lower price. Such a lower price for the product will mean a decreased value of the new marginal units which the factors of production are making; in other words, the marginal product of each factor will have diminished. This process will continue until the marginal products are equal to the prices of the factors.

If in any industry the prices of the factors are greater than their marginal products, the industry will be operating at a loss or, at least, at less than maximum profits, and therefore there will be a tendency to reduce output. The decreased demand for the factors of production will tend to lower their prices, and the decreased supply of the product will tend to increase its price until the prices and the marginal products of the factors of production are again equal.

In actual business experience we will find that full equilibrium is seldom if ever attained. Thus, the demand for different products will change, and before equilibrium under the new situation can be attained, demand may change again. One invention will alter the relative productivity of labor and capital, and before full adjustment can be made, another invention will come on the scene. But we must not ignore the fact that the intervals between such changes are only explainable as an effort of our economic system to readjust itself to a new set of equilibrium conditions. In the subsequent chapters, we shall discover how monopoly and monopolistic competition both in the markets for goods and in the markets for the factors of production not only tend to delay the attainment of equilibrium, but also result in the final equilibrium solution being different from what it would have been had pure competition prevailed.

Before going any further we should understand clearly that the marginal productivity theory is not a justification of the distribution of income as it exists today, nor is it a justification of the income which any individual receives. It is simply an explanation of the way in which our economic system works. However much we may disapprove of the results which are attained, we must have a thorough understanding of the functional nature of the process of distribution. Otherwise, any attempt to reform the system will be likely to give rise to evils and maladjustments which are worse than those that the reform was intended to correct.[8] Unfortunate as it may be, an

---

[8] The Miller-Tydings Resale Price Maintenance Act apparently was designed to inhibit pure competition and to encourage monopolistic competition.

ethical point of view is no substitute for intelligence in this modern world of ours.

Within each firm and within each industry, marginal productivity is the explanation of the demand for the factors of production. The supply of factors of production to any firm or to any industry is explained in terms of opportunity cost (the earnings which the units of the factors could make in other firms or industries). The following chapters deal mainly with conditions of supply and demand which are peculiar to individual factors of production and which lead to some modifications in the application of the principles. The basic principles of marginal productivity and opportunity cost must nevertheless be kept constantly in mind throughout the discussion.

Criticism of the General Equilibrium Theory under Perfect Competition

At its best, the general equilibrium theory as outlined here gives us a picture of what would be required to attain complete equilibrium of our economic system. It also gives us a standard by which to determine whether or not particular changes are working in the direction of this kind of equilibrium. Nevertheless, even the most enthusiastic contributors to the theory do not claim that it represents an explanation of the real world. Rather, it is a schematic point of departure from which, by removing assumptions, actual problems can be approached.

Its worst features are the number of assumptions required which are contrary to actual conditions and the fact that many of these assumptions cannot be removed without in some respects detracting from the theory itself. Many of these assumptions are made simply with the intent to reduce the problem to a set of simultaneous equations from which the mathematical economist can derive useful mental exercise. When the theory reaches this form, it does not mean much more than the simple statement that all prices of factors of production and goods are mutually interrelated; that a shift of demand will result in a higher price for the product whose demand has increased and a lower price for the product whose demand has decreased; and that, given sufficient time, with no other disturbances intervening, a shift in the factors of production will restore these prices to a new equilibrium ratio based upon the change in demand. Some of the most unrealistic assumptions are:

1. Pure competition which is also perfect.
2. Constant cost.
3. No decreasing costs.
4. Standardized products for individual industries.

If the production function even closely approached reality, there would be no need for the separate chapters on wages, rent, interest, and profits which follow.

Most of the special rules which we have to develop when we attack these separate questions by particular equilibrium analysis are the result of situations of monopoly, monopolistic competition, oligopoly, monopsony, and oligopsony. If it can be demonstrated that monopolistic competition is a permanent institution, then the entire set of assumptions of general equilibrium theory under pure and perfect competition would have to be drastically revised.

CHAPTER XIV

Wages[1]

THE FIRST problem which confronts us in dealing with the problems of wages is that labor in general is too broad a category to be considered as a single factor of production. So divergent are the different kinds of skills possessed by different groups of workmen that our third assumption of the preceding chapter is not fulfilled—labor in general is not a homogeneous factor, and there are differences in productive ability between different units of it.

Differences in Skills

So far as differences in kinds of skills are concerned, this problem can be easily met by considering each of the different groups of laborers as a separate factor of production.[2] Our second condition of equilibrium—that the prices of the different factors of production must be proportional to their marginal products—will then apply as between the different groups of labor exactly as it did between labor and capital. For example, carpenters and bricklayers are different factors of production for the purpose of building houses. If the bricklayers' union demands an increase in wages while the wages of carpenters remain the same, then the proportion between the marginal products and wages of brick laying and of carpenter

---

[1] See Hicks, J. R., *Theory of Wages*, The Macmillan Co., 1933, and Taussig, F. W., *Principles of Economics*, Ch. 47, The Macmillan Co., New York, 1921.

[2] Or, should we say that the sale of skills is a sale of differentiated products under monopolistic competition or monopoly.

work will have been disturbed, and the law of substitution will start to work. In simpler language, the cost of a brick house will have risen relatively compared to the cost of a wooden house, and people will tend to substitute lumber for brick in building houses. If the bricklayers' union sticks to its price, bricklaying will be confined to those uses in which the marginal product of bricklaying is equal to its price. Bricks will be used in most houses only for chimneys, where their advantage over wood is unquestioned, and only those few houses will be built entirely of brick whose prospective owners consider that the advantage of a brick house over a wooden house merits paying the new, higher price for brick. The net result is, of course, that some bricklayers will be unemployed. We will reserve a full discussion of this sort of unemployment until later. What we have established here is that different kinds of skilled labor may be treated as different factors of production and that the law of substitution works between them.

Differences in Efficiency [3]

Another difficulty with which we are confronted is that even within the same trade or craft the workers may be of considerably different efficiency. The principle of substitution will apply between individual workers as well as between groups. If wages are the same for all individuals in a trade, employers will attempt to obtain and keep the more efficient men and to discharge or avoid hiring the less efficient. If the less efficient men who find themselves unemployed offer to work for lower wages, some employers may find it to their advantage to hire these men rather than the better workmen, when the difference in wages is sufficient to compensate for the difference in efficiency.

---

[3] Differences in efficiency are closer to conditions of monopolistic competition than are differences in skills. The latter may be marketed under monopoly by trade unions.

In occupations that are more or less standardized, there is less discrepancy between wages and marginal products due to differences in individual efficiency than might be supposed offhand. In the actual world, while there may be a marked difference in efficiency between superior workmen and average workmen, or between average workmen and substandard workmen, there is usually in every trade a sufficiently large number of average workmen whose efficiency differs so little from one to another that a substantially accurate adjustment of wages to marginal products may be attained by paying the entire average group the same wage.

The payment of piecework wages will also tend to narrow somewhat the discrepancy between wages and marginal products due to individual differences in efficiency. Piece wages, however, would compensate completely for all differences in efficiency only in the imaginary case where labor cost was the only cost involved in making a product. For example, if an average worker using a machine can turn out four times as much product as a substandard worker, then, even though both were paid the same rate per piece, the *machine cost* of using substandard workers would be four times that of using average workers. That is, four substandard workers would need four machines to turn out the same amount of product as one average worker with one machine. To allow for this difference so that wages and marginal products would be equal, it would be necessary to pay the substandard workers a *lower price per piece* than the average workers. In some of the complicated wage systems in use today this is actually attempted. But rather than to attempt to explain to the workmen the justification for a differential piece rate, as given above, many firms adopt the simpler expedient of not hiring the substandard workmen if they know them to be substandard and of discharging them as soon as their inefficiency is discovered. As substandard workmen's lack of efficiency tends to become known to the various employers, they will be the last to be hired when business is picking up and the first to be fired when business slacks off again. If regularity of employment may be considered as one form of compensation, then substandard workers are indeed receiving less than average workers.

The superior efficiency of super-standard workmen may be compensated for, at least in part, by some system of bonuses paid by a firm. The adjustment may also take place by a specialization between firms as to the workmen they hire. Thus, some firms may so plan their productive processes as to take full advantage of the superior men's greater efficiency and offer a higher wage to attract them. A motor car assembly line manned entirely by superior workmen may be able to turn out enough more cars per day to justify paying the men a wage much higher than the average, and some manufacturers may adopt this policy. On the other hand, no manufacturer could gain by mixing superior and average men on the same assembly line, as the slower pace of the average men would hold back their faster fellow-workers. Consequently, it will pay some other manufacturers to standardize on average men, paying them the average wage.

For the most part, however, superior men will have to depend on individual bargaining with their employers to secure a better-than-average wage to compensate for their greater efficiency. The absolute maximum which a superior worker can obtain over a long period of time is the full value of his services to the employer who is best situated to take advantage of his superior efficiency. The minimum wage which he can be forced to accept is the wage which the next most eager employer would be willing to pay for his services. Between these two limits there will be a "range of indeterminateness," and the actual wage paid will be a result of the relative bargaining abilities of the employer and the employee. In the case of extremely exceptional individuals, such a "range of indeterminateness" may be fairly wide, particularly if there is only one or a very few employers who are in a position to take advantage of their superior abilities. Thus we used to have the annual controversy in the sport pages in the days of Babe Ruth's glory as to whether he was worth more or less than the salary which the New York Yankees offered him in his new contract each year.

Exploitation of Labor

However, the Babe Ruths, the Greta Garbos, and the Alfred Sloans are so few in number that, for the purposes of an elementary text, we can safely leave them to worry for themselves as to whether they are being paid wages that represent the full value of their services, and concentrate our attention upon the vast majority of workmen who make up the ordinary supply of labor. Nevertheless, there is one rather curious fact that should not escape our attention. If we define "exploitation of labor" as the paying of wages which are less than the full value of a workman to the employer, then exploitation is much more apt to exist in the case of the highest-paid individuals than in the case of the lowest. This is simply due to the fact that in the case of these exceptional individuals there is usually only one employer who is in a position to take full advantage of their exceptional ability. And even though the best-situated employer is paying the individual less than he is worth to the firm, he may be paying him more than what his value would be to the next best-situated employer. Thus, in the case of Babe Ruth, even though there had been no league agreement not to bid competitively for players, the Yankees were the only club in the league with a stadium large enough and located in a city large enough to take full advantage of the Babe's exceptional ability to draw the customers through the turnstiles. Competitive bidding might have saved Ruth from having to accept his $80,000.00 pittance, but competitive bidding alone could never have forced the Yankees to pay him the full value of his services to them.

At the other extreme, take the case of the village half-wit whom I may hire to work in my garden at 15c an hour. If I should hire him, I find that I have to spend so much time and energy supervising his efforts that I prefer to do the work myself. Meantime, my neighbors (who do hire him) are always in doubt as to whether he is worth what little they have to pay him. His wages are low, not because he is being exploited, but because his productivity is so miserably low.

Exploitation is not likely to persist where there is a large group of similarly skilled workmen, because it would increase profits of employers to hire more of these "exploited" men; and, in the competitive effort to hire more, they would tend to drive wages up to the marginal product. This is the case in many of the "sweated" industries. While it would be idle to deny that exploitation often does exist in these trades (manufacture of women's cheap dresses, artificial flowers, and so on), we should not ignore the fact that in a great many cases competition in the use of cheap labor will have driven the price of the product down to so low a point that the value of a worker's product will not exceed his wages, even though those wages may be deplorably low.

Economic Effects of Minimum Wage Laws

While we are on the subject, it might be interesting to observe the economic effects of a legally imposed minimum wage in the above circumstances. If no exploitation exists, such a minimum wage is bound to result in less employment, except where monopsonistic exploitation exists, since the output of the industry will have to be restricted to a point where the higher price to be obtained for a smaller amount of the product will be sufficient to compensate for the higher labor cost imposed by the minimum wage. The fact that some people are working for less than a proposed minimum wage is evidence that they are willing to do so rather than remain unemployed. Consequently, when the minimum wage is imposed, they will be tempted to conspire with their employers to conceal the fact that they are being paid less than the minimum, rather than face unemployment, and the law will be expensive and difficult to enforce. On the other hand, there may be certain classes of people for whom we decide that it is not socially desirable that they be employed. If this is the case, the desired end can be attained better by direct legislation to that effect; that is, by child labor laws, maximum hours for female workers, compulsory medical examinations for workers in hazardous occupations, and so forth. Such legislation, besides achieving the direct end stated by the law, will also tend to raise wages in the trades from which the undesirable labor is withdrawn by decreasing the supply of labor available. Then, too, such legislation is ordinarily easier to enforce than minimum wage laws.

Our zeal for social reform should not blind us to the social cost involved in either minimum wages or specific prohibitions of certain kinds of labor. Such cost can be measured in terms of fewer goods and in terms of the higher prices which the public must now pay. In addition, it may be necessary for society to provide through doles, mothers' pensions, or other forms of poor relief, for the people made unemployed by social legislation. On the other hand, in the case of child labor, at least, it may be that if their minds and bodies are saved from being stunted by too early employment, their increased productivity at maturity may more than compensate for the products they might have made as children. Furthermore, insofar as more children are educated, it will tend to decrease the relative advantage enjoyed by the members of the higher-trained occupations. Thus, there will be, for example, more people qualified as business executives and as engineers, so that the wages in those occupations will tend to be less than they would have been in the absence of such legislation. This will work to the disadvantage of those people who would have attained to the skilled groups in the absence of the legislation, but it will be to the advantage of the rest of the population in that they can obain these skilled services cheaper.

The Supply of Labor

We must now turn our attention to the supply of labor. Here we have no such thing as a definite cost of production of labor governing its supply as we did in the case of the supply of goods. While the rate of wages undoubtedly does have some influence upon the numbers of the population, there are so many other causes at work (sanitation, medical care of infants, accident prevention, birth control, social attitude toward marriage and large families, and so on) that the rate of wages as a single cause becomes of so little importance that we can leave the question to the student of population problems. For our purposes, we may take the numbers of potential workers at any given time as a thing for granted and work from that point.

We may define the supply of labor as the schedule of amounts of work (units of labor) that workers are willing to offer for sale at each possible price. This supply is a function mainly of two variables—the number of workers that are able and willing to work at each possible price, and the number of hours that each one is able and willing to work at each price.

If no worker had any savings and it was simply a question of work or starve, and if under these circumstances all employers conspired together to try to drive wages down to the lowest possible level, there is little doubt that a great majority of workers would be willing to work for a much lower wage than they are now receiving. Considered in these terms, the supply of all labor in general is seen to be extremely inelastic. For a very short period (under these circumstances) the amount of labor offered for sale at a lower price might actually be greater than the amount offered at a higher price. That is, workers who have been accustomed to the products included in a higher standard of living, rather than give them up, might make the first adjustment to a lower wage by attempting to work a greater number of hours. But they would very shortly discover that at least some amount of leisure was worth more to them than the products they would have to give up, and they would adjust themselves to a lower standard of living. Furthermore, no matter how willing they might be, there will be a tendency for the greater number of hours worked to detract from their efficiency, so that a larger number of hours is counteracted by a smaller product per hour. It seems safe to say that, with a given population, the supply of all labor in general will not be very elastic over a long period of time.

If the supply of all labor is inelastic, then the demand for labor will be more important than the supply in determining its price. However, even the absence of trade-unions need not be an occasion for the reader to worry about such a conspiracy among employers as was imagined above. If such a conspiracy were formed, as wages were driven below the marginal products of labor, a profitable opportunity would be presented for certain laborers to quit the ranks of labor and become employers (provided they could obtain capital), thus breaking the monopoly power of the conspiracy. Furthermore, as wages were driven down, it would pay any employer to start substituting labor for capital and to employ more laborers by paying higher wages to get them away from the other employers. Thus, each and every employer in the conspiracy would have the strongest of motives to violate his agreement, and the conspiracy would fall of its own weight.

However, the wages that are being paid today are in fact

determined not so much by the demand for and the supply of labor in general as by the demand for and the supply of labor in particular occupations and particular industries. In this connection, the general demand for labor is important only insofar as it affects the supply available for any one occupation or any one industry. Thus an increase in the demand for structural ironworkers, by offering either higher wages, steadier employment, or both, may induce more youths to enter that occupation rather than learn the plumbing trade. A general increase in the demand for unskilled and semiskilled labor (such as occurred during the war) may, if the wages offered are high enough, induce many young men to go to work at these jobs rather than to spend their time in school learning to be pharmacists and accountants, thus decreasing what would otherwise have been the supply of labor in these skilled occupations. As soon as all labor is employed for the maximum number of hours they are willing to work, the supply becomes completely inelastic.

Causes of Differences in Wages

If all men were of identically the same mental and physical abilities in all respects, if all occupations were equally easy to enter, and if the conditions of work (other than wages) in all types of occupations were equally attractive or equally distasteful to all people, then, in a perfectly competitive labor market, the wages of all classes of labor would tend to be equal. Business executives and bricklayers, geologists and garbagemen, college presidents and dogcatchers would all be receiving the same salaries. The income they received from interest on investments might be different, but the wages received for work performed would be the same for all of them. However, none of the "ifs" above are fulfilled in actual life; consequently the relative scarcity of men in certain occupations serves to keep their marginal productivity so high that they can command a higher wage than those in other occupations in which the supply is greater relatively to the demand. We shall examine for a moment some of the conditions that give rise to this scarcity:

(1) In the first place all men do not have equal educational opportunities. To make such educational opportunities absolutely equal, not only would tuition, board, and room-rent have to be free through high school, college, and graduate, technical, or professional school, but also children of poorer parents would have to be freed from the necessity of going to work at an early age to help augment the meager family income. Other things being equal, the relative scarcity of men who are able to obtain an advanced education will tend to make the earnings in occupations requiring higher education higher than in those requiring less training. There is no guarantee, however, that this will happen at any one time in any one profession. If all, or a vast majority, of college graduates decide to become lawyers, the average lawyer might be earning $10.00 a week while the average carpenter was earning $40.00.

(2) The second element that contributes to the relative scarcity of men available for certain types of occupations is the unequal natural endowment of different individuals with different skills. This is a scarcity which even completely free education would not overcome. Thus, even of the numbers who graduate from medical schools today, comparatively few possess the combination of mental ability and manual dexterity necessary to a really first-rate surgeon. By allowing a free education to all members of the population who possess these peculiar natural abilities, the number of first-rate surgeons would certainly be increased somewhat, and earnings would tend to decline. However, so long as the demand for surgeons' services continues to be what it is at present, or increases, it may be doubted whether education could increase the supply of surgeons sufficiently to reduce their earnings to that of less skilled labor. It should be noted that there is no "intrinsic" value of the sur-

geon's skill per se which enables it to command such a price as it does. It is true that the surgeon "saves lives"; but so does the tenant farmer who raises foodstuffs. It is simply the relative scarcity of men who have both the skill and the training of qualified surgeons which enables them to charge $200.00 to $2,000.00 for an hour's work in an operating room, as it is the wide distribution of farming skill which makes the number of farmers so great proportionately to the present demand for them that a tenant farmer might count himself lucky if he earned 50c an hour. The sole effect of skill in determining wages is the extent to which it may be a cause of scarcity in the number of men available for certain occupations.

(3) Another element that will contribute to cause differences in wages in different occupations is the relative social esteem in which these occupations are held. Thus, if two occupations require equal skill and training, but one is generally considered to be a more "respectable" or "dignified" employment than the other, workers may be induced to enter the more "dignified" employment at a lower wage than it would take to induce them to enter the less highly regarded trade. This accounts, in considerable measure, for the comparatively low wages of many so-called "white-collar" jobs. I have heard many a shipping clerk and timekeeper complain bitterly, "Those dumb birds out in the factory are getting paid more than I am for work that I could do better than they do." But when I asked them why they did not request the boss to give them employment in the factory rather than in the office, the usual answer was that they "considered such work beneath them." The lower wage was the price which they were paying to maintain a real or imaginary dignity.

(4) The great hazards or dangers of a particular occupation may cause workmen to be sufficiently reluctant to enter it so that a wage higher than that which prevails in other jobs of equal skill may have to be offered to attract them into the

hazardous occupation. But such a difference in wages will amount to full compensation for the hazards involved only to the extent that all prospective workmen are fully acquainted with the nature and frequency of the danger involved and make full allowance for it. For the most part, it will often be found that workmen are either insufficiently acquainted with the dangers involved or are too optimistic in believing that they individually will not be the ones to be killed or maimed, so that a hazardous occupation can usually obtain workers at wages only slightly higher than those paid in less dangerous work. This is one argument for compulsory workmen's compensation insurance as against voluntary individual accident insurance.

(5) Another source of inequality in wages lies in the chance of large earnings for a few successful men in certain occupations. The existence of these few large prizes may be sufficient to attract many more men into an occupation than could be induced to enter it by the expectation of receiving only the average salary. Thus, if anyone could be certain that he would have to spend his entire life as a $25.00 or $30.00 a week law clerk, he might not attempt to enter the legal profession. But the large earnings of a small minority of lawyers who are highly successful acts as such a powerful inducement to strive for these prizes that the profession tends to become "overcrowded" until the lowest 60 per cent of the lawyers are earning less than the average plumber, and many lawyers who started out with high ideals finish as "shysters," ambulance chasers, and professional politicians. The fact that the salary of a congressman is greater than what a lawyer could earn in his home town is the explanation of the demagogery employed by many in trying to keep their jobs. This element of wages is somewhat analogous to the principles on which a lottery is run. If the top prizes are small, there will have to be a great many of them so that there is a reasonable chance of winning one. If the top prizes are

extremely large, people may be induced to participate even though the odds are hundreds or thousands to one against them.

(6) The regularity of employment is an important factor influencing wages. A trade where employment is highly irregular will ordinarily have to offer a higher rate per hour to attract workers than a trade requiring similar skill where the employment is steadier. This explains much of the difference between the wages in seasonal and casual trades (for instance, shipping on the Great Lakes, harvest hands in the Wheat Belt, and longshoremen) and wages for similar occupations in factories which run the year round. Some of this labor is cared for by seasonal migration, but a much better solution would be the establishment of off-season industries.

Short-Period and Long-Run Supplies of Labor for Special Occupations

During short periods, an increase in the demand for any one kind of labor will tend to raise the wages in that occupation. The short-run supply of any one kind of labor is ordinarily very inelastic. As soon as all average workmen are employed, the only immediate sources of an increased amount of labor consist in working overtime, increased effort on the part of the existing working force, and the hiring of substandard workers. Obviously, increases in the amount of labor offered from these sources in response to higher wages cannot be very great, and successive increases in wages will bring about smaller and smaller increases in the amount of labor offered. The short-run supply of labor to an industry is essentially inelastic.

Effect of Shifts in Demand for Goods on Price of Labor

Any one employer, however, can obtain an increased supply of labor for himself by offering slightly higher wages than other employers in the industry; that is to say, the supply of labor to the single firm is more elastic than the supply to the whole industry. If the increase in the demand for the product is felt generally by all employers, each of them will be motivated to attempt to obtain an increased amount of labor in this fashion, and wages will be bid up competitively to the full amount of the higher marginal product occasioned by the increase in the demand for the commodity. Even if the increased demand is felt by only a part of the employers, the same result will take place. As workers are drawn away from those employers the demand for whose products has not increased, the marginal productivity of the remaining workers to their present employers and their importance to the employers will have increased, so that it will start to be desirable for these employers also to begin raising wages rather than to lose the remainder of their working force.

Some workers may find it easier than others to shift from one employer to another. Thus, single men may be able to move more easily than married men, and married men with houses on short leases can move more easily than those who have long leases or who own their own homes. Older workers who expect a pension may be more reluctant to change employers than younger men; and so on. This suggests one possible source of exploitation. An employer may grant wage increases only to those workmen whom he knows to be willing and able to leave him if he refuses, and he may refuse to give the increases to the other workers who will not be so likely to leave.[4] This is sometimes done. The more intelligent employer will, however, weigh against the gains of this kind of exploitation the possible decline in productivity on the part of the workers who feel that they have been unjustly treated, and the possibility that he may find it difficult to obtain high-class workers in the future if he earns for himself the reputation of being an unfair employer.

In a particular occupation, high wages due to an increase in

---

[4] Discriminating monopsony.

demand for the product can persist only for the length of time that it will take for workers in other occupations to be induced by the high wage to shift over and train themselves for this occupation, or for the oncoming generation to be induced by the higher wage to enter this occupation in greater numbers than before. This length of time will vary, of course, with the length of time it takes to learn the trade. Ordinarily, workers will be reluctant to shift from one trade to another if they have any reason to suspect the high wages in the new occupation to be purely temporary. In order to augment the supply of labor very rapidly in a certain industry, wages must therefore be either extremely high or give promise of continuing to be higher over a considerable period of time than they were before.

In any event, the long-run supply of labor to any occupation will be much more elastic than the short-run supply. After all the elements making for differences in wages which we discussed above have been taken into consideration, any wage that more than compensates for these elements will be sufficient to attract a greater amount of labor into an occupation if a sufficiently long time is allowed and no impediment to entry exists. The long-run supply curve of labor for any one industry or any one occupation will have an upward inclination due solely to the fact that as more and more labor is attracted into any one industry it must be drawn away from other industries where its marginal product will be increasing as more is withdrawn.

However, a mere shift in demand for goods by the public from one industry to another will not in itself be sufficient to give rise to an upward inclination of the long-run supply curve of labor for the industry the demand for whose products has increased. For example, if people demand more suits of clothes and fewer pairs of shoes (perhaps because in driving cars they wear out the seats of their trousers faster than their shoes), the demand for labor in the clothing industry will increase. The temporary effect will be an increase in the wages of garment workers. On the other hand, since the demand for shoes has decreased, the marginal productivity of shoe-workers will decline, and shoe factories will either lower their wage rates or reduce their working force at the prevailing wage. So, in the long run, other conditions being equal, the clothing industry would not necessarily have to offer higher wages than it did before the change in demand to attract the necessary number of workers away from the shoe industry. If the same conditions persisted long enough, the mere fact of steadier employment in the clothing industry might be sufficient inducement for the workers to make the change. Under these conditions, the long-run supply curve of labor to the clothing industry would be a horizontal straight line at the previous wage; that is, supply of labor to the industry would be infinitely elastic.

On the other hand, a shift in demand for goods may cause the expanding industry to encounter a long-run supply curve of labor that is less than infinitely elastic. If the product whose demand is increasing required a greater proportion of labor and a smaller proportion of capital than the product whose demand is declining, then the expanding industry will require more labor than the declining industry is willing to release without bidding up wages. Thus, in our illustration above, if it requires more labor and less capital to make $100.00 worth of clothing than it does to make $100.00 worth of shoes, then the marginal product of labor in the shoe industry—in spite of decreased demand for shoes—will start to rise before the clothing industry has obtained the full number of additional workers needed. Consequently, the shoe industry will start to raise wages to avoid losing more workers than it cares to part with, and the clothing industry will have to increase wages to attract the full amount of needed labor away from the shoe industry or away from other industries.

If the expanding industry requires higher trained or better

educated labor than the contracting industry, then it will have to offer higher wages to induce a greater number of men to train themselves for the work. (Some companies meet this problem by maintaining their own schools and paying new employees to attend them. This is simply another form of additional compensation.) If the expanding industry requires workers in socially "undignified" or disagreeable jobs (for example, slaughtering cattle), it will attract to itself first those workers whose objections to the employment are least; but as it attempts to obtain still more workers, it will have to offer higher wages to induce the more priggish and the more fastidious workers to enter the employment. The same will be true of any expanding industry offering a more dangerous employment. At first it will be able to employ workers who underestimate the danger, but an increasing number of workers will have to be drawn from those who are more insistent on being compensated for the risks involved.

In all these cases of rising supply price of labor to an industry, under perfect competition among employers the workers already in an industry will be able to command the same wage as that necessary to induce additional workers to enter the industry. If their present employer refuses to raise the wages of old workers, other firms in the industry would be willing to pay the same wage to them as they would to attract workers from another industry. Indeed, because of their greater experience in the trade, they would be more readily hired. Thus these workers will be able to obtain a wage higher than that at which they would have been willing to work if the demand for the product had not increased.

Imperfections of the Labor Market

We must now turn our attention to those situations in which the competition among employers for labor is less than perfect and which in consequence give rise to the exploitation of labor. We have already considered some of them in the case of individuals of exceptional ability. Most exploitation results from inequality in bargaining power between the employer and the employee. The deficiency in bargaining power on the part of the workman is usually due to two causes: lack of knowledge of the value of his services to an employer, and lack of ability to hold out for a wage if he does know his worth.

The only common way in which a worker can obtain even a rough estimate of his value to one employer is by knowing what other employers are paying for the same type of work. But this criterion is valid only if marginal products of labor are the same for both employees. Where the different firms are widely scattered geographically, this information may be extremely difficult for him to obtain. Moreover, the mere knowledge of money wages in variously located firms will not be sufficient unless the worker knows also the costs of living in different localities. Thus, in order for a worker to know whether it would be worth his while to move from Chicago to Pittsburgh for a certain difference in wages, it will be necessary for him to know what Pittsburgh wages will buy in Pittsburgh as compared to what Chicago wages will buy in Chicago.

In those instances where an employer refuses all wage increases, so that a worker actually has to leave his employment to better himself, the immobility of labor will act to its own disadvantage in bargaining. A worker may know that another employer in a distant city is offering better wages, but he cannot be certain that he individually will be able to obtain a job with the other employer, or to keep the job if he does obtain it; thus he may remain where he is rather than take a chance on being unemployed for a time. Another element that contributes to immobility is the cost of moving from one place to another. Closely coupled with this is the uncertainty as to how long a wage difference will persist. If it costs a worker $100.00 to move his family from one town to another, a wage difference of $2.00 a week would have to persist for one year for the worker to recover the cost of moving and break even; it would have to last for longer than a year for him actually to gain much by moving. With a given cost of moving, the smaller the difference in wages, the longer the time the difference will have to continue in order to make it worth while to move. Under these circumstances, if the difference in wages is small, workers may remain with their present employer, either in the hope that he may raise their wages, or through a fear that wages in the other town may fall before they have recouped themselves for the cost of moving.

The worker who is unemployed and seeking a job is subject to certain other disadvantages in bargaining power as an individual. The only recompense which he has if he does not work today is a day's leisure. For most men a day's leisure spent in pounding the pavements and worrying about employment is not a particularly happy alternative to work. On the other hand, the employer who does not hire the man will lose only the difference between the man's wages and the value of his services. The closer the wage that the workman demands approaches his marginal product, the smaller this difference will be and the less the employer will lose by not hiring him. The employer may thus be able to hold out for some considerable time before hiring any one workman at any particular wage, until he can be assured that there is no other workman who would be willing to work for less. The ability of the workman to hold out for a wage will depend upon how much savings he has to carry him until he can find a job elsewhere and how long a time he thinks will be necessary for him to find a job with another employer who may offer more than the one with whom he is trying to bargain at present. The reader will remember that we are treating here with cases of imperfect competition of employers on the labor market.

By refusing to deal with those workmen who show themselves capable of bargaining shrewdly, and by taking only those men who appear to be in most need of a job, it may be possible for an employer to obtain his working force at times for a wage that is less than that which his competitors in the industry are paying. As a deterrent to this practice, however, stands the fact that workmen who feel that they are underpaid may resent it and may turn out a much smaller amount of product than they would be capable of doing if they received what they considered a "fair" wage. Furthermore, any employer who becomes notorious for "beating down" wages may find himself unable to obtain labor at times when the demand for labor is brisk, which will be precisely at those times when the opportunity for profit is greatest. Then, too, workers who believe that they are underpaid will leave at the first opportunity that presents itself. Even though the employer may be able to find a continual stream of workers to take the places of those that are leaving, the "cost of labor turnover" (costs of hiring and breaking in new men) will be greater for him than for other employers who have a more contented working force.

The longer the fairly similar conditions persist, the less will be the danger of exploitation, simply because the forces of competition in the labor market—both among employers in the same industry and between different industries—will have time to exert their full effects. It is the rapid changes of the business cycle—and particularly of short cycles—that make exploitation more feasible. The employer who refuses to increase wages as rapidly as marginal productivity is rising (owing to increased demand for the product) in the upward movement of the business cycle may discover that before his workers have had time to leave him the business cycle enters the downward movement again and their opportunities to leave are lost.

Trade-Union Wage Determination

We must now examine the economic implications of trade-union activity in determining wages. The foremost economic function of a trade-union is the prevention of exploitation. This is accomplished by collective bargaining. We have considered above the reasons why an employer might be little concerned about losing the services of any one workman. But when all of his employees are banded together in a body ready to leave at the same time, the loss of his entire working force will be a matter of serious import, and the employer may be forced to give far more consideration to the demands of a union than he would to any one employee. Moreover, when a trade is fully unionized, the knowledge that none of his fellows will work for less than the union scale of wages may enable any unemployed union workman to hold out for such a wage better than if there was a danger that some other workman would offer to work more cheaply. The payment of "out-of-work benefits" by unions will also strengthen such bargaining power.

Even where competition would eventually eliminate exploitation, there are some cases in which trade-union activity will be an economic benefit. Thus, where there is a temporary oversupply of labor for a certain industry and labor is being exploited through a maximum wage agreement among the employers in this industry, and where the mobility of labor is less than the mobility of new firms, the first effect of competition might be a rush of new firms into the industry, causing the price of the product to decline greatly, but not raising wages materially. Exploitation, as we have defined it, would then be eliminated, simply because at the low price of the product the marginal product of labor would be equal to the low wage. After labor has had time to shift into other industries which pay better, the increased number of firms will no longer be able to continue in the industry if they have to pay wages which are equal to those that workers can obtain elsewhere. As a result some firms will have to close up, and the fixed capital invested in them will be lost. A higher wage, imposed at the start by a trade-union, would have prevented the needless expansion of the industry. Against this, however, must be set the disadvantage that at the higher wage many workers would have had to remain unemployed until they could shift into the other industries. Unemployment might be a more powerful force than low wages to make them leave the overcrowded industry, but it will lose some of its force if out-of-work benefits are paid by the union. We should have to examine each individual case on its merits to determine which was worse, exploitation or unemployment, in order to determine to what extent the prevention of unnecessary expansion in the industry represented a net gain.

As far as all labor as a class is concerned, the benefits conferred by any particular trade-union cease with the prevention of exploitation. The fixing of a wage, by a trade-union, which is above the marginal product of the existing number of workers in the trade will force employers to contract output and discharge laborers until a higher price for the product is reached, at which wages and marginal products are again equal. The laborers who are thrown out of work because of the higher wage will have to seek employment in other trades, and their addition to the supply will tend to depress wages in those other trades. At the same time, all other workers will have to pay a higher price for fewer goods made by the high-wage trade-union labor. Limitation of membership by a trade-union in a highly paid trade is a denial of opportunity to other workers. Monopoly wage levels are no more justifiable than monopoly commodity prices. There are, however, some conceivable circumstances under which it would be possible for a trade-union to take some of the monopoly profits away from a monopolist.[5]   If this is the case, and neither output, price of the product, nor number of persons employed would be affected by the outcome, then the general public can sit disinterestedly on the side lines and cheer their favorites in battle.

---

[5] In order to do this without affecting output and number of persons employed, the trade-union would have to adopt a peculiar technique.   It would have to set an extremely high price for a few workers, a lower price if the employer would employ more, and so on, so that the employer could not gain by restricting output or restricting employment.

CHAPTER XV

Interest

INTEREST is the price paid for the use of loanable funds. Loanable funds may be used either for the purchase of consumers' goods or as capital in the process of production. It is with the latter use that we shall be chiefly concerned, although we cannot overlook the fact that the demand for loans for consumptive purposes will have an influence on the rate which producer-borrowers must pay.

Money capital is demanded chiefly because it confers on its possessor the power to command the services of the means of production. Such power may be used to buy the services of the *original* means of production—land and labor—through the payment of rent and wages; or it may be used to buy *intermediate goods* such as raw materials, semifinished goods, and buildings and machinery, in which the past services of land and labor are embodied. Such intermediate goods are often called *capital goods.*

When capital is invested in payments to various kinds of labor, or in raw materials and semifinished goods, in such a way that it *will be fully recovered when a unit of the product is sold,* it is ordinarily called *circulating capital or working capital.*

When capital is invested in plant, machinery, and equipment, or in labor devoted to maintenance and upkeep, so that *only a part of such capital will be recovered in the sale of a unit of the product,* then such capital is usually called *fixed capital.*

The fact that the businessman must be able to recover such investments (either quite soon in the case of circulating capital, or in installments over a period of time in the case of fixed capital) in order to induce him to remain in business and to continue at the same rate of output is too obvious to need further explanation. It is true, of course, that quite often either a part or all of the invested capital is lost. But no one would invest, either in his own business or by loaning to others, if he were certain in advance that such losses would occur. When sad experience demonstrates that investment has been ill-advised, the attempt is made to contract or withdraw such investment in such a manner as to involve the least loss possible.

What does require an explanation is the fact that many businesses, even highly competitive ones, return *more* than the capital invested. We must therefore explain why, after all other costs have been met, there is a surplus in the form of *interest* that is either paid to those from whom capital has been borrowed or pocketed by the owner if he has invested his own capital.

Physical Productivity of Capital Goods Does Not Explain Interest

The services of land and labor, used in such a way that they are employed partly in the making of capital goods and partly in combination with capital goods, yield a greater *physical* product than the same amounts of land and labor services would yield if they were used entirely in making a product without the use of capital goods. This is an obvious technological fact which we can leave to the physicist and the chemist for explanation. For the purposes of economics, we can take it for granted that a man can catch more fish if he first takes time to make a pole and line or a net than if he devoted his entire time to trying to catch fish by hand.

Similarly, we know that a greater physical product will result from agriculture through the use of farm implements and
fertilizer than through the use of labor and land alone. Many
kinds of products could not be turned into their present form
at all without the use of at least some capital goods. Thus
blast furnaces are required to make steel, stills to extract gasoline from crude petroleum, and so on. The *value* of the marginal physical product must at least equal the price.

None of this, however, constitutes a satisfactory explanation
of why the use of capital goods should yield a *value* return
over and above the cost of the services of labor and land embodied in the capital goods used by a competitive industry.
Unless there is some force which restrains all competitors, we
should naturally expect them to expand output, by using capital goods, up to the point where a declining price of the product is just sufficient to cover the costs of the services of labor
and land involved in making the capital goods and those used
directly in making the product. If lenders were willing
to loan unlimited sums of money without interest, this would
indeed be the case, and there would be no limits, except purely
technological ones, to the extension of the use of capital goods.
Capital goods would be substituted for labor in existing industries to the limits of mechanical feasibility, and new enterprises requiring tremendous amounts of investment would be
undertaken. (Interest on invested capital would not be a cost.)

Why Interest Must Be Paid

If it can be shown, however, that interest is a cost that must
be considered by all businessmen, then we will have found a
brake which stops this expansion of output and this extension
of the use of capital goods. If interest is a cost that must be
paid, then competitors in an industry will cease to expand output at that point where a falling price is just equal to all costs
including interest, and they will not expand output to such

a point that the lower price of a larger output fails to cover interest charges. As long as interest must be paid on all borrowed money capital, all competitors are safe in so restricting output, since no new competitor of equal efficiency who enters the field with borrowed money capital can afford to cut prices below theirs. Even if some few competitors who were using their own funds should decide that they did not care to earn interest on their money, they would find that, unless they could supply the entire market, other people who bought goods from them at a price which included no interest could resell those goods at a price equal to that charged by the interest-paying competitors. Indeed, interest-paying competitors would themselves be likely to be the first to take advantage of such an opportunity to buy goods at a lower cost than their own and to resell them at a profit.

If it can be shown that interest must be paid on borrowed funds anywhere at all in the economic system, then we shall be able to show that interest must be considered as a cost by all men who attempt to start a business enterprise. Even though there might be some lenders who would be willing, if no other opportunity presented itself, to loan at zero interest, so long as any borrower is willing to pay interest, these lenders will naturally prefer to loan to such borrowers as pay interest rather than to those who do not.[1] Indeed, even though some lenders would be willing to loan without interest if they had to, so long as anyone is willing to pay interest, even these lenders insist on receiving it. This is simply another way of saying that as long as the amount of funds demanded is in excess of the amount that would be offered at zero interest, there will be interest charged on all loans. Furthermore, as long as interest is being paid on borrowed funds, anyone who invests his own capital in his own business will have to con-

---

[1] If funds were obtainable at zero rates for unlimited amounts for an unlimited time, it would be worth while to build a bridge across the Atlantic.

sider the *opportunity cost* of doing so. Thus, if someone is willing to pay me interest for the use of my money, I will want to make sure that it will earn at least an equal rate of interest before I invest it in my own business.

Time Preference and Liquidity Preference

We have now to explain why most people insist on being paid interest and would not loan at all without it. The answer to this is found in what is known as *time preference*[2] and *liquidity preference*.[3] Time preference is the preference to have an equal amount of goods and services at one time rather than at some other time. We shall find that most people would rather have an equal amount of goods and services in the present rather than in the future, and that they would rather have such goods in the near future than in the distant future. We say that such people have a *positive* rate of time preference. If it should so happen that some people prefer to have an equal amount of goods in the future rather than in the present, we say that such people have a *negative* rate of time preference. Liquidity preference is the preference to have an equal amount of cash rather than of claims against others.

We must now examine the reasons for these time and liquidity preferences. If I were to offer you the choice between receiving one dollar now and receiving one dollar a year from now, probably you would say, "Give it to me *now*." Why is this the case? One reason, of course, is that if I gave you the dollar now, you would be sure of having it, whereas if you waited until next year I might fail to give it to you. This element of risk is one that we shall have to deal with later, but for the moment let us assume that I can give you a satisfactory guarantee that you will receive your dollar next year.

---

[2] Böhm-Bawerk.
[3] J. M. Keynes.

Doubtless you would still prefer the dollar now to the certain guarantee of a dollar a year from now, and this must be explained. The answer is that you can think of very many desirable things for which the dollar might be spent immediately, whereas the wants which might be satisfied by the expenditure of a dollar next year do not seem nearly so important at present. In other words, you have a *positive rate of time preference.*

Now, if I should try to borrow a dollar from you with the guarantee that it will be returned next year, what I am really doing is offering to exchange future purchasing power for present purchasing power. If your rate of time preference is positive, in order to induce you to make such an exchange, I will have to offer to pay you next year some amount greater than one dollar. The greater amount will have to be large enough so that the satisfactions which you think will be derived from spending or having this sum in the future will be at least equal to the satisfactions you give up in the present by lending the dollar to me instead of spending it or keeping it.

Time preference is quite analogous to perspective in space.[4] Whoever has stood on a railroad track has noticed how the ties appear to be shorter the more distant they are from the eye. The same thing is true of the dollar which you will get back one year from now if you lend it to me, except that instead of being distant in space it is distant in time. What I am doing is offering to trade you a future dollar in return for a present dollar. If your realization of your present wants is greater than your anticipation of your future wants, a dollar in the future will not appear as big to you (in its power to satisfy wants) as a dollar in the present. In order to make the future dollar appear as big to you now as the present dollar does (so that you will be willing to make the trade), I must add something to it. That something is interest. Your *un-*

---

[4] I am indebted for this analogy to Prof. J. M. Shortliffe.

dervaluation of future purchasing power as compared with present purchasing power forces me to promise you a greater amount of future purchasing power so that your estimate of anticipated satisfactions from the sum that I will pay you back next year will be at least equal to the present satisfactions which you would give up if you lent me the dollar instead of keeping it or spending it now. The difference between the amount you lend me and the amount I must pay you back, expressed as a percentage of the original sum lent, is your *rate of time preference*. Thus, if you insist on receiving $1.25 next year in return for lending me $1.00 today, 25 per cent is your rate of time preference.

The rate of time and liquidity preference, and consequently the rate of interest at which people could be induced to lend, will be different for different individuals, depending upon their particular circumstances and upon their psychological make-up. Ordinarily, people who are farsighted enough to anticipate fully what their wants will be in the future will have a lower rate of time preference than those who live entirely in the present and take no heed of the future. Many people, indeed, attach so much importance to having goods immediately that, far from being willing to lend, they borrow to buy consumers' goods and pay rates as high as 20 per cent to "loan sharks" or installment plan stores rather than wait until they have saved the cash to pay for the goods. Mere knowledge of what future wants will be is not sufficient to induce a low rate of time preference. In order for his rate of time preference to be low, the individual must have sufficient imagination to anticipate the intensity of his wants in the future. Shipwrecked sailors may know that they will die of thirst before help can reach them if they drink up their supply of water too rapidly, but unless they can anticipate what the pangs of thirst will be in the future, they will clamor to drink all they want today.

Differences in present and anticipated future *income* will also affect the individual's rate of time preference, as well as differences in present and anticipated *wants*. A youth with a small income who expects to receive a large inheritance when his wealthy uncle dies will have a very high rate of preference for present purchasing power over future purchasing power. On the other hand, a man who is working for a good salary at present but who expects to be retired a few years hence, either on half pay or with no pension at all, will have a very low rate of preference for present purchasing power. Indeed, if he anticipates his future wants keenly enough, he may actually prefer a certain amount of future purchasing power to a similar amount of present purchasing power. If he does, his rate of time preference will be negative. If no opportunity for safe investment was available, instead of insisting on receiving interest he might be willing to pay someone to keep his funds safely and to return them to him when they were more needed. In a way, this payment might be considered as a sort of negative interest rate.

Another element that will influence an individual's rate of time preference is his expectancy of life. If he anticipates that he will not have long to live, he may prefer to have his purchasing power in the immediate present when he can enjoy it rather than to defer the use of it until some future time when he may possibly not be alive. A consideration which would tend to offset this in the case of some people would be the desire to leave an inheritance to care for their dependents.

After all other considerations have been taken into account, the preference of any individual for present purchasing power will be greater, the greater the amount which he is lending. For example, there may be a very small part of my present income and cash balance that I am not spending at all or that I am spending for present goods whose marginal utility to me is extremely low. This small part of my income and cash balance I might be willing to lend for no interest on the mere assurance that I would get it back in the future (of course, I would take interest if I could get it, but if no borrower anywhere was paying interest, I would be willing to loan this small sum without interest). However, as soon as I start to consider the lending of still more of my income and cash balance, then the goods which I would have to give up in the present will be those which are increasingly important to me. In other words, the greater the amount of the loan in proportion to total income, the greater the sacrifice of present liquidity and the greater the marginal utility of the present goods whose purchase must be foregone in order to make the loan. At the same time, as I consider deferring more and more purchasing power to the future, the uses to which I anticipate that I can put that future purchasing power will be steadily declining in importance. Thus, the greater the amount of the loan, the less will be my estimate of the marginal utility of the goods which I might purchase in the future or of the dollars which I might care to leave to my heirs. Consequently, the greater the amount of the loan, the greater the rate of interest I will insist on receiving to compensate for my increasing time preference.

Certain elements of liquidity preference must be considered entirely apart from time preference. (1) There is the desire to have a sum of money on hand to meet accidental emergency payments.[5] For example, consider the extra twenty or thirty dollars I may take along on a motor trip to cover possible repairs on the car. I do not want to spend this money and I hope that the occasion for spending it does not arise. Nevertheless, I would much rather have it in the form of cash than to have it in the form of a claim of debt against someone else, since an unfamiliar garage man would probably

---

[5] Hicks explains interest simply in terms of the imperfect "Moneyness" of mortgages, stocks and other "Money substitutes."

not be interested in accepting such a claim in payment for his repair bill. (2) A desire for liquidity may be fostered when it is anticipated that interest rates will rise in the near future. For instance, suppose that I buy a bond for $100.00 which pays $3.00 a year interest, and that the market rate of interest for this type of investment then rises to 6 per cent. Nobody would then be willing to pay much over $50.00 for my bond, since he could invest $50.00 at 6 per cent elsewhere and get a return of $3.00 a year. I may receive my $100.00 back if I wait a number of years until the bond is due, but meanwhile I shall have to be content with 3 per cent on my bond while others are earning 6 per cent, or if I sell out, I will be compelled to sell at a loss. If I anticipate any such rise in the interest rate, I would do well to keep my funds in the form of liquid cash until after the rise.

Supply of Loanable Funds

Time and liquidity preference, then, determine the amount of loanable funds which will be offered by lenders at each possible rate of interest. It will also determine the amount of owned capital that an individual will invest in his own business. In this respect he may very properly be considered as loaning to the business, even though he owns the capital himself. Thus, if I use my own money to pay the workmen in my business, I will not be able to get it back until I can sell the goods which they have made, and I am deprived of using it for myself exactly as if I had loaned the money to someone else for the same period of time. If my own time and liquidity preference is lower than the market rate of interest, I will invest my own funds in my business rather than borrow capital. Obviously, however, I will not starve myself to provide capital for the business. If the business shows a profitable opportunity for the investment of a greater amount of capital than I can provide without stinting myself, I will borrow the extra capital required and will still retain some of my own funds for personal expenditures and personal cash balance.

If we know the rates of time and liquidity preference of each individual for various amounts of funds that he might loan, then we can draw up individual supply schedules of the amount of money that each individual lender would loan at each possible rate of interest. By adding together the supply schedules of all individuals, we obtain a supply schedule of

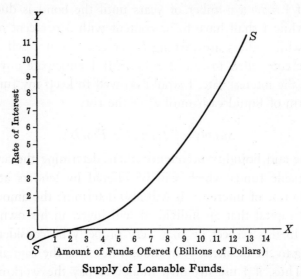

Supply of Loanable Funds.

loanable funds for the general market. We can represent this as a supply curve exactly as we did with the supply of any other commodity.

In the diagram, SS represents the imaginary supply curve of loanable funds. Note that it starts below the zero line, thus indicating that some few people would be willing to loan a small amount at negative rates of interest. This curve co-incides with the zero line, indicating that there are some people who would be willing to loan at least a part of their funds at zero interest on the mere assurance that they will get their money back. It then starts to slope upward and keeps on increasing its slope, thereby indicating the rates of interest necessary to induce the same people to loan more of their funds and to induce other people with higher rates of time preference to start loaning. It may even curve backwards.

If the supply of loanable funds were determined by the rate of time and liquidity preference of lenders, then the market rate of interest would be determined by the amount of funds which the borrowers wish to obtain. The market rate of interest will be that rate at which the amount offered by lenders is exactly equal to the amount borrowers will take. The market rate of interest is therefore a market price for loanable funds, quite analogous to the market price of other commodities. It is a sensitive market price, owing to the extreme ease with which money can be transported from one place to another, and hence the money market is apt to be far more competitive than many commodity markets. If the supply of loanable funds happened to be that shown in our diagram, then, if all borrowers wanted a total amount of only two billion dollars, they could obtain it without paying interest at all. If they wanted nine billion, they would have to pay 5 per cent for it. If they wanted twelve billion, they would have to pay 9½ per cent; and so on.

Bank Influence on Supply of Funds

We have been assuming up to this point that the only source of supply of loanable funds was from savers. Where a banking system exists, however, the chief source of loanable funds will be the banks rather than savers. Furthermore, it will be shown in the chapter on banking that the banks are able to *create* money for the purpose of lending it. What the bank ordinarily lends is not coin or currency but claims against itself in the form of bank deposits or bank notes. With a given amount of cash, the banks in a banking system may loan in the form of bank credits many times the amount of cash on hand. Such cash may come from savers, but there are many other ways in which the banks receive cash. All this will be made clear in the chapter on Credit Control and Banking Mechanism.

The important point for us to note here is that where there is a banking system, borrowers will not have to borrow from savers but may borrow from banks. Moreover, the amounts that banks are lending may be, at times, greatly in excess of the amounts which are saved by individuals. The banks themselves will have no time preference; their choice is merely between lending or having idle lending capacity that is earning them nothing. The more that they are able to lend at any given rate of interest, the greater will be their earnings. This situation results in "involuntary" saving due to changes in price levels caused by bank lending and expansion of deposit currency.[6]

While banks will have no time preference, they will be governed by liquidity preference. A certain part of the claims against banks must be paid in cash on demand. No bank willingly puts itself in the position of being unable to meet such claims. Consequently, if a bank anticipates that cash will be difficult to obtain in the future, it will raise its rate of interest so as to discourage further loans and thereby put itself in a more liquid position. Moreover, if a bank anticipates that the rate at which it can lend will be higher in the future, it will be less anxious to lend now. When this situation exists, it will usually be found that the bank rate on short-term loans is much lower than on long-term loans.

There are certain factors of monopsonistic competition in the borrowing of funds. Thus, certain persons who are known to be good credit risks, those with wealthy parents and those with some influence at the bank, may obtain loans at lower interest rates or with less difficulty than others.

---

[6] See pages 401–404 for an explanation of "involuntary" saving.

Demand for Loanable Funds

We must turn, then, to the demand side of the market and find out what it is that determines the amount of loanable funds that borrowers would take at various possible rates of interest. As far as those who borrow for consumptive purposes are concerned, the rate of interest they would be willing to pay for any particular amount of money depends on their time preference. If their present wants seem very much greater to them than their anticipated future wants, they will pay a high rate of interest in order to add to their present purchasing power, even though they know that their future purchasing power will be diminished by the necessity of having to repay the amount of the loan and the interest. As we shall see later, due partly to the fact that lenders consider this type of loan more risky, borrowers who use funds for increasing their consumption will have to pay a higher rate of interest than other borrowers.

The great bulk of loanable funds, however, is borrowed for investment in production. The rate that borrowers for this purpose will be willing to pay will depend on the profits above all costs except interest expected from organizing or expanding any business. This rate will depend upon the marginal value product of capital. Anyone who expects to make a profit by investing will, if necessary, be willing to pay for the use of money capital. Furthermore, if no one would loan for less, he would be willing to pay such a rate of interest as would just fall short of taking away his entire profit. Let us imagine, for example, that there is a certain business in which, after all other costs (including my own wages of management) *except* interest have been allowed for, I estimate that $6,000.00 a year profit can be made safely. If such a business requires an investment of $100,000.00, then $6,000.00 represents an annual return of 6 per cent. Consequently, I could obtain a clear net return even *after paying interest,* provided I can borrow the money capital at any interest rate below 6 per cent. Therefore, I would be willing to pay any market rate of interest less than 6 per cent rather than fail to obtain the capital. If the market rate is a full 6 per cent, I will not know whether I should start such a business or whether I should earn my wages of management by working for someone else. If $8,000.00 a year could be made on $100,000.00 capital, I would be willing to pay up to 8 per cent interest; if $9,000.00, I would pay up to 9 per cent, and so on.

The expected rates of returns, then, are the determining factors in setting the rates of interest that commercial borrowers will be willing to pay for loanable funds. However, regardless of his rate of returns no borrower will have to pay more than the market rate of interest; competition among lenders will assure this. It is the marginal borrowers and the marginal lenders who set the rate of interest. The actual rate will be at that point where the amount borrowers are willing to take is equal to the amount that lenders are willing to loan. Notice, however, that where a banking system is in operation, there may be extreme variations in the supply of loanable funds from time to time.

Yet no rate of returns in excess of the market rate of interest can persist long in any industry. In any industry where competition is possible, any rate of returns above the market rate of interest will tend to attract more firms into the industry. This competition will make its effects felt in three ways: the greater output of product will cause a decline in the price of the product that will decrease the rate of returns; the greater demand for suitable means of production will cause a rise in cost that will decrease the rate of returns; and the increased number of borrowers demanding money capital will tend to raise the rate of interest, and the increased amount of capital used will tend to lower its marginal physical product. Where competition increases in response to excess profits in one industry alone, most of its effect will be felt in the decline of returns in the industry, and little or no effect will be observed on the interest rate. But when a number of industries are showing profitable opportunities for investment, the interest rate will tend to rise. If some time must elapse before the output of the new competitors in these industries can be put on the market, the interest rate will be likely to rise before any fall in the price of products occurs.

Notice that what we have been saying is merely that the returns in a business must *promise* at least to equal the interest rate in order to induce borrowing and investment. *After* the investment has been made, there is no guarantee that even interest charges will be earned, as many businessmen and lenders have learned to their sorrow. If, attracted by large returns, too many competitors rush into an industry in ignorance of the fact that others are doing the same, their combined output may drive the price so low that no one is able to earn his interest charges.

Disinvestment of Capital

In such circumstances, if the capital is invested in fixed forms of capital goods suited only to the particular industry (such as specialized machinery and equipment), it may be found impossible to withdraw invested funds from the business without encountering a greater loss than would be occasioned by leaving them in that business. Actually, the only way to get such funds out immediately is to sell the capital goods in which they have been invested. But if the price of the product is such that a machine cannot be used to earn its interest charges, no one else who buys the machine would be likely to be quite so foolish as to pay what the machine originally cost (or even the original cost less depreciation).

Anyone who calculated correctly and who bought the machine at secondhand would pay only such a price for it as would allow him to earn interest charges on it at the present low price of the product. Consequently, the owner of the business may be equally well (or badly) off if he keeps the machine in operation until it can return a part of its original cost through the sale of the product.

At first sight, it would appear that working capital could be withdrawn from a business far more easily than fixed capital, and in general this is true. Whatever part of the working capital is recouped in the price of a unit of the product when it is sold need not be re-invested by paying wages or buying a stock of goods or raw materials, unless the owner so desires. However, when there is a large amount of specialized fixed capital in the business, the owner may find it necessary to re-invest very nearly the same amount of working capital in order to recover some part of the value of the fixed capital by using it in production. (Machines need labor to run them and raw material on which to work.) For this reason, retail stores can go out of business completely much more easily than manufacturing establishments, simply because the retail stores have most of their capital invested in the form of circulating or working capital rather than fixed capital.

When any business does not pay its interest charges, the creditors can legally take the business away from the owners by foreclosure or bankruptcy proceedings, but this merely makes the former creditors the new owners of the business. Unless they can manage the business better than the former owners did, they will receive no more interest than they did before the foreclosure. As owners, they may get only 2 per cent on their investment while the market rate of interest may be 6 per cent. Nor will there be anything they can do except either to continue running the business or try to withdraw their investments at a loss in the manner outlined above. If they (or someone else to whom they may sell the business) continue to operate it, the amount of product that they put on the market will help to keep the price depressed so that the other competitors in the industry will be in no better position to earn their interest charges than they were when this particular firm was in the original owner's hands.

Once industry has fallen into a condition wherein all of the firms are failing to earn their interest charges, there are only a very few things that could happen to restore their collective ability to earn interest. These are: (1) for some of the firms to leave the industry completely, *not* merely to change ownership; (2) a fall in the rate of wages; (3) a fall in the price of raw materials; (4) an increase in the demand for the product. If any of these things occurs (and no new firms enter the industry meanwhile), the rise in price of the product or the fall in costs may again enable the firms to earn the market rate of interest. The hope that some of these eventualities will take place may keep many of the competitors in business far longer than the circumstances justify. Interest is a promise, not a certainty, but it is a promise necessary to induce the investment of new funds.

The Risk Element

For many loans there is a serious risk that either interest or principal or both will not be repaid. How does this affect our problem? In actual practice we will find that there are different market rates of interest for loans estimated to represent or involve different degrees of risk. The market rate of interest will therefore cover two things: (1) the rate of interest based on time preference and (2) a payment for the risk involved. If the reader will look on the financial page of a newspaper, he will find quotations such as the following:

Issuing Company	Rate	Maturity	Price	Yield
Blank Company	3.50	1965	107¼	3.26%
John Doe Company	4.00	1961	101¾	3.93
Richard Roe Company	5.00	1950	82	6.09
State of Ruritania	6.00	1963	56	10.71

The column headed *Rate* shows the number of dollars per year the company will pay on each bond. The column called *Yield* shows the actual rate of interest the lender is supposed to receive when the bonds that carry the given "rates" are sold at the prices shown. The differences in yields are based on the estimate that the market places on the ability and willingness of the issuing organizations to repay the loans and the interest. The higher yield shows that there is more doubt that the loan and nominal "rate" will be paid in full.

Note that the higher yield is in no sense an insurance premium to guarantee the repayment of any individual loan. However, if it is the normal experience that, on the average, $1.00 out of every $100.00 invested in a certain type of company will not be repaid, then any bank or investment company which has an equal amount invested in 100 *different* companies of this type will recover its losses by charging each borrower an additional 1.01 per cent interest, and the remainder of the yield will be pure interest. As far as any individual lender who invests in only one company is concerned, if that company fails he will lose all or a part of the loan. To him the higher yield represents a mere bait necessary to induce him to take a greater gamble with his funds.

Short-Term Loans

If the reader will turn to another part of the financial page of the newspaper, he will find a column headed "Money Rates" or "Bank Rates" which shows the rates of interest that banks are charging on short-term loans. Here again he will find different rates of interest on different types of loans. Ordinarily, the shorter the length of time for which the loan is made, the lower will be the rate of interest; hence "call money" (loans on which repayment can be demanded any day the bank desires) will bear the lowest rate of interest. Only in a small part do these differences in rates represent differences in risk. Extremely short-term loans (such as 30-day loans and call loans) are usually made with funds which the banks would not dare to use for long-term loans because they may need such money on very short notice. Consequently, unless this money can be loaned for short periods, it will have to remain idle in the banks. Therefore, the banks will ordinarily be glad to take any rate of interest, even as low as a small fraction of 1 per cent, rather than have the funds remain idle and earn nothing. There is also another advantage of short-term loans which tends to make them lower priced. If a bank extends a loan for 30 days and the market rate of interest suddenly rises from 3 to 5 per cent, at the expiration of 30 days the bank can demand that the borrower pay 5 per cent to have the loan renewed, or it can loan the money to someone else at the higher rate of interest; but if the loan had been for six months, the bank would have to wait the full six months before it could start charging the higher rate of interest on this particular loan.

On the other hand, in times of financial panic it will be found that call loans carry much higher rates of interest than other loans. In part this will be deceptive, because while long-time loans may have rates quoted, no bank may be willing to make new long-term loans at such a time. Moreover, in times of stock market panic, call loans have a peculiar advantage for the borrower. Thus, if a man wishes to borrow for only one day in order to hold on to his stock in hopes of a price recovery, call money at 21 per cent per year would cost him only 1/365 of this rate or about six cents per day for each $100.00 he wished to borrow. On the other hand, if he borrowed time-money for six months at 12 per cent per year, it would cost him $6.00 for each $100.00 although he actually needs the money only for a few days.

Nominal and Actual Rates of Interest

Care should be taken in reading interest rate quotations to distinguish between nominal rates of interest and the rates that actually are paid. We saw this in the case of the bond quotations, the "rate" being the nominal rate and "yield" being the actual rate. Such differences will be also found occasionally in the rates charged by banks. Thus, a bank may say that its rate is 7 per cent. But when a man tries to borrow $10,000.00, it may require him to borrow $20,000.00 at 7 per cent and leave $10,000.00 of it on deposit with the bank. He is then paying interest on the $20,000.00 but has the use of only $10,000.00, and the real rate of interest on the money he has to use is 14 per cent and not 7. The same falsity of the nominal rate of interest will appear where, in addition to the quoted rate, the borrower is charged a "commission" for the granting of the loan.

A similar deceptiveness exists in the way interest is charged on installment plan purchases. For example, I may wish to buy a refrigerator the cash price of which is $120.00, but the dealer tells me that I can pay $11.00 a month for 12 months, making a total of $132.00. He also tells me that this represents a 10 per cent interest charge. But does it? One dollar per month amounts to $12.00 per year. The first month when I am borrowing the full value of the refrigerator ($120.00), the actual rate is 10 per cent. However, each subsequent month I reduce the amount which I am borrowing by $10.00, but I *still pay $1.00 per month* (a rate of $12.00 per year) on the progressively decreasing sums which I am borrowing. For each month, if we divide $12.00 by the amount of the unpaid balance, we will derive the actual annual rate of interest which $1.00 per month represents, as shown by the table.

This table shows what it really costs to "pay as you use," as the advertisements tell you to do. Using a similar method,

	Unpaid Balance (Amount actually borrowed)	Interest ($1.00 per month or $12.00 per year)	Actual Annual Rate of Interest on Balance Due
1st month	$120.00	$12.00	10.00%
2nd month	110.00	12.00	10.91
3rd month	100.00	12.00	12.00
4th month	90.00	12.00	13.33
5th month	80.00	12.00	15.00
6th month	70.00	12.00	17.14
7th month	60.00	12.00	20.00
8th month	50.00	12.00	24.00
9th month	40.00	12.00	30.00
10th month	30.00	12.00	40.00
11th month	20.00	12.00	60.00
12th month	10.00	12.00	120.00

Weighted average rate on unpaid balances.............. 18.46%

one can find the true rate of interest on any installment plan purchase, or on a loan from a "small loan company" which is repaid in small installments.

Bank Discount

Another source of confusion as to the actual interest rate is the practice of bank discount. This is used on many short-term loans. If the bank discount is 5 per cent, instead of charging interest as a separate item, the bank will take your promise to pay $100.00 one year from now and give you $95.00 today. Actually you have the use of only $95.00 and you pay $5.00 for it. The actual rate of interest is then 5.26 per cent.

Cash Discounts and Trade Discounts

The reader may have had occasion to notice on the bills sent to retailers by wholesalers or manufacturers the phrase "2% ten days" meaning that the retailer may deduct 2 per cent from the bill if he pays within ten days. This is not intended as an interest charge but as a penalty for failure to make prompt payment of the bill. If the retailer bought and sold the same amount of goods twelve times a year, 2 per cent on each turnover would represent 24 per cent a year on his working capital, so he is encouraged to borrow from the banks at 4 or 6 per cent in order to take advantage of this discount and pay cash to the wholesaler. In certain products where the manufacturer's catalog is to be shown to the consumer, the prices quoted are retail prices, and then from these prices the retailer is allowed to deduct a discount ranging sometimes as high as 40 or 50 per cent to cover his own selling costs and profit. These discounts as well as the cash discounts are not interest rates; they are merely different ways of quoting the prices of goods.

Valuation of Income-Producing Property

Regardless of the nature of income from property, whether it be interest, rent, or profits, the principles which govern the determination of the value of such income-producing property are the same. In order to determine the value of any piece of property which yields an income, at least two things must be known: the amount of the annual income and the market rate of interest.

Capitalization of Earning Power

With any property that may be expected to yield the same unchanged income perpetually, a knowledge of the above two elements alone will enable us to determine its present value. We would find out what sum of money invested at the market rate of interest would yield the same income as the piece of property in question. That sum of money will then be the value of the property in question. To find this sum, we divide the annual income expressed in dollars by the market rate of interest. For example, let us assume that there is a certain piece of land which we know will yield an income of $6,000.00 a year forever, and that the market rate of interest is 6 per cent. Dividing $6,000.00 by .06 gives us $100,000.00, which is the sum we would have to have invested at 6 per cent in order to yield us an annual income of $6,000.00. The value of the land under the given conditions is $100,000.00.

We notice that a change either in the interest rate or in the annual earnings will change the value of the income-yielding property. Thus, if the annual earnings remained the same ($6,000.00) but the interest rate declined to 3 per cent, the value of the property would be doubled, since twice as great a sum would have to be invested at 3 per cent to earn $6,000.00 as was the case at 6 per cent. On the other hand, if the annual earnings decline while the rate of interest remains constant, the value of the property will decline proportionately; and, likewise, if the annual earnings increase for any reason while the rate of interest remains unchanged, the value of the property will rise proportionately.

The above method of figuring values is sometimes called *capitalizing the earning power*. This method may be used to find the maximum value at which a share of stock should sell. It will be found, however, that in stock market "booms" stocks often sell for many times their capitalized earning power. Sometimes such valuations are based on anticipated future earning power. In this case, the valuations are no sounder than the forecasts of increased earnings on which they are based. Often, however, the prices of stocks exceed any valuation based on any reasonable forecast of future earnings. In these instances the prices are usually due to the sheer ignorance of the speculating public which believes that, because a stock has already risen fifty points, it will rise fifty more. Actually, in sober truth, every point that a stock rises above its capitalized earning power is just that much more reason to expect a decline in its price. When we reflect that excessively high prices of stocks usually occur at the peak of the business cycle when corporate earnings are known to be abnormally high, prices that could be justified only by still greater earnings are obviously fictitious.

Valuation of Terminable Income Property

We must now turn our attention to the valuation of other income-yielding property which will yield an income not in perpetuity but only over a definite period of time. We find the method in this case somewhat different from that shown above. Our procedure is to take the annual income for each year until the income-yielding capacity is exhausted, and then to discount (deduct interest from) each year's installment of income for the length of time that we would have to wait for the property to yield the income. The total of these discounted income payments will then be the present value of the income-producing property.

The present value of any future payment is given by the formula:

$$P = \frac{1}{(1+r)^n} \times A$$

where P is the present value, r is the rate of interest, n is the number of years that will elapse before the payment is to be received, and A is the amount of the future payment.

An example will help to make this clear. Suppose that there is a coal mine which will yield a net return over operating costs of \$1,000.00 a year for a period of ten years, but that at the end of that time the coal will be exhausted, so that no more income will be obtainable from the mine. Suppose also that the market rate of interest is 5 per cent. The computation of the value of the mine is given in the following table:

(1)	(2)	(3)	(4)	(5)
Net Return	Present Value of Each Year's Net Return	Value Still in the Mine at End of Year	Amount of Interest Received	Amount of Principal Recovered
1st year $1,000.00.......$	952.38	$7,107.82	$386.09	$613.91
2nd year 1,000.00........	907.03	6,463.21	355.39	644.61
3rd year 1,000.00........	863.84	5,786.37	323.16	676.84
4th year 1,000.00........	822.70	5,075.69	289.32	710.68

(1)	(2)	(3)	(4)	(5)
Net Return	Present Value of Each Year's Net Return	Value Still in the Mine at End of Year	Amount of Interest Received	Amount of Principal Recovered
5th year 1,000.00........	783.53	4,329.48	253.79	746.21
6th year 1,000.00........	746.21	3,545.95	216.47	783.53
7th year 1,000.00........	710.68	2,732.48	177.30	822.70
8th year 1,000.00........	676.84	1,859.41	136.16	863.84
9th year 1,000.00........	644.61	952.38	92.97	907.03
10th year 1,000.00........	613.91	....	47.62	952.38

$7,721.73 Total Present Value

To obtain the value of the first year's return, we have used the formula to find the sum which would have to be invested at 5 per cent for one year in order for the principal and interest combined to equal $1,000.00 at the end of the year. Substituting in the formula:

$$P = \frac{1}{(1 + .05)^1} \times \$1,000.00 = \$952.38$$

The present value of the second year's return is $1,000.00 divided by $(1.05)^2$; and so on. The total of these values gives the present value of the mine.

Careful consideration of the table will save us from a common error. We must not consider the entire return of $1,-000.00 as a net income. Part of it is income and part of it is return of capital invested. At the end of the first year, the mine has declined in value by $613.91 (at the end of the year the mine is only a nine-year mine, so that its value is shown by the total of the first nine items in column 2). Only $386.09 is a true income; and the other $613.91 represents a repayment of the principal. At the end of the second year, the mine will have declined in value by $644.61 more, and only $355.39 is a net income; and so on. To keep our capital intact so that we would continue to earn the same amount of income, we should need each year to re-invest, in some other enterprise earning 5 per cent, that part of the $1,000.00 which constitutes a return of capital. This process of reinvestment to earn a constant return is sometimes called *amortization*.

The term *amortization* is also used to describe the reinvestment of a part of its revenue by a business corporation (rather than paying this revenue out in dividends) so that it will be able to repay a bond issue when due.

If the reader bears this principle of limited income yield in mind, he will not confuse the comparatively high rates of return on the stocks of oil- or gas-producing companies or mining companies as being a higher net income than is yielded by stock in some other companies in which the income-yielding resources are not being exhausted by depletion. (Some companies of this nature do set aside a "depletion allowance" to allow them to repurchase new sources of supply when their present ones are exhausted. To the extent that this allowance has been figured accurately, the dividends paid then do represent a true net income which can be spent by the recipient without fear of impairing his principal.)

While we have confined our illustration to extractive industries, the same principle of declining capital value would apply to any manufacturing unit that was allowing its plant and equipment to wear out without setting aside a fund for its replacement and that was paying what should be the depreciation allowance as a dividend to its stockholders.

To return to our illustration of the mine, the accuracy of our valuation is really dependent on two sets of forecasts—one engineering and one economic. The engineer may estimate for us how long the coal will last at its present rate of extraction. If we can accept his estimate as accurate, the remainder of the problem is economic. For the value to be as we have calculated it, three things must remain the same over the ten-year period: the price of coal must remain the same, and its cost of extraction must remain the same (or, if they change, both must change in the same direction and by the same amount) in order that the net return remain unchanged; and finally, the interest rate must remain unchanged. Changes in any of these elements would tend to increase or decrease the value of the mine.

We have said nothing about the cost of plant and equipment in connection with the value of a manufacturing unit or in connection with any other kind of income-producing property. This is because such costs have ordinarily no significance in determining the value. Whether the factory cost a certain amount originally or whether it would cost a certain amount to reproduce it at the present time ordinarily enters very little into the calculations of an individual who is considering buying the factory as a going business. It is true that he would ordinarily not pay more for a factory than it would cost him to duplicate it by building another himself, and hence duplication cost sets an upper limit to the price he will pay. The prime interest of the prospective buyer is not in the cost of the factory but in its capacity to yield income. No matter how much machinery and equipment may have cost originally or how much it would cost to duplicate them, if they cannot be made to yield an income in operation, their value is no more than what they will bring as junk.

Valuation of Public Utilities

The discussion thus far should give us an insight into some of the difficulties which confront Public Service Commissions, the Interstate Commerce Commission, or other bodies that have the task of regulating the rates or prices which public utilities are allowed to charge. The law ordinarily specifies that such public utility companies be allowed to earn either a specific rate of interest or a "fair rate of return" on the value of the investment in them. The regulatory body cannot use the method of "capitalizing the earning power," which we have discussed above, in order to determine what is the "value of the investment," since whatever rate it allows the company to charge will in itself be the principal factor which determines the earning power, or at least which will set a maximum to the earning power. For example, if the demand for city water is quite inelastic, the higher the rates a water company is allowed to charge, the higher will be its earnings, and consequently the higher will be the value of a property which is capable of making such earnings. On the other hand, if the company is allowed to charge only very low rates, the value of the company based on its earning power would be extremely low.

Deprived of the method of capitalizing earning power as a means of establishing the value of public utilities on which a rate of interest is to be allowed, the regulatory bodies are forced to fall back on the cost of plant and equipment as a means of setting the value on which the allowed rate of return is to be calculated. Here a controversy instantly arises as to which cost—original cost or cost of replacement—shall be the cost basis on which earnings are calculated. Usually, in times of depression (when original cost is higher than replacement cost), the utility companies insist that original cost should be the basis used for valuation. But when prosperity returns and replacement costs are higher than original costs, it is replacement costs that they insist on as the basis for valuation.

The fact that the Interstate Commerce Commission spent years of time and millions of dollars attempting to value the railroads, and still did not arrive at a valuation which could be fully sustained in the courts, is evidence of the difficulties involved.

As if the problem of valuation were not enough, the regulatory body is also saddled with the additional difficulty of determining what may and what may not be considered as legitimate operating costs to be deducted from gross revenue when earnings are calculated, to see if they exceed the earnings allowed by law. For example, if the president of a company were also the majority stockholder, he might vote to pay himself an extremely large salary and insist that this was a cost which must be deducted before the earnings of the company were computed. The regulatory body would be then faced with the problem of determining whether the president was really worth this sum to the company and, if not, what should be a fair salary for his services.

Since all public utility companies are monopolies, there are no competitive businesses rendering the same kind of services with which they may be compared to find even a partial answer to the above problems. Regardless of our political affiliations, we may sympathize with the desire to find a "yardstick" with which to measure public utility companies. Whether or not the T.V.A. power development is really a proper yardstick is, of course, another question.

CHAPTER XVI

Rent

THE TERM *rent* in popular speech implies a payment made for the hire or use of any material good. We shall do well to forget this definition for the time being, since in economics the term has a very different meaning, and we shall find that it is only in certain very peculiar circumstances that *economic* rent is also rent in the sense in which that term is used in common speech.

Inelastic Supply of Factors of Production

In economics, whenever any unit of a factor of production is receiving a greater income than the minimum amount necessary to induce that factor to remain in its present occupation, the *surplus* of receipts over its minimum supply price may be called an *economic rent*. Thus we have seen [1] that some savers would be willing to lend a part of their funds at zero interest. Nevertheless, because the amount of funds required by borrowers is greater than the amount which would be supplied at zero interest, these savers will be able to charge the full market rate of interest on sums that they lend.

We can find the same type of surplus, or rent, in the incomes received by some units of the other factors of production. Thus, if some workers in a trade would be willing to work for $10.00 a week, but the demand for the product is such that

---

[1] Interest as well as the price of other factors is determined at the margin.

it is necessary to induce other workers into the trade who will not work for less than $15.00 a week, the first workers (who now receive $15.00 also) will be receiving a rent of $5.00 a week —the difference between what they would have been willing to work for and the amount they can actually get because of the greater demand for their services.

It will be seen, then, that rent can arise only when the supply of any factor of production is less than perfectly elastic.[2] If the supply were perfectly elastic, then by definition the supply prices of all units of the factor would be the same. The market price of the factor would be exactly equal to the supply price; an increased demand would merely call forth more units at the same price. But when the supply of a factor is less than perfectly elastic, the units of the factor which have the lowest supply price will be used first. So long as only these units are used, there will be no rent. As soon as the demand increases to a point where it is necessary to employ higher-priced units of the factor, rent will arise on those units of the factor whose supply price is lower, since in a competitive market they will be able to demand the same market price as is received by those units which are just forthcoming at the market price.

It is, however, in connection with surplus income from land that the term *rent* is most often used by economists. Indeed, many economists reserve the term *rent* for uses in connection with land alone, and employ other terms for the monopoly gains we have noticed above. It is not necessary, however, for us to quibble over the use of these terms. By whatever name they are called, the nature of these incomes is the same: they are a return made possible because the supply of the factor is less than perfectly elastic and because the demand for the factor is sufficient to require the use of more units of it than would be offered at the lowest supply price of any unit.

---

[2] Robinson, Joan, *Economics of Imperfect Competition,* Ch. 8, The Macmillan Co., London, 1934.

Rent from the Social Point of View

Considered from a social point of view, all income derived from the uses of the services of land is an economic rent. We have defined land as including all natural resources (all natural raw materials, all natural sources of non-animal energy, and standing room). By definition, these natural resources are the free gifts of nature; they have no cost of production and consequently no supply price based on cost of production. Furthermore, the physical laws of the conservation of energy and the indestructibility of matter assure us that the efforts of man cannot add to or subtract from the total amount of such resources. From the point of view of society as a whole, any payment for the use of matter and energy in their original natural forms is a surplus over supply price, and from the point of view of society as a whole the rent of land is not a cost of production. How, then, can we explain the payments which are made to those who happen to own land?

In the first place, while matter and energy as such exist in unlimited quantities, the quantities in which they exist in their present form are not unlimited. Furthermore, some forms of matter and energy are adaptable for human use with far less cost of labor and capital than are other forms. Thus, carbon in the form of coal can be obtained with less effort and cost than carbon from the atmosphere or from sea water; the latent energy of a waterfall can be harnessed for human use for some purposes at far less labor cost than energy from the sun or the tides. Nitrogen already present in a particular piece of soil is available for use as plant food without any additional expenditure of labor or capital such as would be required to bring nitrates from Chile or to extract them from the atmosphere for use in another piece of soil that lacked nitrates.

But the mere fact that natural resources in certain forms can be used in production with less cost in labor and capital than natural resources in other forms is not, in itself, a sufficient explanation of the reason why the owners of the land in which these resources are embodied are able to demand a payment for the use of such land. To explain successfully the rent of land, we must be able to show that the services of land are sufficiently scarce relatively to the demand for such services that a payment will be made for their use. (It does not matter whether such a payment is received by the landlord as a surplus over other costs by using the land in production himself, or whether he leases the land to someone else for a cash rental.)

To start our analysis in the simplest case possible, let us assume that all land is capable of producing only one product and that all land is of equal productive power (equal fertility, and so forth). In these circumstances, under pure competition, an increasing demand for the product will be met by an increasing number of firms, each producing at the point of minimum average total unit costs, until all the land is in use. Production for the industry is under conditions of constant costs. Until all land is in use, land is not a scarce factor of production. Price will be equal to minimum average total unit cost of all firms in the industry, and there will be no surplus over cost to go to the landowner as a rent. If the landowner uses the land in production himself, the total revenue from the product will cover only wages, interest, and wages of management. No one else would pay to use the land, since the total costs would likewise be equal to total revenue and they would have nothing left with which to make the payment.

Now, what happens when all the land is in use and the demand for the product increases still further? Output can no longer be expanded by adding more land, but only by using other factors in greater amounts in connection with the fixed amount of land in existence. The law of nonproportional outputs will now operate to bring about increasing marginal and average costs as expansion of output is attempted. The law

of nonproportional outputs we stated as follows: Whenever
any factor of production is held constant in amount, as successive units of other factors are used in combination with it,
the output of the product will not be in continuous proportion
to the amount of variable factors used, but will increase to a
maximum proportion; after this point, additional output per
unit of variable factor added will decline.

When land is the fixed factor which is held constant in agricultural production, the working of the law of nonproportional
outputs is easy to observe. For instance, let us assume that
we have but one acre of ground on which to raise corn. As
we attempt to use more and more seed, we will soon reach a
point where the plants are crowded and an additional pound
of seed will result in a smaller addition to the crop than resulted
from the previous pound of seed. As we hire more and more
labor to hoe the corn, we will very shortly reach a point where
an additional hour's labor in hoeing will result in a smaller
addition to the total crop than the previous hour of hoeing
labor. Similarly, the use of additional pounds of fertilizer will
begin to show diminishing proportional outputs. A similar
point will be encountered in the use of additional farm tools.
With the prices of the variable factors given, the least cost combination of variable factors with a fixed acre of land can be
determined as shown in the chapter on "Equilibrium of the
Industry."

After the least cost combination has been attained, the attempt to expand output by adding more of any or all of the
variable factors will result in increasing marginal and average
costs, even though the prices of the variable factors do not rise
when more of the units of the factors are used. For example,
assume that the wages of farm labor are 50c an hour and that
we can obtain all the labor we want at that price; that the price
we pay for seed-corn is 2c a pound and that the price of fertilizer is also 2c a pound. Further assume that at the least cost
combination the addition of the last hour of labor and of the

last pounds of seed and fertilizer has added three bushels of corn to the total crop. The marginal cost of the added output is $54 \div 3$ or 18c per bushel. Now, let us add one more hour of labor and one more pound each of seed and fertilizer. We find that this adds only two bushels of corn to the total crop. Marginal cost per bushel is now $54 \div 2$ or 27c. Thus, the cost is rising as more units of variable factors are added, simply because of decreasing output per unit of variable factor, although the prices of the factors remain unchanged.[3]

When all land is in use, if people want more of the product than can be produced at the least cost combination, they will have to pay a price for it which is equal to marginal cost. Each producer will expand output to the point where price is equal to marginal cost. But at this output average total unit cost will be less than the price of the product and total revenue will be greater than total cost. Here is a surplus return over costs. Each firm will be in equilibrium because marginal revenue (under pure competition the same as price) is equal to marginal cost. The *industry* will be in equilibrium because no new firms can enter to take advantage of the surplus, since there is no more land for them to use. This surplus is economic rent of land. The owner can earn this economic rent by using the land himself in the production of the product. If the landlord does not care to use the land himself, he can offer it for lease to others. Competitive bidding for the use of the land will then

---

[3] All of the above is simply another way of saying that the elasticity of substitution of labor and capital for land is less than infinite. When we hold the amount of land constant and attempt to add more labor and capital to it, instead of increasing the amount of land used also, we are really attempting to substitute labor and capital for land in the process of production. As we have seen above, there are limits to the profitability and, eventually, to the physical possibility of such substitution. As a bright undergraduate once remarked, "If it were not for the law of nonproportional outputs, the food for the entire world could be grown in a flowerpot." If it were not for the law of nonproportional outputs, an ever greater output could be obtained merely by using more and more capital on small pieces of land best suited for any kind of production. In other words, the elasticity of supply of services of land would be infinite as far as the purposes of production were concerned. An ever-expanding output could be produced without encountering scarcity of land, and there would be no rent of land.

force whoever does obtain the use of the land to pay the full amount of the economic rent for it. Even if there is only one bidder, the landlord can refuse to lease the land for a smaller rent than he could make by using it himself to produce the product. (Note that even though the landlord were to decide to make no charge for the use of the land, economic rent would still arise. The freeholding tenants would then themselves produce to the point where price was equal to marginal cost, and pocket the economic rent themselves.)

Differential Rent

In the preceding discussion we made the assumption that all land was of equal productivity or fertility. We shall now remove that assumption, recognizing that for most purposes there are different grades of land. This introduces no contradiction, but merely an elaboration of our previous analysis. When there are different grades of land, the best (most productive) grade will be used first before recourse is had to the poorer lands. So long as the demand for the product is so small that all the best grade land is not needed to produce the output, the situation will be the same as above when there was only one grade of land and not all of it was in use. Price will be equal to minimum average total unit cost and there will be no rent. When all the best grade land is in use, further increases in the demand for the product will be met first by more intensive cultivation of this best land. Price will be equal to marginal cost and greater than average total unit cost, and rent will arise on the best grade land, exactly as before.

As demand increases still further and output on the best land is expanded, a point will be found where the rising marginal cost on the best land is just equal to minimum average total unit cost on the next best grade of land. At this point the second grade of land will be brought into use. It will be earning no rent (with the price equal to minimum average cost), but

farmers would be exactly as well off using this land and receiving no rent from it as they would be if they leased the best
grade land from others and paid the full economic rent for
its use.

After all of the second grade land is in use, if the demand
for the product increases still further, output will be increased
on the second grade land beyond the point of minimum costs
(and output on the first grade land will be expanded still
further). Price will now be equal to marginal cost and greater

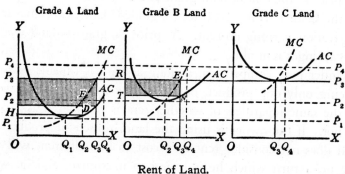

Rent of Land.

than average cost on the second grade land, and the second
grade land will now start to earn a rent, although not as
large a rent as that on the best land. As demand increases
and price rises further, a point will be found where rising
marginal costs on the two grades of land are exactly equal
to minimum average cost on a third grade of land. At this
point the third grade of land will be brought into use with
results similar to that on the second grade; and so on with
successive price rises for as many grades of land as there are
in existence.

The diagram illustrates the emergence of rent on different
grades of land. *MC* is marginal cost (not including rent) and
AC is average total unit cost (not including rent) on each
of the three grades of land. P_1, P_2, P_3, and P_4 are various

possible prices of the product, and Q_1, Q_2, Q_3, and Q_4 are the outputs which would be produced at these prices.

At price P_1 there is no rent. Between prices P_1 and P_2, the situation is the same as if grade-A land were the only land in existence: price will be equal to marginal cost, and the difference between marginal and average cost, multiplied by the output, will constitute rent. At price P_2 rent on grade-A land is shown by the area P_2FDH. At price P_2 it will be noticed that grade-B land is brought into cultivation but earns no rent. At price P_3 the rent of both grade-A and grade-B land is shown by the shaded areas. At price P_3, grade-C land also comes into cultivation, earning no rent. At price P_4, grade-C land would be earning a rent also.

Under pure competition, so long as land is capable of producing only one product, output of the individual firm will be the same regardless of whether rent is considered as a cost or not. If the owner is using the land himself in production and does not consider rent as a cost to himself, rent will be the net return which he is trying to maximize, and he will produce up to the point where price is equal to marginal cost (not including rent), as we have seen above. If a tenant hires the land and pays full economic rent for it, rent will be a fixed cost and will not determine output. Furthermore, at any given price for the product, minimum average cost (including rent) will be the same as marginal cost (not including rent). This may be seen in the diagram.

At price P_3, on grade-B land:

EQ_3 is marginal cost (not including rent) at output OQ_3;
NQ_3 is average cost (not including rent) at output OQ_3;
total rent is the shaded area $RENT$.

Average rent per unit of product, at output OQ_3, is given by the height of the shaded area EN.

But $EN + NQ_3 = EQ_3$; that is, average cost (not including rent) plus average rent is equal to marginal cost (not including rent).

For a fixed cash rent equal to RENT on Grade B land:

At any output less than OQ_3, average rent per unit of product would be much greater than EN, since total rent would be divided by a smaller number of units; hence, average cost (including rent) would be greater than EQ_3.

At any output greater than OQ_3, although average rent per unit of product is falling, average cost (not including rent) is rising so rapidly that when the two are added together, average cost including rent is greater than EQ_3.

Therefore, EQ_3 represents *minimum* average cost, including rent. (This is not a peculiarity of this diagram, for it can be shown by calculus that these relationships hold for any set of marginal and average-cost curves.)

As far as we have gone in our analysis, it would appear that rent is purely a result of the price of the product and is not a cost factor that will help to determine output and price. This would be true if there were only one product that land was capable of producing (the assumption which we made). Our analysis of rent can stop here for any land which has only one use. Wherever land has only one use, the rent will be a result of the price of the product and will amount to the difference between the price of the product and the labor and capital costs of production on each unit of output.

Regarded from the point of view of society, all rent of land is of this nature, that is, the total amount of all land in existence is fixed, and the amount of land cannot be increased or decreased by its owners in order to obtain a price for it. The elasticity of supply of land in general might be said to be zero. Landowners will offer all the land they own in return for whatever income they can get for it.[4]

Rent Within an Industry

However, looked at from the point of view of a single industry, at least a part of the rent of that land which has more

---

[4] From our point of view, it makes no difference whether the landlords receive rent by leasing the land to others or by using the land themselves in production; the supply of land for the purposes of production will be the same.

than one use enters into the cost of production and helps to
determine output. In order to obtain land for any particular
use, an industry will have to pay a rental that is at least equal
to that which the land could earn in other uses. As the industry expands and it becomes necessary to draw land away from
other uses in which it is increasingly valuable, the price which
this industry will have to pay for the use of the land will rise.
The minimum supply price of each piece of land to the industry
will be the amount which the land could earn in its most valuable alternative use. Such a price may be called the *opportunity
price* of the land, since it is the price necessary to cause the land
to be transferred for use in this industry.

The price of the product will be determined at the point
where price is just equal to marginal cost (*including* transference price of land) on the highest cost land which is to be retained in the industry. It should be noted that from this point
of view, the marginal land (that land which will leave the
industry first if the price of the product falls) need not be the
least efficient nor the poorest land in use. Thus, land which
is best suited for the production of wheat may also be best suited
for dairy farming. And this land might be the first which
would be withdrawn from wheat production and turned to
dairy farming if the price of wheat falls.

When the opportunity price of land is considered as a cost
of production to the industry, there is still the possibility of a
surplus which we may call *economic rent within the industry,*
if the transference price of land to the industry is rising as
more land is used. The firms using the land with the lowest
opportunity price will be able to obtain the same price for their
product as the firms using the highest cost land. They will,
of course, expand output to the point where marginal cost is
equal to price, but a surplus return will remain on the intramarginal lower cost units of output. If the firms using the
land with the lower opportunity prices have taken the land

on a long-term lease before the industry expanded, or if they have bought the land, they will be able to pocket this surplus for themselves. If not, the landlord will be able by threatening to lease the land to others to insist that they pay the full economic rent as soon as their lease expires.

Rent from the Point of View of the Individual Firm

From the point of view of the *individual firm,* all rent of all factors must be considered as costs of production. If the firm leases land from others, the cash payment of the rent is obvious as a cost. If the owner of the land uses it himself in production, the full payment that he could have received had he leased the land to others will be an opportunity cost. While this will not be a cash expenditure which the owner must pay out, unless he considers rent as a cost he will be deceiving himself as to the source of his income and may be overlooking the opportunity to make a greater income. Thus, if I am farming my own land, and the returns which I receive after all other costs (including interest and wages of management) are accounted for do not equal the amount which I could receive by leasing the land to someone else, I would be neglecting the opportunity to make a greater income.

The rent that arises because of differences in the opportunity prices of land might be called an *intra-industrial* rent. It is a surplus which can be earned by using the land in this industry rather than in its next most valuable use. This part of the payment for the services of the land will not influence the output of the industry, since the land will be retained for use in this industry so long as it is earning at least its opportunity price.

However, the consideration of all payment for the services of land (including intra-industrial rent) as a cost to the individual firm (either a money cost or an opportunity cost) will help to determine which firm is to obtain the land for use within the industry. Thus, if I own a particular store location which can earn much more in use as a shoe store than for any other purpose, I will be able to demand for its use the full payment of what it can earn *as a shoe store* (including intra-industrial rent), and I will not have to be content with the lesser earnings it could make as a grocery store. If the first tenant to whom I happen to lease the location proves to be a poor shoe store manager and cannot make the store yield the full amount of this payment, I will not have to lower the rental, because if he fails I will be able to lease the store to a better manager who is able to take full advantage of the location. The maximum amount of rental that I can receive will lie somewhere between what the best manager and what the second best manager are willing to pay for the use of the location. But in no case can the rental I receive exceed the rental on the next best shoe store location by more than the difference between what the best manager could earn by using my location and what he could earn by using the next poorer location. If I try to run the shoe store myself and find that I am not a good manager, I will be able to receive more by leasing it to someone else who is.

Location Value

The rent of land as we have explained it is a *value* surplus left over after other costs have been accounted for. This surplus depends upon the amount received from the sale of the output and upon the costs necessary to produce that output. A given piece of land can command a rental either because costs of production on it are low, or because the receipts from the sale of its product in the particular location are high. We have already examined the influence of differential costs of production upon rent. We must now turn our attention to the influence of location.

Of two pieces of land equally productive (that is, on which costs of production are the same), the one located nearest to the market for the product will command the higher rental.

This will be due to the differences in the cost of transporting the product to the market. Thus, a dairy farm located within 100 miles of New York City will receive a higher total revenue, after freight charges are deducted, on the same quantity of fluid milk sold in New York City than would be received by a dairy farm 200 miles distant from the city. The full amount of this difference will be an addition to the economic rent of the better located farm. The additional rent due to the location of the land might be called its *location value*.

The location value of retail store sites requires further explanation. A particular store location can earn a high rental either because people are willing to pay high prices to trade in that location or because a large volume of business can be done in that location. The high rentals paid by many so-called "exclusive" shops on Fifth Avenue are due to the fact that the district is considered a fashionable place in which to buy, and in consequence the wealthy people who trade there allow themselves to be charged higher prices than they would pay for the same goods if they were displayed and sold on Tenth Avenue. On the other hand, the high rental earned by some other stores is due to what is called the high "rate of turnover" which is possible in these stores, or to the volume of business which can be done at a low price. The "rate of turnover" is the number of times a year that the same value quantity of goods can be bought and resold. A store with a high rate of turnover can do a greater volume of business on the same amount of invested capital than a store with a smaller rate of turnover; consequently, since its interest costs are less, there will be a greater surplus left as rent. The total volume of business which a store can do is also a factor in determining the rental. A store which is empty of customers for a great part of the time will still have to maintain a sales force to care for customers when they do come in, so that the cost of salesman's wages per unit of goods sold will be high. On the other hand, a better located store may have a sufficient number of customers coming in all the time, so that its salespeople are fully occupied and its selling cost per unit of output is lower. The latter store will then be able to earn a higher rental than the poorer located store. For these two reasons—volume of sales and rate of turnover—a United Cigar Store located at Times Square pays a higher rental than a similar store located in the Bronx, even though cigars and cigarettes sell for the same price in both places.

Another element in location value closely related to the above is the lower advertising costs which may be necessary to do the same volume of business in different localities. Thus, a store that is so located that a large number of prospective buyers pass it every day may use its windows for display purposes and sell a large volume of goods without further advertising cost. A store so located that buyers are not in the habit of passing it will have to incur a much greater expense for advertising in order to do the same volume of business. The better-located store would command a greater rental than the one in the poorer location.

Urban Site Rent

The difference between the nature of the location value of agricultural land and the location value of urban sites must be recognized. The location value of agricultural land is due to its distance from a competitive market and is mainly a function of transportation costs. The location value of urban sites contains a distinct monopoly element.[5] Possession of a particular site carries with it a partial monopoly of the trade of a particular group of people insofar as people are motivated by habit or laziness in trading in those localities which are most con-

---

[5] Chamberlin, E., *The Theory of Monopolistic Competition*, Appendix D. Harvard University Press, 1935. John Ise presents an interesting contrary view in the *American Economic Review*, February, 1940.

venient to them.   If all people would buy only from the dealer who offered goods at lowest prices regardless of his location, no retail store location could command a higher rental than any other in a city, except as differences in transportation costs were different in different locations.   If people were content to buy all products by mail order, transportation costs would be the only element that could give rise to a location value on the sites of the warehouses from which they were served.

One other source of location value should be noted that may be present in the rent of either agricultural land or manufacturing sites.   If the wages in a particular community are much lower than those that prevail in other communities but the workers refuse to move out to localities where they could obtain better wages, then farm land in the low-wage locality will be able to earn a higher return than farm land of equal fertility and equal transportation costs in other localities.   The same would be true of factory sites in the low-wage locality.   If the land available for farm land in such a low-wage farming community is limited, or if the land available for factory sites in a low-wage manufacturing community is limited so that competition for workers will not raise wages, then the excess location value due to low wages will persist until such time as workers move out of the community.   The high rental values of mines and the low wages of miners in certain isolated mining communities can be explained only by the inability or unwillingness of the miners to move elsewhere and seek other occupations.

Before leaving the subject of agricultural rent, certain causes must be noted which may decrease the rent of agricultural land. The discovery of a new and cheap fertilizer may make some land available for use in agriculture which formerly could not be used at all and may lower the cost of production of larger outputs on land previously in use.   While the new land may then start to yield a small rental, the increased output of the product will cause the price to fall and consequently reduce the rental on what were previously the more fertile lands. To the extent that the fertilizer will give a greater amount of product with the same expenditure for labor and capital on all lands, the total output will be increased, the price of agricultural products will fall, and the general level of agricultural rents will decline. In effect the available supply of agricultural land has been increased. A similar result follows from the discovery of any improved agricultural methods which are generally adopted.[6]

Changes in dietary habits may also cause agricultural rent to decline. As people consume less food, the decrease in the demand for foodstuffs will lower agricultural rents. Even a shift in dietary habits from animal products to vegetable and cereal products may tend to reduce agricultural rents, since a smaller number of acres of land will be necessary to feed a population subsisting more upon vegetables and cereals and less upon animal products.

There are no grounds on which to prophesy that either agricultural or urban rents will increase over a long period of time. Agricultural rents will increase only if the demand for agricultural products increases more rapidly than new methods of agricultural production are discovered and adopted. Urban rents for business purposes will increase only as people concentrate more and more of their buying in a given locality. New means of transportation that cause population to be decentralized, and new methods of marketing, may offset this tendency.

Quasi Rent

Investments in durable capital goods often yield a return which is quite analogous to the rent of land. Once such invest-

[6] The effect on agricultural rents and land values of the newly developed method of growing vegetables in tanks of water filled with appropriate minerals, will be interesting to observe.

ments have been made, they are in the nature of "sunk costs."
Once the capital goods are in existence, the owner has no recourse except to make whatever return on them that is possible
under the circumstances. Their original cost will not be a
determinant of the price of the product, since the owner will
continue to use the capital goods in production as long as price
is greater than average variable costs. The minimum supply
price of capital goods already in existence may be said to be
zero in the same sense that the minimum supply price of land
is zero. Consequently, any return on these goods is in the
nature of a rent. The name *quasi rent* has been used by some
economists to designate this return.

While we have just said that the cost of *existing* capital goods
is not a determinant of the price of the product, nevertheless
if demand for the product increases, in order to induce the
construction and use of *new* capital goods, the price of the
product must be sufficient to promise a return at the market
rate of interest on any new funds which are to be invested.
Consequently, if either the rate of interest or the cost of production of capital goods has risen, the old capital goods that
were previously in existence may earn a rate of return greater
than that which was anticipated by the owners when the goods
were originally purchased. This situation is quite similar to
that which occurs in the purchase or long-term lease of land.
Subsequent events may operate either to raise or to lower the
actual return from that which was contemplated at the time the
lease or sale was made.

CHAPTER XVII

Profits

PROFITS are the net income accruing to the owners of a business after all costs are accounted for. What we are to class as profits depends upon what we consider to be the costs of a business. We have classed wages, rent, interest, and wages of management as costs. Profits, according to our definition, will thus be any income in excess of these costs.

We have already seen in the chapters dealing with price that, under perfect competition, there will be no profits in the long run. Any pure profits that we discover will have to be either profits arising from a monopoly position or profits of a temporary nature.

Monopoly profits, as we have seen, *arise through the ability to control output so that price will not fall to a point where it is only equal to cost.* In addition to the ability to control output, another condition must also be implied: namely, the nature of the demand for the product must be such that at some possible point of output price will be in excess of costs. Even the profits of monopolies may prove to be of a temporary nature, as we shall find when we examine the implications of these conditions more fully.

Sources of Monopoly Power

If the demand curve for a product is known, the source of monopoly power lies in the ability to control the output of an industry. Such power to control output is really based on two conditions: (1) the power to regulate the output of the single firm or small group of firms which comprise the industry at present; (2) the power to prevent new firms from entering the industry. We shall now examine some of the more common sources of this power.

In the first place, the exclusive right to render a certain service in a particular market may be granted to one firm by a charter or franchise issued by a government. This is usually done in the case of industries called *public utilities* such as streetcar lines, gas and electric companies, water companies, railroads, telephone and telegraph companies, and so on. The services which public utilities provide are usually called *legal monopolies,* since competition in producing them would be so wasteful and inefficient that it is considered advisable to grant the exclusive right to perform such services to one company. In return for such a grant, the chartering government usually reserves the right to set the maximum rates that may be charged for these services. The setting of rates by a government agency then acts as a limitation upon the amount of monopoly profits that may be earned.

The usual procedure followed by a regulatory body in setting maximum rates is to allow the company to earn a certain percentage on the value of its investment. This gives rise to the very difficult question as to what is the proper value of the investment. We have already given some consideration to this question.[1] What interests us now is that while such a regulatory agency may *allow* a certain rate of return on the investment, it cannot *guarantee* such a return, unless the public is to be taxed to make up any possible deficits, and this, of course, is seldom done. It follows that even the limited profits allowed by the regulatory body are not necessarily a permanent source of income. Thus, competition by busses and trucks may so decrease the demand for the services of a particular railroad

---

[1] See the chapter on "Interest."

that it cannot earn a profit, no matter what rates it is allowed
to charge. The widespread use of automobiles in a certain
locality may completely destroy the earning power of a streetcar
line. A cheap source of electricity may cause people to cease
using gas, even for heating and cooking, at any price that would
be profitable to the gas company. Even when supported by a
government franchise, monopolies are dependent on the demand for their product in earning monopoly profits.

Another source of monopoly power is the possession of patent
rights issued by the government upon a product or upon the
machinery or process used in the manufacture of a product.
The possession of such patent rights will serve to prevent direct
competition in the manufacture of the product, so that output
can be controlled for the duration of the legal life of the patent.
Here again, however, the amount of monopoly profits and the
length of time they will continue will depend upon whether
successful competing substitute products are introduced and
upon the nature of the demand for the product. If it could
always be known in advance what the monopoly profits on a
patent were going to be, and if the market in which these
patents were sold was perfectly competitive, the inventor could
always obtain the full value of these monopoly profits for himself by selling or leasing the patent rights, and there would be
no profit left over to go to the owners of the business who
merely used the patent. But in the absence of these conditions
in the actual world, we sometimes find inventors being exploited by being paid less than their patents are worth, or they
are overpaid when the invention does not prove as profitable
as was anticipated when the patent was purchased. The use
of trade marks may serve to prolong the profit-yielding monopoly value long after the patent expires.

The net returns arising out of the exclusive ownership or
control of a source of raw materials or water power should not

be considered as monopoly profits at all but as a rent on the land in which these scarce resources are embodied. If other conditions are the same, the owners of these resources can obtain no more by using the resources themselves in production than by leasing them to others. It may be considered a monopoly profit if there is only one owner.

Another source of monopoly power and monopoly profits lies in the agreements that are sometimes made between firms that would otherwise be competitive to restrict output or to maintain prices. Trusts, pools, cartels, and "gentlemen's agreements" are some of the commoner names given to monopolistic organizations of this sort. Unless these agreements are given sanction by government (such as was the case with the German Cartels and the N.R.A. codes during their brief existence), they will be unenforceable and consequently will last only so long as each and every member considers it to his own self-interest to keep the agreement. If prices are to be fixed for even a short period, the agreement will have to provide some means of restricting the output of each of the constituent firms. Otherwise, as soon as a profitable price is set, it will be to the interest of each of the member firms to produce all that it can to sell at that price. If very many of the firms try this, the total output of the industry will soon be so great that it cannot be sold at the price fixed in the agreement, and there will be a temptation for each firm to cut prices to dispose of its output. Furthermore, any monopoly profits achieved by an agreement of this sort are apt to be shortlived unless some means exists for preventing the entrance of new firms into the industry (for example, control of patent rights or of raw materials). In the absence of obstacles to the entrance of new firms into the industry, the setting of a profitable monopoly price will act as an inducement for new firms to start competing with the "trust" for a share of the excessive profits.

Profits of Monopolistic Competition

By far the most common source of monopoly profits lies in what we have called product differentiation. As we have seen, when a product is successfully differentiated in the minds of a group of buyers either because of the services which are rendered with it or because of the impression which past advertising has made on the minds of the buyers, the firm will have a limited monopoly of the trade of a certain group of buyers. The good will of the business consists in the ability to retain customers, either while charging a higher price than that charged by competitors, or by selling at a price equal to that charged by competitors although lower selling costs than those incurred by competitors are enjoyed. As we have seen in the discussion of cost and price, there is no way of telling how long the profit-yielding advantage of product differentiation will persist. New competitors may attempt to duplicate as closely as possible the services offered by an old firm, or they may offer superior service to a particular group of the old firm's customers. Profits of the old firm may then be reduced or eliminated by a reduction in the demand for its products, by increased cost of production on a smaller output, or by increased selling costs; or by two or more of these causes acting in combination.

For some firms in some industries, however, the monopoly profits arising out of product differentiation and good will may persist for a considerable number of years. This is most likely to be the case in the manufacture and sale of those products that require a large volume of output to attain low unit costs, or in those that require a heavy expenditure on plant and equipment to produce even a small output. Wherever a heavy initial cost must be incurred to start a firm (whether a cost of production, a selling cost, or both), it will tend to act as a deterrent to the entrance of new firms into the industry, since there will naturally be some hesitancy about risking the necessary amount of capital. Product differentiation and the possession of good will by the existing firms in the industry will tend to increase such a risk and give it greater force as a deterrent to the entrance of new firms.

Profits of Innovation

There is another source of profits which may appear either in combination with product differentiation or in a perfectly competitive industry. We may call this type of profits the *profits of innovation*.[2] Thus, the first firm or firms to introduce a new product, even though the product is unprotected by a patent, may make a profit for a time until competitors start to duplicate or imitate the product, thereby forcing its price down to a point where only competitive costs of production are covered. Similarly, the first firm or firms to adopt a new lower-cost method of production in a competitive industry may make a profit because they will have lower costs than their competitors until such time as the improvement is adopted generally by the industry. Thus, the first wheat farmers to use tractors and gang plows in extensive wheat farming made a profit by so doing; but as the tractor came to be generally used, the decline in the price of wheat eliminated this source of profit.

The opening of a new market for a product may also give profits of innovation for the first firms which start to sell in that market until competition wears away these surplus gains. The discovery and utilization of a new and cheaper source of raw materials will likewise give profits of innovation to the first firms that take advantage of it.

All of these sources of the profits of innovation are purely temporary sources of profits. They will persist only until such time as competitors adopt the same methods or duplicate the product. The opportunity to make such profits may exist for

---

[2] Schumpeter, J. A., *The Theory of Economic Development*, Ch. II, Harvard University Press, 1934.

a long time before anyone realizes it, either because businessmen are in ignorance of the opportunity or because they are doubtful of the possible success of the new method. Once the method has been put into practice by one firm, however, and the profits are actually shown to exist, imitators may rush in to follow the lead of the successful innovator. If no obstacle exists to the adoption of the new method by competitors, competition will continue to the point where the profits of innovation are eliminated.

When it is possible to combine innovation with one of the monopoly elements we discussed above, the profits arising out of innovation may continue for a long period of time. Thus, a firm which manufactures a new product may control the patent rights either on the product itself or on its process of manufacture. Such a patent, however, will be a guarantee only against exact duplication of the product by competitors. Once the innovator has demonstrated that there is a market for such a product, the product may be closely imitated or even improved upon by competitors without necessarily infringing the original patent. Thus, we have seen one electric refrigerator after another put on the market, each differing somewhat from the other in design, but all competing with each other in the market for refrigerators. The degree of monopoly power conferred by a patent varies from one product to another and depends to a considerable extent upon the breadth of the claims allowed in the patent.

As important as (and sometimes more important than) patent rights, in the prolongation of the profits of innovation, is the possibility of building up good will for a trade mark or brand name in connection with an innovation. A firm that puts a new product on the market may be able to obtain a great deal of free advertising in the news columns of the papers simply because the product has "news value," whereas subsequent competitors may have to pay for all the advertising necessary to introduce their variety of the product to the public. All of the competitors who are first in the field will be able to take advantage of the old axiom that "a satisfied customer is the best advertisement." The competitors who enter the field later will have to struggle to overcome this advantage of the first firms. For example, any of us would probably be far less hesitant about buying any of the so-called "standard" makes of cars which are on the market than we would be about buying a new make of car whose manufacture was just started this year. This advantage of good will is apt to be greatest in those products of which the buying public is unable to determine the merits by inspection. In any event, the advantages of good will and the profits accruing from it will last only until competitors are able to make serious inroads on the business of the older firms.

All of the sources of profits which we have discussed thus far have depended for their existence upon some monopoly element. Even the profits of innovation may be classed as profits of partial monopoly, since they are dependent upon the smallness of the number of firms which first adopt the innovation.

Windfall Profits

We must now turn to the consideration of profits that may arise from time to time in purely competitive industries. In general, these may be classed as *windfall profits*,[3] since they are not anticipated by the firms in the industry and since they arise from sources which are entirely beyond the control of the firms.

One of the commonest sources of windfall profits is the advance in the price of a product due to currency inflation, whether such currency inflation is a part of the "recovery" and

---

[3] A term used by J. M. Keynes in *A Treatise on Money*, Vol. I, p. 125, The Macmillan Co., London, 1930. Our analysis here, however, is considerably different from that of Keynes.

"prosperity" phases of the business cycle or is deliberate inflation of the currency by the government. When the price of a product is rising because of currency inflation, those firms which have a stock of goods on hand that have been manufactured or purchased at the previously prevailing lower costs will be able to sell the goods at a profit. Similarly, if they have contracted for labor and raw materials at the previous low prices that were based on the then prevailing low price of the product, they will make a profit by using this labor and raw material to manufacture a product which sells at a higher price than that which was anticipated when the contracts were made.

Note that while one or two firms may anticipate such a rise in the price of the product, it cannot be generally anticipated by the industry, or no such windfall profits would arise. If the full extent of the price rise were known in advance by all firms in the industry, then each would be so eager to accumulate a stock of goods to be sold at the higher price that competition between them would drive up the price of labor and raw materials to a point where no profits remained.

There is some question as to whether this type of windfall profits should be considered as profits at all. If we consider profits as the average earnings above cost for a long period of years, most, if not all, of these profits will tend to disappear. Over a long period of years the unanticipated losses due to falling prices will have to be deducted from the profits which accrue in years of rising prices. Since the losses will be unanticipated [4] as well as the profits, there is no reason to expect one to exceed the other. Careful accounting might consider these windfall profits as reserves to be set aside to cover the losses from bad years and would then consider as a pure profit only the amount by which the profits exceeded the

---

[4] The losses must be unanticipated or they can be avoided. If a firm knows that the price is going to fall, it can avoid or minimize the loss by getting rid of its stock of goods on hand and making no more contracts until costs have been adjusted to the new low price level.

losses.[5] What we call a profit will depend upon the length of time for which we are drawing up the accounts of a firm or an industry.

Another source of windfall profits may lie in sudden increases of demand for a product not occasioned by monetary causes. When demand increases, the existing competitive firms in an industry may all make a profit for a time until new firms enter the industry and supply is increased again to the point where no profits remain. Such a change in demand might be occasioned by a change of taste, by the development of a new use for an old product, or by a change in the distribution of income among the population.

A shift in the location of population may also be a source of temporary profits. Thus, when a new industry employing a large number of men starts up in a small town, the existing retail stores may make a large return temporarily by selling to the employees of the new company. A part of this return will, of course, be an increased economic rent on the enhanced location value of the stores. But the rest of it will be a temporary monopoly profit because only a few stores will be in a position to supply goods for the increased demand. As soon as new competing stores can be set up to cater to the larger demand, this profit will tend to disappear, and the enhanced economic rent alone will remain.

Profits and Risks

Another source of profits arises in connection with the risks involved in a business enterprise. If the production of a certain product involves a considerable degree of risk that the capital invested in such an enterprise will be lost, then the price of the product will have to be high enough to induce the

---

[5] Anyone who buys a business, or a share of stock in a business, in a prosperous year in the expectation that the level of windfall profits represents the permanent earning capacity of the firm, is bound to come to grief.

owners of capital to take such a risk of investment. If any firm in such an industry is then fortunate enough to experience *less* than the average anticipated losses, it will be making a profit, since the price of the product is based on the average expectancy of loss.

This element accounts for the larger profits made by certain successful maritime adventurers before the development of marine insurance. Thus, if it was the general experience that one shipment out of every ten resulted in a total loss of both ship and cargo, freight rates and the prices of imported goods would have to carry at least an additional 10 per cent and probably more to induce shipowners and shippers to take such risks. Any shipowner or shipper who experienced no such losses would be making the 10 or more per cent as a profit, and any who experienced less than 10 per cent of losses would make a proportionate profit.

Whenever any risks of this sort are covered by insurance, the profits arising from the risk element will disappear. The principle of insurance involves the taking of a small loss by everyone, in the form of the premium paid, in order to avoid a possible greater loss. The risks which can be covered by insurance will not act as a deterrent to the investment of capital in the industry. The normal price of the product will then have to cover the insurance premium as a cost, but there will be nothing left over as a profit. Wherever risks can be eliminated either through insurance or through any other methods open to all the firms in an industry, the profits due to the risk element will disappear.

We have discovered, then, that business profits are the most uncertain and unstable of all forms of income. For profits to persist for any appreciable length of time, there must be a monopoly element that gives rise to them. Even monopoly profits will last only until competition of successful substitutes or a decrease in the demand for the product eliminates them.

CHAPTER XVIII

Monopolistic Competition and General Equilibrium Theory

WE HAVE had, earlier, an exposition of general equilibrium theory in terms and under conditions of perfect and and pure competition. In the intervening discussion of the markets for the factors of production, we have had to take into account certain "imperfections" of these markets (presumably conditions which would disappear if sufficient time were allowed to elapse with *no new disturbing elements* intervening).

On the other hand, we noted certain elements of monopolistic competition which might be expected to continue even after market imperfections were removed (if they ever could be). These elements would force those of us who accept the doctrine of monopolistic competition either to *reject* the theory of general equilibrium as stated under the conditions of pure and perfect competition or to *alter* that theory so as to take account of the various forms of product differentiation and degrees of monopoly which exist in the actual world.

The Conditions of a State of Equilibrium

We may restate our conditions or requirements for a state of general equilibrium: (1) No opportunity for firms to profit by expanding or contracting output. (2) No profitable opportunity for new firms to enter an industry, and no necessity for any existing firms to leave an industry. (3) No profitable

opportunity for changes in the proportions of factors of production used by a firm or an industry. We may allow for a
"moving equilibrium" by taking into account changes due to
an expanding population. Our discussion of how well these
conditions may be fulfilled under monopolistic competition
will occupy the rest of this chapter.

Divergence of Marginal and Average Revenue

The removal of the assumption of pure competition forces
us immediately to re-examine the conditions of equilibrium
which were based on that assumption. The rule of proportionality between prices of factors and their marginal products
still holds. The owner of the monopolistic firm has the same
motives and follows the same process in seeking the least-cost
combination of factors as does the purely competitive owner.

The greatest difference comes in the concept of the marginal
product.[1] Under pure competition the marginal revenue
product consists of the number of units of the product added
by the last unit of a factor employed, multiplied by the selling
price per unit of product. This follows from the fact that
under pure competition the individual firm accepts the price
of the product as a given condition which it cannot alter and
hence does not consider changes in its own output as a factor
which may affect price. Under monopolistic conditions, however, the effect upon price of the increased output must be
accounted for. The marginal revenue product then becomes
the increase in the number of units produced by adding one
more unit of a factor of production, multiplied by the price
of the product *minus* the loss in revenue on all previous units
of output which is occasioned by the decrease in price necessary to sell the increased output. Under monopoly and monopolistic competition, the marginal revenue product will al-

---

[1] See Chamberlin, E. H., "Monopolistic Competition and the Productivity Theory of
Distribution," *Explorations in Economics,* pp. 237 ff., McGraw-Hill Book Co., New
York, 1936.

ways be less than the marginal value product for any unit of a factor of production.

Duplication of Services

Total employment of any factor or factors in an "industry" (roughly defined as a group of closely competing firms) may or may not be less than that would prevail in a similar industry operating under conditions of pure competition. If total employment is the same, or greater, the implication is that there are a larger number of firms, operating at less than optimum output, than would be the case under pure competition. This is the typical Chamberlinean solution. An important question arises here as to the nature of the cost curve which we have in mind. If the cost curve which is used is dependent for its declining slope upon some elements of fixed investment by the individual firm, then the solution is only a first approximation, and not a position of long-run equilibrium. It would then be possible over a period of time for the size of the fixed investment to be reduced and a new cost curve substituted for the old one, which new curve would represent least cost conditions at the saleable output. If the resulting profits attract more new firms to the industry, which duplicate the products of existing firms as far as possible, the individual demand curves of the old firms will tend to become more elastic. Repetition of this process would give an ever-closer approach to the conditions of pure competition. To the extent that selling costs are a necessary element, however, costs and prices, even in the final solution, will be higher than those under pure competition.

Definition of Firm

If Chamberlin's cost curve is a "planning curve" (most of his discussion would lead us to believe that it is a planning curve), then the declining phase of the cost curve for the individual firm must be explained by the indivisibility of the

units of certain factors of production. It may be remarked
that Chamberlin draws most of his illustrations from gasoline
stations and other retail establishments, where the proportion
of indivisible units to total factors of production employed is
probably much higher than in most manufacturing establishments. We should not be misled by what at first sight appears
to be indivisibility of the "natural" units of the various factors
of production. It is true that we cannot hire half a man, but
in many lines men can be and are hired for part time or for a
few hours. Half a machine is of no use, but in some lines
machines need not be owned but may be rented for only the
time they are required (harvesting machinery, for example).
In chain store organizations it is possible to divide the services
of high-salaried purchasing agents, advertising managers, and
merchandisers among a large number of individual stores in
the chain. In a strict economic sense, the entire chain must
be considered as one "firm." Nevertheless, from an accounting viewpoint, at least, it is entirely proper to consider each
individual store as a "firm" in competition with various independent and other chain unit stores in its particular locality,
charging a portion of the services of the general management
to each individual chain unit as if they were hired services from
an outside agency. The so-called voluntary chains are actually
operated much in this manner. Individual ownership of
stores is retained, but buying is placed in a pool, and advertising and some other services are performed by a central organization for the membership. If monopolistic competition leads
to chain store organization, and we regard the entire chain
as the "firm," then Chamberlin's conclusion must be reversed.
The typical "firm" instead of becoming smaller is much larger.

Employment of Factors

If total employment of factors of production under monopolistic competition is less than it would be if the industry were

operating under conditions of pure competition, then the excluded units of the factors must seek employment in other industries. Presumably the marginal productivity of these units will be less in the other industries to which they are forced to turn. Thus they will have to accept a lower price or wage than they could have obtained if the monopolistic industry were operated under conditions of pure competition.

It does not necessarily follow that factors of production which are excluded from one industry when conditions of monopolistic competition develop will have to seek employment in industries whose products are sold under conditions of pure competition. They may be absorbed in other monopolistic industries. In either case, however, they must accept a wage which is low enough to induce the new employer to make use of their services. To the extent that the monopolistic industries are maintaining rigid prices for their products, the purely competitive industries with more flexible prices are apt to prove able to absorb the excluded factors more readily. The movement of population from cities to farms during the last depression (although it was not caused primarily by monopolistic competition) is evidence of the ability of purely competitive industries to absorb workers at low wages. (In most cases these were not cash wages, but the children returned to the farm, and the farm supported more people on a lower standard of living.)

It must be noted that whenever monopolistic competition results in reduced employment in an industry, not only do the excluded units of factors themselves have to accept lower wages, but also they tend to drive wages down in the industries into which they are absorbed. This situation is occasioned not only by the direct competition of the excluded factors for employment, but also by the fact that expansion of output in any industry which employs them will tend to drive down the price of the product and therefore to decrease the marginal revenue product of the previously employed factors in the expanding industries.

The preceding discussion has reference to the development of conditions of monopolistic competition in an industry which had previously been purely competitive. If an entirely new industry starts up under conditions of monopolistic competition, then the entire employment offered by this new industry may be a net addition to the total opportunities for employment of factors of production. The result, then, is simply that these new opportunities for employment are smaller than they would have been if the new industry had sprung up under pure competition. It may be, however, that the new industry would not start at all without the inducement of possible monopolistic profits. In this latter case monopolistic competition must be given credit for the full amount of created employment.

Selling Costs and the Problem of Distribution

Under monopolistic competition the use of factors of production in ways that represent selling costs may easily result in a larger output for a firm (and perhaps even for the industry) than would be the case under pure competition. Lower production costs for the expanded output will result only where the individual firm, or the industry, is operating under conditions of decreasing costs. Even in these cases, it is possible that some other combination of price cutting and lower selling costs might yield better results.

For the economy as a whole, selling costs must result in a purchase pattern different from that which would prevail under pure competition (aside from that represented by the spending of their own salaries by advertising men and salesmen) or the whole expenditure would be a sheer waste. If advertising and selling efforts by each firm and each industry simply "cancel each other out" and leave the public taste for products no different from what it would have been without these efforts, then the entire expenditure is a waste, *both* from the point of view of the individual firm and of society as a whole.

If we grant that selling costs do result in a purchase pattern different from that which would have prevailed without them, then it remains to be shown that such a pattern is better than the one which would have prevailed without selling costs. Any such judgment must be made, however, largely on the basis of noneconomic criteria. Even by other standards, the issue is by no means clear-cut. On the ground of public health, the friends of advertising may point with pride to the increased sale of oranges. On the same grounds, the opponents may point the finger of scorn at the sale of fraudulent patent medicines. On the grounds of aesthetics, the pros may point to the improved design of many articles of common use, while the cons will deplore the excessive standardization of other articles which results in mass ugliness. Sponsored radio programs make both education and insidious propaganda available to the masses. The reader must choose between the conflicting claims as best he can.

Monopolistic Competition in Supply of Factors of Production

Many industries that are purely competitive, or that approach the conditions of pure competition in the markets in which they sell their products, may be dependent for some of their factors of production upon sources of supply which are more or less monopolistic in character. Agriculture offers perhaps the best example of this type. The primary markets for many farm products usually give a close approximation to the conditions of pure competition. On the other hand, farm machinery is now supplied by an oligopoly, which at times has approached a pure monopoly. Moreover, owing to the importance of patents, oligopoly with differentiated products is probably the greatest degree of competition that may be expected in the supply of farm machinery. Fertilizers, cotton bale ties, binder twine, barbed wire, and other farm capital goods have been subject to varying degrees of monopoly control.

We have many examples of industries operating under monopolistic competition which buy their supplies or stock of goods from other firms which in their turn are monopolistically competitive. At one time the most important function of the retailer was to bargain for the best merchandise at the lowest prices, and customers relied on his buying ability to obtain good merchandise for them. Today, however, the tendency is for the retailer simply to buy the brands which his customers have already been induced to ask for by national advertising, and the retailer's function approaches that of being merely a convenient display and delivery place for nationally advertised goods.

Diversion of Monopoly Profits to Suppliers of Factors

There are many interesting trade practices connected with the situations outlined in the two preceding paragraphs. Here, however, we are most concerned, not with these practices in themselves, but with their effect upon the distribution of income. The first effect which we notice is the diversion of what might otherwise be a retailer's profit into the hands of the manufacturer of the nationally advertised brand. Whenever a nationally known brand obtains a sufficient hold upon the public taste, retailers are practically forced to stock the article, whether or not they wish to do so. No cigar store can afford not to handle Lucky Strikes, Camels, and Chesterfield cigarettes. Any grocer can name you a few score of "regular brands" of goods which he could hardly do without and still hope to remain in business. When this situation exists, the manufacturer can advertise a retail price for his product and then charge the retailer a price which leaves him practically no operating margin. This leaves the retailer only one source of profit on this type of article. He may try to stock up heavily during periods of advancing prices and reduce his stock before prices decline. Such planning, of course, requires a considerable amount of forecasting ability, but even this source of profits disappears if the manufacturer maintains a policy of rigid prices.

On some types of articles where the customers are not so strongly affected by advertising and may be influenced by the retailer's suggestions, a different policy may be followed. The retail price may be advertised by the manufacturer, but the retailer is permitted a larger markup in the hope that he will "push" this particular brand of goods. The manufacturer really regards this wider markup as a form of selling cost used perhaps instead of a greater expenditure on advertising. This is not the same thing as increasing sales by a lower price to the consumer, where the whole effect would be dependent upon the retailer's efforts.

In this situation some retailers may act as expected and simply push the sale of the product at the advertised price. Other retailers may see an opportunity to obtain a large volume of sales without so much effort by cutting a few cents off the advertised retail price. If this actually results in increased volume, it would appear that the manufacturer should have no objection. Quite often, however, there will be other stores in the same community which are not volume stores and which ordinarily require a higher markup. They may then be in a position where they either have to meet the price cut or incur some ill will on the part of their customers. Such a situation leads to the whole controversy over resale price maintenance by the manufacturer.

Secondary Monopoly

Wherever monopoly exists in the supply of any factor of production, whether the factor happens to be a nearly complete consumers' good or some form of raw material or labor, the

effects of monopoly practices are felt all along the line up to
the sale of the finished product. For example, the building
contractors in a certain city may happen to be honestly competitive with each other, but if there is a monopoly of certain
building materials or of building labor, then the contractors
will have to accept the price of the building material or labor
as cost data in figuring their bids. The effects in restricted
output are exactly the same as if the building supply company
or the labor union were themselves setting the prices for
finished buildings. The monopoly elements will be reaping
the monopoly gains, the competing contractors being forced to
restrict output against their will. If, on the contrary, the contractors happen themselves to have a monopoly through agreements for collusive bidding, then the building supply firm or
labor union may be simply taking some of the monopoly
profits away from them. Even here we cannot ignore the
effect upon cost curves of the monopolistically supplied factors.
The monopoly prices charged by a contractors' "ring" are apt
to be higher and the output lower if they in turn must buy
some of their supplies at monopoly prices.

Monopolistic Elements in the Purchase of Factors of Production

Sometimes we encounter situations in which there is a monopoly element in the market for factors of production on the
buying side. One firm may be the sole employer of labor in
a community, or it may employ a vast proportion of the labor.
One firm may be the sole purchaser of a certain type of mineral.
Often a chain-store organization or a large automobile manufacturer may buy the entire output of certain factories.

It is quite commonly assumed that firms in a monopoly position of this sort will proceed to exploit the factors of production of which they are the sole buyers. (We have defined
exploitation as paying factors less than the full value of the
marginal product.) Undoubtedly much exploitation does

take place, but we should not ignore the elements which may tend to prevent or limit such exploitation. Above all, the firm is vitally interested in maintaining a continuous and reliable supply of the factors of production. A chain which builds up a market for a certain product cannot afford to have the manufacturer go out of business. He may in some cases force the manufacturer to integrate with him. A firm which exploits a cheap labor supply may some time find that workmen are leaving the town. Thereupon they may have to offer very high wages to induce other workmen to move in, or they may have to go through a costly process of moving to another locality. The greater the amount of fixed investment, the greater will be the danger of loss in this situation.

Exploitation by a monopsony (single buyer) may take the form of price discrimination. That is, instead of paying the same price to all units of a factor, each unit will be taken at the lowest price it is willing to accept. This practice is most easily followed in a situation where the various sellers are not in a position to compare prices with one another. In the case of labor particularly, discrimination may engender so much ill will as to cancel much of the gain from its practice.

Some Aspects of the Theory of Bilateral or Successive Monopoly

We have been deliberately discussing some examples of bilateral or successive monopoly in order to acquaint the reader with the nature of the problem involved. The exact theoretical statement of this problem has been given us by Dr. A. C. Hoffman, of the Bureau of Agricultural Economics, United States Department of Agriculture.[2]

"As an hypothetical example of bilateral monopoly, we may take the case of two firms, one having complete control of the processing of a food product and the other of its retailing. For

---

[2] Monograph No. 35, "Large-Scale Organization in the Food Industries," Temporary National Economic Committee, 76th Congress, 3rd Session.

simplicity it will be assumed that no other handling operations are involved, or that if they are involved, they would be competitive.

"To illustrate the first principle which would govern the outcome in such a situation, it will be convenient to refer to Figure 1 of the diagram. In this diagram, $D^1 D^1$ has been derived from the consumers' demand curve by the deduction of the retailing costs, and similarly SS represents the farm supply curve plus the unit costs of processing the product. Equilibrium under competition would, of course, obtain at point P, with quantity OQ produced and offered to consumers. If either processing or retailing were monopolized while the other remained competitive, equilibrium would come at point P^1, with the supply (OQ^1) now equal to half that under competition.

"Suppose now that separate and independent monopolies developed in each field. The most profitable policy for both, assuming that they could hit upon some method of dividing the total quantity of monopoly profit to be derived, would be to offer quantity OQ^1. This is, of course, the same outcome as that under single monopoly.

"But it is quite improbable that the monopolists would be able to agree on how to divide this total profit. Jockeying between them would almost certainly develop, each trying to obtain a larger share of the profit by widening his profit margin per unit. To see what would happen now, let us turn again to Figure 1.

"We may start by assuming that the processor is first in the field with his monopoly, in which case he is offering a supply of OQ^1 to competitive retailers at a price of Q^1P^1. All the monopoly profits are his. But now some firm contrives to get control of retailing. Obviously the retail monopolist will not permit equilibrium at point P^1, since this would leave him nothing above his actual costs of doing business.

"On the expectation that the processor will maintain his price at Q^1P^1, the retailer will put his margin above his costs equal to P^2p^2, which will maximize his total profit under the given conditions.

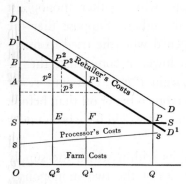

FIG. 1.—In no event would the food supply be larger under successive monopoly than under single monopoly, and it would probably be much smaller.

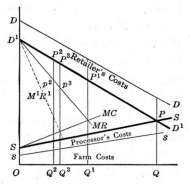

FIG. 2.—The greater the number of successive monopolists and the less they conspire together to increase their combined profit, the worse will be the plight of farmers and consumers (Figures 2, 3, and 4).

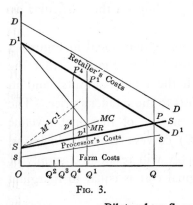

FIG. 3.

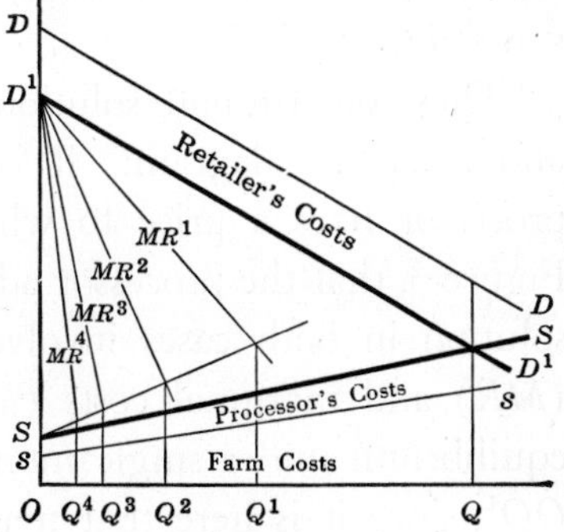

FIG. 4.

Bilateral or Successive Monopoly.

"But see to what this leads: Supply will be restricted to OQ^2 [half that under single monopoly and only one-fourth that of competition, using straight-line relationships as has been done in this diagram (with curvilinear relationships, the results would be qualitatively the same, however)]. Clearly everyone is worse off than before, except the retail monopolist who now has some profit represented by ABP^2p^2 in Figure 1.

"The unfortunate result just demonstrated is not changed in principle by different assumptions which either monopolist might make as to the price of the other. Suppose that the processor, after seeing what happened when he tried to maintain a price of Q^1P^1, decided to lower it somewhat, the retailer now making his profit margin P^3p^3. This will result in slightly larger supplies, and everyone is better off than before, but supply is still more restricted than it would have been under single monopoly.

"We have now defined the limits within which the supply will vary, depending on the policies of the two monopolists. But we do not need to drop the matter here. If the two monopolists act independently of each other, there appears to be a determinate solution from which neither monopolist would find it to his advantage to deviate. Or, rather, there are several determinate solutions, depending on the particular assumptions made.

"These determinate solutions are demonstrated in Figures 1 and 2 of the diagram. It is assumed in Figure 2 that the processor fixes a price to which the retailer adjusts; and in Figure 3, that the processor adjusts to the retailer's price. The solution in both cases involves the use of marginal revenue (MR) and marginal costs (MC) curves. In both diagrams, equilibrium under single monopoly will result in a supply of OQ^1, since it is here that marginal cost is equal to marginal revenue for the monopolist.

"When the second monopolist (the retailer) comes onto the scene, he will presumably find the processor selling at a price of Q^1P^1 (Figure 2). The retailer would then try to maximize his profit by fixing his profit margin at P^2p^2 (where his marginal revenue as described by MR is just equal to the price of Q^1P^1 fixed by the processor). Supply is then limited to OQ^2, which, as we have already seen, is the lower limit of restriction for two successive monopolists.

"The processor will now find it to his advantage to lower his price slightly so as to increase his total profit. This he would do until final equilibrium would result in a supply of O^3Q^2. From this point it will not pay the processor to deviate, since here his marginal costs will equate the return which he can expect from the retail monopolist.

"If it is assumed that the retailer fixes the price to which the processor must adjust, the solution is that shown in Figure 3. The processor, being a monopolist, will adjust his operations so as to offer varying quantities of supply at prices described by his marginal cost curve (MC). The marginal costs of the product to the retailer are then shown by M^1C^1, which is derived from MC as MC was from SS. The retailer will thus seek equilibrium at the point where his marginal return equates M^1C^1, which in Figure 3 results in a supply of OQ^4.

"The outcome so far as farmers and consumers are concerned is about the same in Figure 2 as in Figure 3, and it would have been exactly the same if the slopes of D^1D^1 and SS had been equal in both cases. The effect on the monopolists themselves, however, is vastly different. When the processor was assumed to fix the price to which the retailer was forced to adjust (Figure 2), the retailer got only a small part of the monopoly profit; but when the assumption was reversed (Figure 3), it was the processor who got the lesser share.

"Instead of assuming that the monopolists fix the prices at which they buy and sell to each other, it might be assumed that they fix their margins. In this case the equilibrium outcome would be slightly different from the one we have described above, but the basic principle would be the same.

"Three or More Successive Monopolists

"We pass now to the case of three or more successive monopolists, one above the other. The principles according to which the outcome is finally determined are much the same as those we have just deduced for the case of two successive monopolists, except that supply is almost certain to be limited even further.

"The solution for three or more successive monopolists is shown in Figure 4. Again we use marginal revenue and marginal costs curves, as in Figures 2 and 3. As we have shown, equilibrium for a single monopolist would give a supply of OQ^1. If a second monopolist enters the picture, supply will be further limited to OQ^2.

"Now suppose we introduce a third monopolist. In order to get some share of the profit, the third monopolist will increase his margin, and in doing so he will tend to limit supply still further. He will not get much profit because, according to our assumption, he must operate within the restricted limits of supply left to him by the first two monopolists. The final outcome for three monopolists as shown in Figure 4 will find supply limited to OQ^3 (or thereabouts, depending on the relative slopes of consumer demand and supply costs).

"On the assumption that the first monopolist fixes a price to the second monopolist, and the second to the third, the third monopolist will get the least profit. The advantage among the monopolists would be reversed (as we have shown in Figures 2 and 3) if the fixing of price ran in the opposite direction.

"The same sort of solution could be shown for any number of successive monopolists, with the situation becoming progressively worse for farmers and consumers as more monopolists managed to insert themselves into the marketing system.

"A Modification of the Assumptions

"It may be objected that the assumption of complete monopoly at successive stages in the marketing system is very unrealistic, and so it is. But so, for that matter, is the usual textbook assumption of horizontal monopoly.

"The highly restrictive tendency of successive monopoly

would be modified, but not changed in principle, by the assumption of monopolistic competition rather than of complete monopoly in any or all of the marketing functions.

"Suppose, in our earlier example, that retailing were carried on under conditions of monopolistic competition. The retail margin would then be determined in accordance with the principles of ordinary oligopoly, which means that it would vary from that of competition to that of complete monopoly, depending on the assumptions each firm made as to the effect of its actions on the others. Similarly the processing function might also be only partially monopolistic, which would lead to a further modification of the outcome. Under these conditions supply might be less restricted than under complete monopoly in each function, but more restricted than if the oligopolists were vertically integrated.

"Theory of Successive Monopoly Contrasted to That of Oligopoly

"The solutions shown for successive monopoly are vastly different from those demonstrated by Chamberlin and others for horizontal monopoly and monopolistic competition. Those familiar with the main outlines of theory will recall that under oligopoly the outcome as to price and supply will vary from that of monopoly to that of pure competition, depending on the assumption each firm makes as to the effect of its policies on those of its competitors. It is unnecessary for our present purpose to go into the various refinements of this principle. Its import for us here is that in no event would the public be worse off under oligopoly than under complete monopoly, and that in most cases it would fare much better.[3]"

---

[3] This statement may be correct under the peculiar assumptions stated by Dr. Hoffman, but there may be some situations under which a horizontal monopoly might achieve greater output and set lower prices than an oligopoly. This point, also, ignores the possibility of monopoly under some form of reorganization which might be expected to result in lower prices than those charged under oligopoly with a differentiated product.

Monopsonistic Competition

We may define monopsonistic competition as a situation in which sellers prefer to sell to one buyer rather than another even though all buyers are offering the same price. Like monopolistic competition, it is non-price competition, but on the buying side of the market. Several elements may account for this preference of one buyer over another. One buyer may have a better credit rating. One buyer may have a better reputation for accepting goods when delivered, or he may not make claims for minor or non-existent damages when other buyers are in the habit of making such claims. A buyer who is a "steady customer" and may be counted on for more business in the future may be preferred to one who buys only occasionally. A buyer who is willing to take prompt delivery may be preferred to one who attempts to postpone deliveries. A buyer who purchases in large volume may be preferred to one who buys smaller orders.

These elements might be considered as contributing to a "good will" on the buying side of the market quite similar to the good will which a firm may possess among its customers. In many ways this good will may be a distinct advantage to the firm which possesses it. When supplies are limited at current prices, but sellers are not quite ready to raise prices, the favored buyers will obtain the available supply at the low prices. Favored customers may be warned in advance when a price increase is about to take place. In times of brisk business, favored customers may receive prompt delivery on their orders, while less favored customers may find their orders delayed. Favored customers may find that more care is taken to see that their orders are filled carefully, and that the goods are better inspected before they leave the sellers' hands. Many of these practices may seem of small moment when considered alone, but, added up, they may contribute importantly to a favored firm's profits or to its ability to remain in business in the face of keen competition. Although we have called these firms "favored," it should not be implied that there is anything unethical or uneconomic in this sort of favoritism. The fact that a firm is favored because of its reputation for honesty or for paying its debts promptly could hardly invite censure from even the most violent opponents of the present economic system. There are, of course, other forms of favoritism that are less legitimate.[4]   Nor can we even assume, without exception, that "honesty is the best policy" in this instance. In some industries firms that are notorious for breaking their contracts during periods of falling prices still survive and prosper.

Monopolistic Competition and Final Equilibrium

Under pure competition we described a state of stable equilibrium as one in which no firm had any motive to expand or contract its output or to enter or leave any industry, and in which all resources were fully employed. There are also no pure profits in a state of equilibrium, although there will be rent for scarce factors.

If we regard these as the criteria for stable equilibrium regardless of the nature of competition, then monopolistic competition offers us some very difficult problems. An industry may be in full equilibrium in the Chamberlin sense—that is, each firm is operating with its average revenue curve tangent to its average cost curve and at zero profits. This need not mean, however, that no new firms will enter the industry. Even though existing firms are making no profits, a new firm may start up with somewhat different selling methods and actually show a profit.

We might attempt to squirm out of this difficulty by so

---

[4] For example the old secret rebate system.

formulating our definition of an industry that each firm with a differentiated product would be considered a different industry. This is no solution to the problem, for it simply leaves us with the possibility of new "industries" springing up *ad hoc* in the same manner as new firms emerged under the concept of industry as used in the previous paragraph.[5]

Another solution might be to rule out any changes in selling methods in the same manner and on the same grounds that we rule out changes in methods of production and new inventions from the concept of equilibrium under pure competition. When we consider, however, that so small a difference as the personality of the storekeeper may be the element which gives rise to successful product differentiation, we must be arbitrary indeed to rule this out as a new method of selling.

Alternative End Results of Monopolistic Competition

1. *The monopoly solution.*

We might accept Triffin's thesis of regarding each firm as being an industry in and of itself if this would lead us simply to a situation of universal monopoly. We might then, as has been pointed out, recast our general equilibrium theory in terms of the classic theory of general equilibrium as explained in the earlier chapter. To have this solution consistent, however, the entire competition should be directly for the consumer's dollar, but the individual firms which we are calling individual monopolies under this approach are not by any means so unconscious of the activities of rival sellers as to make a perfect monopoly solution possible. As long as many of the firms are producing goods that are closely substituted for each other, they will not act as if they were competing solely for the consumer's dollar, but will in fact take some account of the actions of their nearest rivals. This leaves us in a world which

---

[5] C. F. Triffin's *Monopolistic Competition and General Equilibrium Theory,* Harvard University Press, 1940.

is partly a close approach to pure monopoly and partly a situation which is typical of Chamberlin's solution to the problem.

2. *Duopoly with and without product differentiation.*

From this point on, as well as in the preceding section, our whole problem hinges largely on the degree of successful product differentiation.

If the two firms in a duopoly have important enough differences in their products, then they may, for a considerable range in output, depend upon consumers bound to them by the production difference which exists. To the extent that this is true, there is no point in treating two such firms differently from any other two nearly perfect monopolies. To the extent that the product is standardized or that the differentiation makes no impression on the minds of the buyers, we are forced back upon the pure duopoly solution which, according to many economists, can become stable only by the merging of the two firms into a single monopoly.

3. *Oligopoly with standardized products.*

This is a situation which must be regarded as extremely unstable. Its continuance is dependent upon some means of prevention of entry of new firms; otherwise, the privilege of free entry would reduce the situation to one of pure competition. If there is some means of preventing entry (such as control of raw materials), then there are strong possibilities of eventually combining into a single monopoly, with perhaps some attempt at apparent competition whenever and wherever the public attitude against monopolies happens to be strong.

4. *Oligopoly with differentiated products.*

This condition, while somewhat more stable than that of the oligopoly with standardized products, again cannot be considered as stable unless there is some means of preventing the entry of new firms. If such means exist, the oligopoly may persist for some time; but there is always a danger, at least as far as ownership is concerned, of a merger among the firms which would lead it in the direction of monopoly ownership, although to the extent that the differentiated product had sufficient individual market appeal, the separate brand names and other distinguishing features might be retained.

If there is no effective barrier to the entry of new firms, the existence of profits may be sufficient to allow the entry of some firms which partly duplicate the services of the old firms and/or differentiate their production still further. The end result here would, of course, be monopolistic competition.

5. Monopolistic competition.

What we are assuming here is monopolistic competition in a perfect market. Therefore, we are ruling out all of the "economic friction" or market imperfection which was considered under the classic general equilibrium theory to be an important element in preventing eventual complete adjustment to the pattern of the theory. However, for monopolistic competition to attain its equilibrium situation in the Chamberlinean sense (tangency of average revenue to average cost curves with no profits), it must be possible to prevent the entry of still more firms into the industry.

Summary and Conclusion

We have noticed that the indispensable condition of equilibrium in each of the situations we have discussed is that no new firms be induced to enter the industry, or, if you prefer to consider the firm and the industry as identical, that no new firms offering closely competing products be encouraged to start up. If the existing firms are making no profits, this fact is considered an adequate deterrent to the entry of new firms under the classic equilibrium theory. The very existence, however, of the concept of differentiated products which are close substitutes, an integral part of the doctrine of monopolistic competition, violates the possibility of this solution.

Even though all firms or all industries (depending upon the definition) are making no profits, it is still possible for a new firm to spring up, offering a slightly differentiated product and employing selling methods that may actually enable it to make a profit.

The more we go into the problem, the more we are forced to conclude that perfect equilibrium is an impossibility under conditions of monopolistic competition. The best we can hope for is a neighborhood of equilibrium where the motives to change will be few and small. It may still be found that firms making losses will tend to drop out of their industry, and that industries, whether making profits or not, may be subject to competition by new firms. Since monopolistic competition tends somewhat to obscure the immediate effect of changes in demand, it might be expected that the situation would result in fluctuations of wider amplitude in employment of resources and in smaller price changes than those associated with pure competition.

If we are to choose between the classic general equilibrium theory and an attempt at an equilibrium theory under monopolistic competition, neither solution is apt to be satisfactory to us in the present state of development of our science. The classic theory makes so many unrestricted assumptions that it becomes a mere "thinking tool." The monopolistic competitive doctrine faces boldly the difficulties which are evaded or avoided by the classic doctrine. At its present state of development, it can be considered to be a more accurate theoretical analysis of the conditions of the economic world, but it is not so far consistent with any perfect equilibrium solution. This should not discourage the reader. Rather, it should lead him to realize that there are many problems of economic theory which are still unsolved, and to which he can devote his own attempts at solution.

CHAPTER XIX
Credit Creation and Banking Mechanism

I N THE previous discussions of value and price and distribution we have practically ignored any independent influence of money upon our analysis. For us, so far, money
has been merely a convenient common denominator in which
to express the prices and costs of goods and services. It also
served as a medium of exchange and a means of making payments which avoided the difficulties of barter. It was more
simple for us to do this in order to concentrate our attention
on the factors in price determination which are peculiar to
individual commodities.

It is now necessary to remove this assumption. We may
define money as *anything which is commonly accepted as a
medium of exchange, measure of value, or standard of deferred
payments*. It also sometimes serves as a store of value. We
must recognize, however, that money can be created or destroyed and that the efficiency of money in making payments
can be increased or decreased. The next chapter will deal
with the results of such changes in the effective quantity of
money. The present chapter deals with the means by which
the quantity of money may be increased or decreased.

The most obvious way in which money may be created is
for the government to print additional paper money to pay
for its current expenses instead of paying for them by taxation or by borrowing. Nearly always in the past this process,
once begun, has led to the printing of excessive amounts of
paper money with disastrous results. This is the definition of

"inflation" which registers in the mind of the man in the street. Most governments, consequently, are very timid about using this particular way to increase the quantity of money. If they do use it, they try to cover up their tracks by exchange control and other means such as are in use in Hitlerian Germany, so that the people will not realize the extent to which the currency has been depreciated.

Another way in which money used to be created far more commonly than it is now is by the unrestricted issue of bank notes by private banks. A bank note is a piece of paper bearing the words: *The ——— Bank promises to pay the Bearer* $5 *in lawful money on demand.* These notes have generally been printed to resemble the paper money of the national government as closely as possible. In the early part of our history, often called the period of wildcat banking, these notes were issued by many banks in amounts far beyond their power to redeem them. When too many of the notes were presented for collection to a bank at one time, the bank simply closed its doors and suspended payments, more often than not going bankrupt. In those days of slow communication, the worthless notes of a closed bank often continued to circulate long after the bank had failed. As a result of these and other abuses, the privilege of note issue by individual banks has been abolished in most countries. Note issue is usually confined to the Government Bank, if there is one, or to a bank which is semi-governmental and acting under close government supervision.

Certain forms of government borrowing also create money, but we will leave this complicated subject for later consideration.

The most important source of money in the United States is the money created by the lending operations of commercial banks. In order to understand this better, we will review briefly some of the features of the banking mechanism.

At the very outset we must eliminate many popular and

erroneous notions concerning banking. It is often said that "a bank is an organization which lends money." This is a very dangerous half-truth, particularly when coupled with the other popular notion that the government is the only organization that issues money. It is true that some few loans are made in the form of government money, but the bulk of business of the modern commercial bank is in loaning *not* government money but *bank money*. This bank money may be in the form of the bank's own notes but is usually in the form of a deposit credit subject to check. Both of these are the promises of the bank to pay government money on demand. So long as people have confidence in the ability of the bank to keep its promise, checks will be accepted instead of government money as a means of making payments. Thus, the bank's ability to lend is confined not to the stock of government money which it has on hand, but rather to its ability to *create claims against itself* in the form of deposit accounts without having too many of these claims presented for redemption in government money at any one time.[1]

Another popular delusion that we must guard against is the idea that a bank deposit is "money that is put in a bank." This is not true. A bank deposit is a *claim against a bank,* that is, the *right* to demand money from the bank either immediately (as in the case of a checking account) or after a notice of a specified number of days (in the case of a savings account). It is true that you may have this claim because you have made a cash deposit in the past. But when you make a cash deposit, the money is no longer yours; it now belongs to the bank. What you have really done is to have bought a claim against the bank to pay you a similar sum (payable on demand in the case of a "checking account," or after a specified

---

[1] What we have called "bank money" is called "money substitutes" by some authors. By whatever name they are called, however, bank notes and bank deposits constitute an addition to the effective quantity of money. Arthur D. Gayer and W. W. Rostow use the more apt term "check book money" (Public Affairs Pamphlets No. 45, *How Money Works*, p. 2).

notice period in the case of a "savings" or "time" deposit).
Legally, the banker could take the money you have paid in,
change it for silver dollars, and throw them across the Potomac,
as long as he was prepared to pay you a similar sum when re-
quested. *No specific cash* in the bank is represented by your
deposit. All that you have is a general claim against the assets
of the bank.

In business transactions such deposit claims arise far more
often in exchange not for actual money deposited but for the
businessman's promise to pay. In other words, the bank makes
a loan to the businessman, but instead of lending him cash, it
grants him the loan in the form of a deposit credit. Instead
of giving him cash, it gives him the right to draw checks on a
deposit account which it *creates* [2] for him. We can understand
this better if we examine the organization of a bank and trace
the effects of various transactions on the bank's balance sheet.

The Bank Balance Sheet

The bank's balance sheet is a statement of its assets and liabilities. An *asset* is either wealth owned by the bank or a legal
claim which the bank has against someone else. A *liability*
is a claim which someone else has against the bank.

Let us assume that the bank is started by the sale of $100,-
000.00 worth of its own stock. The balance sheet will then
appear as follows:

FIDELITY BANK

BALANCE SHEET

Assets	Liabilities
Cash on Hand........$100,000.00	Capital Stock.........$100,000.00

Capital stock is here listed as a liability. This is because the
sum is owed by the bank [3] to its stockholders. As we progress

---

[2] The power to create deposit credit is, however, not entirely a discretionary power
of each individual bank. It arises from the workings of a *banking system*.

[3] An incorporated bank is legally an entity separate and distinct from its stockholders.
Hence it has financial responsibilities to its owners as well as to its creditors.

in our analysis, we will find the items "Surplus" and "Undivided Profits" in a similar category. These items are sometimes called collectively the "Owner's Equity" in the bank. The bank is considered to own nothing for itself. Everything that a bank has is owed either to its creditors or to its stockholders.

Our bank must now acquire a place in which to do business, as well as a safe and other banking office equipment. Let us suppose that these cost $25,000.00. The balance sheet now reads:

FIDELITY BANK

BALANCE SHEET

Assets		Liabilities	
Cash on Hand	$ 75,000.00	Capital Stock	$100,000.00
Building and Equipment	25,000.00		
Total	$100,000.00	Total	$100,000.00

Assume now that our bank does its first item of business. It loans $5,000.00 for two months at an annual rate of 6 per cent to the Brown Clothing Company, which wishes to buy a stock of goods. The Brown Clothing Company gives the bank its promissory note, payable two months from now, for $5,000.00. The bank discount (interest charged in advance) on $5,000.00 for two months at a 6 per cent annual rate is $50.00, so the bank deducts this and gives the clothing company a deposit on its books of $4,950.00 and the balance sheet now reads:

FIDELITY BANK

BALANCE SHEET

Assets		Liabilities	
Cash on Hand	$ 75,000.00	Capital Stock	$100,000.00
Building and Equipment	25,000.00	Deposits	4,950.00
Loans and Discounts	5,000.00	Undivided Profits	50.00
Total	$105,000.00	Total	$105,000.00

The bank's cash has been neither increased nor diminished by this transaction. What has happened is that a *created* deposit has been given in exchange for Brown Clothing Company's promissory note. If the Brown Company buys its stock from a manufacturer who is not a customer of this bank and gives a check in payment and the check is then presented to the bank to be cashed, the bank would immediately lose cash. In that case, if the check were for $3,000.00, then $3,000.00 would be deducted from the item "Deposits" and $3,000.00 from the item "Cash on Hand." But if the clothing manufacturer also happened to be a customer of this bank and if, when he received the check, he deposited it to his own account, *no item in the balance sheet would be affected.* The $3,000.00 would merely be deducted from Brown's deposit account and credited as a deposit to the clothing manufacturer. Total deposits would remain the same, the bank merely owing $3,000.00 to the clothing manufacturer and the remaining $1,-950.00 to the Brown Clothing Company. "Cash on Hand" would not be affected at all.

As a result of the transaction, we also notice another new item; "Undivided Profits $50.00" appears on the balance sheet, being the amount of discount on Brown Company's note. This represents the difference between the $5,000.00 that the Brown Company has agreed to repay to the bank and the $4,950.00 deposit against which the Brown Company is allowed to draw checks. Properly speaking, this $50.00 will not be a profit until two months have elapsed and the note falls due, since, if the bank needed cash and tried to sell Brown Company's note to someone else, it could not obtain the full $5,000.00 for it. Another bank to whom the note might be sold would itself deduct a discount for the time remaining until the note fell due. (In banking terms, this process of selling a discounted note is called *rediscounting*.) We have said that the discount will not become a profit until the bank earns it by holding the note until its due date. Some banks indicate this by entering as "Undivided Profits" only such discounts as have actually been earned in the past. They then make a separate liability item called "Unearned Discount" to account for the difference between the asset value assigned to the note and the deposit liability created in exchange for the note. As the discount becomes "earned" (by holding the note to maturity), the amount is deducted from "Unearned Discount" and added to "Undivided Profits." But since this involves a considerable amount of calculation, the more usual bank practice is to draw up the balance sheet in the form which we have used above, paying no heed to the fact that some part of the undivided profits may be "unearned" at the time the statement is drawn up.

Without going through all of the steps in detail, let us now assume that our bank has grown and is doing a fairly large volume of business. The bank statement might then appear as follows:

FIDELITY BANK

BALANCE SHEET

Assets		Liabilities	
Cash on Hand	$ 50,000.00	Capital Stock	$100,000.00
Building and Equipment	25,000.00	Surplus	50,000.00
Loans and Discounts	250,000.00	Deposits	500,000.00
Real Estate Mortgages	150,000.00	Undivided Profits	25,000.00
Bonds	150,000.00		
Due from Banks	50,000.00		
Total	$675,000.00	Total	$675,000.00

We now find several new items in the statement which need explanation. "Real Estate Mortgages" shows the amount which is due to the bank from loans it has made on real estate. "Bonds" shows the present market value of securities of various industrial corporations, which the bank has purchased. "Due from Banks" includes the sums which our bank may have on deposit with other banks (perhaps to take advantage of the clearinghouse facilities of another bank in another city), and also the amount of checks drawn on other banks which have been received by our bank and which are in the process of collection.

The new item which we find on the liability side is "Surplus." This surplus was previously undivided profits. At regular intervals the bank's directors meet and decide what to do with the undivided profits. Some are paid out as dividends and the remainder may be kept in the bank as a surplus to allow the bank to keep its investments intact. "Undivided Profits" is not a cash item but a mere bookkeeping difference between the total of assets and the total of all other liabilities. If the bank's present amount of cash is sufficient only to meet its reserve requirements, it would have to *sell* some of its other assets in order to pay a cash dividend.

The Reserve Ratio

We may calculate the *reserve ratio* of the bank from the above balance sheet. The reserve ratio is the ratio of cash on hand to deposits expressed as a percentage. In this case $50,-000.00 cash on hand is 10 per cent of the $500,000.00 deposits, so we say that the bank's reserve ratio as shown by this statement is 10 per cent. Whether a minimum reserve ratio is prescribed by law or whether this is left up to the bank's own discretion (as is done in some countries), any bank which desires to avoid the embarrassment of having to suspend payments will keep a careful eye on its reserve ratio to try to prevent it from going below the necessary minimum. There is no bank in such a position that it does not have to meet some requirements of its customers for at least a small amount of cash every day. Some people need cash for making payments to those who do not care to accept checks. Cash is used for making change in the retail stores. Some firms pay their employees in cash. A working reserve must be large enough to meet the peak demand for cash which is likely to occur on any one day.

We may note the effects of certain types of transactions on the reserve ratio. If, with the above statement showing the bank's position, the bank were to make an additional loan to someone of $25,000.00 in the form of a deposit credit, it would reduce this ratio to only a little over 9.52 per cent. On the other hand, if the bank made a loan of the same amount in cash, it would reduce the reserve ratio to 5 per cent. Or, if any depositor should ask to have a check cashed for $25,-000.00, this withdrawal of cash would reduce the ratio to 5 per cent. Two such withdrawals would exhaust the bank's cash completely and force it to refuse payment to the next person who came to the window.

Adjustment of Bank Reserves

To avoid such eventualities as this, the bank tries to adjust its business so that the amount of cash flowing into the bank will equal the amount going out. One way of attempting to do this is to set a maximum limit on the amount of the deposit which any one individual or firm may carry at the bank. If the bank has a large number of small or medium sized deposits, the amount of cash flowing in from some depositors is likely to be roughly equal to the amount of cash withdrawals by others, and it will not be faced with the danger of large withdrawals by any individual customer. Furthermore, most banks know from experience on what days, or at what seasons of the year, the demands on their cash will be the heaviest. A bank must be prepared to meet these periods by attempting to conserve cash in a number of different ways. The most common way for the banks to provide cash for these periodic needs, however, is to have on hand a fairly large amount of first-grade securities for which it is anticipated that there will always be a ready market. The bank may then sell these bonds or use them as security on which to borrow the needed cash. These bonds are therefore sometimes called the bank's "secondary reserve."

It should not be forgotten, however, that these bonds serve the purpose of a "secondary reserve" only when merely part of the banks in a country desire to sell securities and to obtain cash. Under these circumstances, banks needing cash may sell securities without occasioning much, if any, decline in security prices. But should all the banks of the country try to obtain cash in this same way (as they did in the panic of 1929–33), then the decline in the price of securities (due to the fact that all banks are selling and none buying) will mean that none of the banks will be able to obtain the value in cash at which these securities were listed in the balance sheet before the decline took place. (In the panic of 1929–33, the value of securities held by some banks declined to one quarter of their former value because of the fall in stock market prices.) In other words, this "secondary reserve" fails to act as a true reserve if all of the banks in the country attempt to convert securities into cash at the same time.

Solvency and Liquidity

Attention should be given here to the difference between the terms *solvency* and *liquidity*. A bank is solvent if the amount of its assets exceeds the amount of its liabilities to all claimants other than its shareholders. But a bank is liquid only to the extent that it can turn its assets into cash to meet the demands of depositors and other creditors as rapidly as they are presented. Many a bank which is solvent is not liquid. Its assets may exceed its liabilities to creditors, but the assets may not be in such a form that they are readily convertible into cash. When a bank's assets are largely in the form of real estate mortgages or in the form of claims which are not readily salable or which cannot be sold immediately without serious losses, the bank is said to possess *frozen assets*.

Every bank operates upon the theory that not all of its depositors will withdraw their deposits in cash at the same time, although technically and legally all depositors have the right to do so. Most of the time this presumption is justified. As long as each depositor is satisfied that the bank is able to meet his claims on demand, he will make no attempt to withdraw his deposit except in such amounts and at such times as it is needed for ordinary business purposes. But once a doubt creeps into the minds of the depositors about the bank's ability to pay, then they begin to test that ability by all attempting at once to demand their deposits in cash. This collective action results in a "run" on the bank. There is no bank in the country that is liquid enough to meet such a run unaided. One of the reasons for which the Federal Reserve System was founded was to provide a "banker's bank" at which the member banks could borrow cash in emergencies. Thus the Federal Reserve bank may turn a solvent member bank into a liquid bank either by buying assets from the member bank or by making loans upon the security of the member bank's assets, in the event of a run.

The Federal Reserve banks are themselves liquid enough so that they can turn any single solvent bank into a liquid bank, or even a large number of such banks may be made liquid at the same time. But even the Federal Reserve banks are not strong enough to withstand a concerted run on all of their member banks at the same time. Furthermore, not all of the banks of the country are members of the Federal Reserve System, so that they cannot all take advantage of the System's facilities. It was the threat of a general run on all the banks of the country that occasioned the declaration of the "bank holiday" by President Roosevelt in March 1933. We shall have more to say about the Federal Reserve System later.

The Clearinghouse System

We must now turn our attention to one of the most important ways in which the banks conserve cash, by use of the clearinghouse system. The bank clearing system operates on the principle of mutual cancellation of debts. We can understand it best if we start out with a situation between two banks in the same town where no clearinghouse exists. These two banks will each, in the course of the day's business, receive checks drawn on the other bank. Of course each of these checks might be presented for redemption to the bank on which it was drawn. This method would be awkward and cumbersome, and would involve a continual running back and forth with checks and cash between the two banks. This is avoided in practice by saving the checks until the end of the business day, at which time each bank presents the checks to the other bank and only the *difference* between the two amounts is paid in cash by the bank against which the greatest amount of checks has been drawn. If the two amounts should happen to be equal, no cash payment would be necessary by either bank, the two debts simply cancelling each other.

The clearinghouse system is merely an elaboration of this principle. Where there are a number of banks in the same town, even the cancellation method outlined above involves lost motion and unnecessary movements of cash. For instance, Bank *A* might have a net balance in its favor due from Bank *B* and at the same time a balance against it is due to Bank *C*. It would then be necessary to get the cash from Bank *B* and hand it over to Bank *C*. But Bank *C* might then owe a balance to Bank *B*, so that the cash would travel back to Bank *B* from which it originated. Such a movement of cash would be avoided under the clearinghouse system.

The clearinghouse assumes the position of creditor to all

debtor banks and debtor to all creditor banks. Among clear-inghouse members, a particular bank collects the checks which it has for collection not from the other banks but from the clearinghouse. The bank also owes the clearinghouse, rather than the other banks, for the checks which have been drawn against it. If a bank has more checks drawn in its favor on all other members than against it, it *collects* the *difference* from the clearinghouse. On the other hand, if more checks are drawn against the bank than it holds against the other banks, it *pays* the *difference* to the clearinghouse. Thus, the only occa-sion for a bank to pay out cash is when the *total* checks drawn against it and held by all other banks are greater than the *total* amount of the checks it holds against all other banks. The only occasion for it to receive cash from clearings is when these totals are reversed. In each case, only the *difference between the totals* is paid or received. The economy in the use of cash is obvious.

A bank which is not a member of a clearinghouse (usually an out-of-town bank) can make use of clearinghouse facilities by maintaining a deposit account with one of the members. The member bank is usually called the "correspondent" bank of the out-of-town bank. The member bank collects checks drawn on the other members for the out-of-town bank by pre-senting them to the clearinghouse; and it agrees to accept checks drawn on the out-of-town bank and held by other clear-inghouse members.

The existence of a clearinghouse system results in a smaller proportion of a bank's cash being paid out with a given volume of deposit credit than would be the case were there no clearinghouse. All that the bank will have to pay out will be the net *difference* between the checks drawn in its favor and the checks drawn against it. If the other banks are expanding deposits at exactly the same rate, this difference will be close to zero, and little or no cash will be lost. Some of the effects of this extension of credit on our economic system will be discussed in the following chapter.

The Federal Reserve System

In 1914, after a long history of bank failures and financial panics, the Federal Reserve System was established in the hope that it would remedy these conditions. We all know that the Federal Reserve banks did not prevent the inflation of the 1920's nor the subsequent panic deflation of 1929–33. To what extent this was due to lack of powers on the part of the Federal Reserve banks and to what extent it was due to failure to exercise the powers that they did have is still a debatable question.[4]

Membership

There are twelve Federal Reserve banks, each located in what was considered the leading financial center of a Federal Reserve District at the time the system was established. (There are four main acts under which the Federal Reserve System operates: the Federal Reserve Act of 1913, the Emergency Banking Act, the Banking Act of 1933, and the Banking Act of 1935. Our discussion will have reference to the provisions of the latest of these acts which is in effect at present.)

The Federal Reserve banks have often been called "bankers' banks." The member banks own the Federal Reserve bank of their district. All member banks are required to buy stock in the Federal Reserve bank of their district in the amount of 6 per cent of the member bank's paid-up capital and surplus, except mutual savings banks, which must buy stock in the amount of 1 per cent their total liabilities. The dividends on

---

[4] Those who are interested in this and other earlier questions of the Federal Reserve System will find them well discussed in Harris, Seymour, *Twenty Years of Federal Reserve Policy*, Harvard University Press, Cambridge, 1933.

this stock are limited to 6 per cent, as the banks were not intended to operate for profit but rather to serve as a support for the banking system. All national banks were required to become member banks or lose their charters, and other banks were encouraged to become members provided they met certain minimum requirements. Another more important reason for the name "bankers' banks" is that the Federal Reserve banks make loans to member banks in much the same way that member banks and other commercial banks make loans to private individuals and firms; that is, in the form of "created deposits," or less often in Federal Reserve notes, Federal Reserve bank notes, or United States Government currency.

Reserves of the System

The member banks do not keep their reserves in their own vaults. The only item which is counted as legal reserve is the deposit of each member bank with the Federal Reserve bank of the district. Member banks in New York and Chicago (called central reserve cities) must maintain such a Federal Reserve bank deposit in the amount of 13 per cent of their own demand deposits. In other large cities (called reserve cities) the requirement is 10 per cent. In smaller cities and rural towns the requirement is 7 per cent. In addition, the banks may maintain a *non-legal* reserve, often called "till-money," of perhaps 5 per cent. On time deposits all classes of banks must maintain a 3 per cent reserve.

As a reserve against the deposits of member banks, a Federal Reserve bank must maintain a reserve of 35 per cent in gold certificates. This is a good point at which to note the possibility of "pyramiding" a large quantity of "check-book money" upon a small reserve ratio. On the reserves of the central reserve city banks, 35 per cent of 13 per cent is only 4.55 per cent. For the reserve city banks, 35 per cent of 10 per cent is 3.5 per cent. For the small town banks, 35 per cent of 7 per cent is only 2.45 per cent. Thus the *minimum legal reserves* against checking deposits of the member banks are really 4.55, 3.5, and 2.45 per cent, or a weighted average of about 4 per cent. Against the time deposits the ratio is 35 per cent of 3 per cent, or 1.05 per cent. This legal minimum, however, is not the actual minimum. The Board of Governors of the system may allow any Federal Reserve bank to drop its reserve ratio below the legal 35 per cent subject to a progressive penalty tax.

On the other hand, the Board of Governors is empowered to double the reserve requirements of the member banks. The Board actually did double the reserve requirements in May 1937. Many people said that this action saved us from a runaway price inflation and speculation in commodities. Many others said that it forced an untimely business recession. Perhaps we can find some basis for an attempted solution of the question in the next chapter.

Control of the System

Although we have said that the twelve Federal Reserve banks are *owned* by the member banks of their districts, effective *control* of the system is in the hands of an independent governmental agency, the Board of Governors of the Federal Reserve System. The Board is composed of seven members appointed by the President of the United States. No members are from the Treasury. The members serve terms of 14 years. The President may discharge the chairman of the Board but he cannot discharge any other members.

The twelve individual Federal Reserve banks are governed by a Board of directors selected in the following manner; three class A directors are bankers; three class B directors represent commerce, agriculture, and industry; three class C directors represent the public. The six class A and B directors are elected by the member banks of the district. The three class C directors are *appointed* by the Board of Governors of the Federal

Reserve System.   The board of directors elects a president *subject to the approval* of the Board of Governors.   It may thus be seen that the Board of Governors is in a position to exert considerable pressure within the Federal Reserve banks themselves in addition to the powers specifically granted by law to the Board of Governors.

A list of the main specific powers of the Board of Governors follows:

1. It may suspend the minimum legal reserve requirements for both Federal Reserve notes and deposits.

2. It may double the original reserve requirements of member banks.

3. If the pressure for loans is uneven as among the Federal Reserve banks in different districts, the Board may permit or *require* some of the district banks to rediscount commercial paper for the banks which need more lending power.

4. It may examine the administrative action of any officer or director of a member bank, and after a hearing may discharge such officer for "violation of the law or unsound practices."

5. It exercises supervision over the rediscount rates charged by the twelve Federal Reserve banks.

6. Through the Federal Open Market Committee (7 members from the Board of Governors, 5 representatives of Federal Reserve banks), the Board of Governors decides whether to buy or sell government bonds on the open market.

We have discussed the organization and powers of the Federal Reserve System enough to see that the Board of Governors of the Federal Reserve System have practically unlimited power to create, or help create, check-book money (provided people want to borrow from member banks), and have fairly strong powers to decrease the amount of check-book money and currency in circulation.   This power is attested in a statement from the Board itself.[5]

"Not only do the Reserve Banks not depend for their lending power on member banks, but they are themselves in a position to increase or decrease the lending power of these banks. When the Reserve Banks buy United States Government securities or make advances, they put reserve funds at the disposal of member banks, and thereby increase their lending power.   And, contrariwise, when the Reserve Banks sell securities or reduce advances, they withdraw funds from member banks and thereby reduce their power to extend credit.   By these means the Federal Reserve banks, as creators and extinguishers of reserve funds, are in a position to exert an influence on the cost and volume of bank credit.   This is, in fact, their principal function as a monetary authority, and the policies pursued in performing this function are determined, not on the basis of the reserves available to the Reserve Banks, but with reference to the economic needs of the country."

The writer just quoted let the cat out of the bag when he mentioned the "economic needs of the country."   The creation of check-book money is, after all, in the hands of the borrowers, and particularly of the borrowers for business purposes.   At any rate of interest below the rate which can be earned on invested capital, the "needs" of borrowers are insatiable.   In 1927, 1928, and 1929 when people erroneously expected profits to increase, even rates of interest of 14 per cent or higher did not discourage them from borrowing.

On the other hand, at any rate of interest above the rate of prospective earnings, the "needs" of business to borrow are zero.   In the depths of the depression, borrowing declined although interest rates declined to fractions of 1 per cent for short-time loans and to about 4 per cent for longer-term loans.

---

[5] *Federal Reserve Bulletin*, February 1941, p. 113.

There is little doubt that the Federal Reserve System can restrict the creation of check-book money, once it is well into the inflationary stage. The question is whether it can and will apply the brakes quickly enough and gently enough to avoid throwing the passengers out of the car. On the other hand, there is still no proof that the system can "cushion" a major depression and still less that it can act as a "self-starter" to bring us out of a depression.

CHAPTER XX
Money

IN THE preceding chapter we discussed several ways in which money and particularly check-book money may be created and destroyed. We shall now try to discover how the value of money is determined and how it is affected by these changes.

The value of money is always expressed in terms of the goods and services it will buy. Money has no *intrinsic value* in and of itself. Even commodity moneys such as gold and silver coins have no intrinsic value except for people who actually make use of those metals in their work. The market value of these metals is somewhat higher than it would otherwise be if governments and central banks were not holding large stocks of these metals in their vaults instead of throwing them on the market. Even with this restriction in supply, the face value of most coins is much higher than the value of the metal in them. Our quarter, for example, has so little of actual silver in it that it pays counterfeiters to use real silver in their counterfeits rather than attempt to substitute a baser metal.

Since money is exchangeable for all other goods and services, the value of a unit of it should be capable of expression in terms of the quantity of goods and services it will buy. Economists for many years have been making explanations of the value of money and of what happens when its quantity changes. The crude quantity theory was one of the earliest and least accurate, but we can profit by using it as a point of departure: *The value of a unit of money varies inversely with the number*

336

*of units of money and directly with the number of units of
goods and services in existence.* This theory has several obvious
defects. Not everyone who holds money wishes to spend it
at once or even at the same rate from one time to another. Not
everyone who has goods to sell would be able to raise his prices
simply because there is more money in existence. Even more
important, the statement ignores the fact that, under certain
circumstances, an increase in money may cause an increase in
the production of goods (loans in the form of created check-
book money used to buy raw materials or pay labor). It also
ignores the fact that increased production and employment may
cause the creation of more money (larger payrolls mean more
spending, and retailers of consumers' goods may borrow check-
book money to replenish their stocks of goods).

A somewhat better statement is given in Professor Irving
Fisher's formula:

$$MV + M'V' = PT$$

where: $M =$ the amount of money in circulation.
       $V =$ the velocity of circulation of M.
     $M' =$ the amount of bank credit in circulation.
     $V' =$ the velocity of circulation of M'.
      $P =$ the general price level.
      $T =$ volume of trade.

Even this is not such a great step ahead of the old quantity
theory. Taken literally, it is a mere truism: the means of payment $(MV + M'V')$ equal the total payments that are made
(PT). It also ignores the time element that is inherent in the
equation. Present means of payment are actually being used to
pay for a volume of trade which occurred some time in the past
and was contracted for at prices which prevailed still further in
the past. It does not tell us either how the cause and effect relationship runs between the different items in the equation, although Fisher himself usually seems to feel that the means of
payment is the most important causal effect and that P is the
principal dependent variable. Whether P or T is affected most

by an increase in $(MV + M'V')$ depends upon the *elasticity of supply* of goods in general. If the supply is elastic, T increases by a greater proportion than P; if the supply is inelastic, most of the increase is concentrated in P.

A better statement of the relationship between money and prices is the following: The value of money varies inversely (although not necessarily in any constant ratio) with the ratio of the *effective quantity of money* to *money work to be done.* The initial change may come from either element.

Factors which may *increase* the effective quantity of money:

1. An increase in bank lending (of check-book money).
2. An increased issue of government money.
3. An increase in velocity of circulation (the number of times in a given period that money passes from hand to hand).
4. Government borrowing of funds that would otherwise have remained idle.
5. An increase in the amount of "book credit" extended by business firms to other firms or to individuals.
6. Dishoarding.

Factors which may *decrease* the effective quantity of money:

1. Repayment of bank loans which are not immediately lent again by the bank.
2. Decreases instead of increases in Nos. 2, 3, 4, and 5 in the list above.
3. Hoarding.

Factors which may *increase* the money work to be done:

1. Greater production of goods.
2. Increased taxes.
3. Separation of previously integrated firms.
4. Entrance of previously self-sufficing farmers into the money economy.
5. An increasing population.

Factors which may *decrease* money work to be done:

1. Integration of a group of firms which previously made payments in successive stages of the process of production or marketing.
2. An increase in subsistence farming.
3. Decreased taxation.
4. Declining population.
5. Extinction of business firms.

These lists do not exhaust the number of elements that might be included under each category. It is not always easy to classify an item as belonging under increase in effective quantity of money or under a decrease in money work to be done. This does not matter, as both tend towards higher prices and lower value of money. Likewise the distinction between items that decrease the effective quantity of money and items tending to increase the money work to be done is difficult to draw and is not particularly important. Both of these kinds of items tend towards lower prices and a higher value of money.

This type of analysis is particularly useful in showing us the difficulties of any authority which attempts to control the value of money. The authority must have the answers to these questions and many others and in addition must be able to do a considerable amount of successful forecasting.

The following section gives an explanation of another theory of the way money works. In many respects it does not differ markedly from the above analysis, and it may be simpler for some readers to grasp.

Cash Balances

We might start by asking ourselves, "What is there about money which necessitates an explanation of a change in its quantity different from our explanation of the change in quantity of any other good?" Our answer is that, unlike other goods, money is never consumed, nor, with the exception of pure metallic currencies, does the cost of production of money have any direct relation to its value. All goods, with the exception of money, eventually become consumers' goods. When consumers' goods are cheap so that people are able to obtain more of them for the same amount of effort, they are able to consume more, and they do so. Not so with money. When a person receives a greater amount of money, there is only one of four things he may do with it: (1) he may spend it for consumers' goods; (2) he may spend it for producers' goods; (3) he may hold it as a cash balance to be used in the future for purpose (1) or (2), or to pay off his debts as they fall due; (4) he may lend it to other people. In any event, money is received only to be passed on again sooner or later.

Each person and each firm determines for itself what the amount of its cash balance will be. The amount of cash balance which is held will depend upon individual circumstances. There are several factors that might influence the amount of cash balance which a person decides to hold. Some of these are: (1) the knowledge that certain payments will have to be made in the near future will cause a person to try to build up his cash balance so that he can meet the payment—thus we regularly find some people holding greater cash balances at the first of the month than at other times; (2) most people regularly try to maintain at least a certain minimum cash balance to meet "unanticipated expenditures"; (3) the possession of assets that can readily be turned into cash (such as a savings account at the bank or the ownership of government bonds) would tend to lower the amount of cash balance which an individual needs to maintain for emergency expenditures; (4) if the payments which an individual receives are fairly well synchronized with the payments which he has to make, he will be able to get along on a smaller cash balance than if these payments were different in timing. Thus, a person on a monthly salary who "charges" goods and pays for them once a month will have a large cash balance only in the brief interval between the time he receives his salary and the time he pays his bills; (5) it is also obvious from the preceding statement that a person who can obtain credit may maintain a smaller average cash balance than a person with the same expenditures who must pay them all in cash. Still other conditions which cause people to maintain a greater or smaller cash balance could be listed.

Given the individual's peculiar conditions and circumstances, as discussed above, there is one element which will always tend to induce him to keep his cash balance as small as possible. This is the fact that his cash balance is always "idle" in the sense that it is not yielding him an income. If he can in any way reduce his cash balance without inconveniencing himself, he may invest the difference in some form of loan which will yield interest and thus increase his income. Or, if his cash balance is in excess of the amount which he requires, he may spend the excess amount on consumers' goods. In either event he will derive greater satisfaction than would be the case if he held the excess balance as idle cash.

Effects of an Increase in Quantity of Money

We must now trace the effects of an increased amount of money upon this situation. Let us suppose that the government prints an additional amount of paper money to pay for its expenditures instead of collecting taxes for this purpose. The people who are relieved of paying the taxes now have their incomes increased by the amount of the tax which they formerly paid. Their other circumstances being unchanged, these people will not add the extra income to their cash balances for any considerable period of time, but will either spend it for more consumers' goods or will spend it for producers' goods by the process of investment.

This spending is really an increase in demand in terms of money for the particular goods or services which these people buy with the additional income. The dealers who are selling these goods may not be aware at first that demand has increased and may continue for a time merely to sell more goods at existing prices rather than to raise their prices immediately. When the full effects of the increased demand are felt and recognized, the price will rise for each good whose demand has increased, the amount of the price increase depending upon both the proportion of increase in demand and the elasticity of supply of each particular good.

The dealers who sell these additional amounts of goods and services and who receive the increased supply of money will in turn not be eager to increase their cash balances over the amount they have previously been holding. They in turn will spend the increased receipts for business purposes or will increase their personal expenditures, or both. The goods and services which they buy in their turn will show the same tendency to rising prices as explained in the previous paragraph. The money will then pass with similar results into another set of hands.

If only this one addition, and no further additions, are made to the amount of money, the effect will eventually dissipate itself and further price rises will be stopped. This will happen because, even though people are receiving greater money incomes, as the prices of the goods which they buy are rising (or have risen before the increased flow of money reaches them), people will begin to decide that they need a larger cash balance to hold for their expenditures. (For instance, if I am in the habit of dropping into a movie any time the mood strikes me, and the price of movie tickets should rise from 25c to 50c, I would now have to carry a half dollar instead of a quarter in my pocket for this purpose.) When the additional amount of money is all retained in the cash balances of various people and not passed on immediately as it is received, the price rises will come to a stop.

During the period of rising prices, some people will gain and others will lose. Those who receive their increased incomes at the start of the period will gain because the prices of the goods they buy will not yet have risen to their full extent; hence those people will be able to obtain more goods for a time than they formerly did. Those whose incomes rise last, or do not rise at all, will lose, because, while they receive the same incomes that they formerly did, the rising prices will prevent them from buying the same amount of goods with their incomes.

We chose as our example an increase in the quantity of paper money printed by the government. We might equally well have represented the increased quantity of money as an increase in the amount of bank credit extended in the form of checking accounts by the banks. In this case the borrowers who obtained the checking accounts would be the first ones to increase their expenditures. However, exactly analogous results upon prices and cash balances would follow upon an increase in "bank money" as would follow an increase in government paper money.

Inflation

There are perhaps nearly as many definitions of inflation as there are people who use the term. A short list of some of them may prove interesting. Inflation is:

1. Any increase in the quantity of money.
2. Any increase in general prices.
3. Any increase in prices not caused by increased consumer preference for the goods or by a decreased physical supply.
4. Any increase in government debt which may affect prices.
5. Any increase in the effective quantity of money.
6. Any increase in the effective quantity of money which is greater than the increase in money work to be done.
7. Any increase in money and prices which does not result in increased output of goods.
8. Any increase in prices which occurs after full employment has been attained.
9. Maintenance of a constant price level when costs are falling.
10. Any increase in capital investment which cannot be continued without a continuous increase in the quantity of money.

11. A situation in which the public loses faith in the ability of money to keep its value and rushes to get rid of money in exchange for commodities or securities which promise to be a better store of value.

Numbers 7 and 8 are the definitions of Arthur D. Gayer and W. W. Rostow. Number 7 they would apply to partial "pure inflation" and Number 8 they would apply to full "pure inflation."

Numbers 7 through 11 may all be regarded as dangerous inflation, although the degree of danger implied in the different definitions might be a matter of dispute among different authors.

The Dangers of Inflation

There is no sacredness about any particular price level. The important point is the relationship between individual prices. By prices here we mean all prices of goods and services and all prices of factors of production. Unfortunately not all prices are equally flexible. Some prices are rigid, some are sticky, and some are extremely flexible. A period of depression generally lasts longer than it otherwise would because of the failure of these prices to adjust themselves to each other. The first effects of a period of recovery brought about by increased activity due to currency expansion (or by increased money due to borrowing from the banks by borrowers with increased confidence) may help to raise some flexible selling prices relatively to some rigid or sticky costs and so increase output and employment.

As the rise in general prices continues, however, these tendencies towards equilibrium do not continue. Flexible cost elements begin to overtake fixed selling prices. Monopoly controls, whether by industry or labor, accept higher prices or wages without much increase in output or employment. Those with fixed incomes are forced to curtail the volume of their buying. This curtailment is not necessarily confined to those industries which are no longer increasing output and employment; it may also result in smaller purchases from those industries which are capable of further expansion. Thus we may have, and have had in the past, conditions of partial pure inflation even before full employment is reached. Speculative purchases of agricultural products, of minerals, of land, and of securities will have been made at prices far beyond any prices except those which it is hoped will be paid by others even more foolish. Eventually the bubble bursts. Banks become doubtful, and either they do not increase or they actually decrease their loans. Individuals and firms who have made profits and are more farsighted than the rest start to repay bank loans and reduce their check-book money. We are then started on the vicious spiral of deflation. Those who have lived through the period from 1929 to 1933 do not need to have the picture painted for them.

If full employment happens to be attained, then any further expansion of money merely results in competitive bidding up of the prices of goods and services without any added production. It may be questioned, however, whether full employment attained by expanding bank credit can be *maintained* if monetary expansion is halted at the full employment level. This does not seem probable if maladjustments have arisen during the expansion phase.

Perhaps the remedy lies in ironing out specific maladjustments at any given price level rather than to hope that they will all come out in the wash of expanding prices.

CHAPTER XXI

Interregional Trade

EXCEPT for the political issues that have centered around the subject, there might perhaps be little justification for a separate chapter on interregional or international trade in a textbook on elementary economics. Economically, the main factors involved are simply an extension and an application of the principles of specialization and division of labor. However, since there is probably no subject within the field of economics about which the general public has been more thoroughly misinformed through misguided patriotism and self-seeking propaganda than the question of international trade and tariff, it will pay us to examine the issues in detail.

Just as we found that the productivity of labor might be increased by specialization and division of labor within an industry, so may the general productivity of a country or of the world be increased by the specialized use of land and labor. California orchard land would certainly be capable of growing some wheat, and North Dakota could raise its own oranges (in hothouses). But obviously, California can obtain more and better wheat by raising oranges, selling them, and buying Dakota wheat; while North Dakota can obtain more and better oranges by raising wheat, selling it, and buying California oranges. Specialization by both of these states results in a greater amount of both wheat and oranges for both states than would be the case if each tried to grow the other's product instead of importing it. If California, however, were still a part of Mexico instead of being a part of the United States, we should probably find some people insisting on a tariff on California oranges. But merely sticking up a flag and drawing a national boundary line does not contravene the laws of economics. There would be exactly as much advantage in trade between California and Dakota if California belonged to Mexico as there is at present.

In the above example the economist would say that Dakota has an *absolute advantage* in the raising of wheat and a *disadvantage* in the raising of oranges, while California has an *absolute advantage* in the raising of oranges and a *disadvantage* in the raising of wheat. However, trade between two regions will be profitable for both even if one region has an advantage in both products, provided that its advantage in one product is greater than its advantage in the other.

The Law of Comparative Advantage

A simple illustration may show us the significance of this principle. Suppose that there is a skilled corporation lawyer who is at the same time a better typist than any stenographer that he could hire. Would it pay him to type his own briefs and legal documents? Obviously not, for he may be able to earn as much as $50.00 or $100.00 an hour devoting his time to the preparation of cases and pleading them in court, whereas he can hire as many good typists as he needs at salaries of $25.00 a week. While the lawyer has an advantage in both typing and in pleading cases, he will gain more by devoting all of his time to the occupation in which he has the *greater comparative advantage,* that is, in pleading cases. He could save himself only $25.00 a week by doing the work of one typist, and he would be losing the time that he might be spending in pleading cases, which yields him a much greater return.

This principle applies to regions or countries and governs the decisions concerning industries on which resources shall be expended just as well as it governs the decisions of the lawyer who is considering in what occupation to spend his time. A numerical example may supply the best illustration of this principle. Let us suppose that country A could produce 30 bushels of wheat with one unit of labor and capital, and 20 pounds of dyestuffs with two units of labor and capital, while country B with one unit of labor and capital could produce only 20 bushels of wheat and with two units of labor and capital could produce only ten pounds of dyestuffs. Country A then has an advantage of two to one over country B in the production of dyestuffs and an advantage of three to two in the production of wheat. If each country tried to be self-sufficient in respect to these two products, the amount received by each and the total product would be as follows:

	Wheat (bushels)	Dyestuffs (pounds)
Country A, using three units of labor and capital	30	20
Country B, using three units of labor and capital	20	10
Total product of both	50	30

But if country A should devote its entire three units to the production of dyestuffs, and country B should devote its entire three units to the production of wheat, the result would be as follows:

	Wheat (bushels)	Dyestuffs (pounds)
Country A, using three units of labor and capital	....	30
Country B, using three units of labor and capital	60	....
Total product of both	60	30

On what basis will trade between the two countries now take place? A will not take less than 30 bushels of wheat for ten pounds of dyestuffs, since by giving up the production of ten pounds of dyestuffs it could produce 30 bushels of wheat for itself. The minimum price of dyestuffs in terms of wheat is therefore three bushels for one pound. On the other hand, *B* will not give more than 40 bushels of wheat for ten pounds of dyestuffs, since by giving up the production of 40 bushels of wheat it could produce ten pounds of dyestuffs for itself. The maximum price of dyestuffs in terms of wheat is therefore four bushels for one pound. The price will be fixed somewhere between these two limits. Let us suppose that it actually happens to be 3.75 bushels of wheat for one pound of dyestuffs. After trading begins on these terms, the account would then stand:

	Wheat (bushels)	*Dyestuffs (pounds)*
Country *A*	37.5	20
Country *B*	22.5	10
Total	60.0	30

If we compare this with the account covering the situation when both countries were self-sufficient, we find that by specialization and trading *A* has gained 7½ bushels of wheat and *B* has gained 2½ bushels of wheat. Note well that although the assumption was that country *A* had an advantage in the production of *both* products, it has nevertheless gained by specializing in that product in which it has the greater comparative advantage and buying the product in which it has the lesser advantage from country *B*.

Limitations of Comparative Advantage

The foregoing illustration, although it brings out the principle involved in the law of comparative advantage, is nevertheless an oversimplification of the problem. The advantage which any one country enjoys (whether absolute or relative) will apply only within certain limits of output. There is no doubt, for example, that the cost of production of wheat on most farms in America *at our present output* is below the cost of production of wheat on most farms in England, France, Germany, Holland, Italy, Spain, and Switzerland. But if the tariffs on wheat were removed in all these countries, it is doubtful if we could supply them all with wheat. We could certainly expand our wheat output quite a bit, and they would obtain wheat cheaper than they do now. But if we undertook to supply the wheat requirements of all these countries, our cost of production would rise because of the higher cost of working our land more intensively, the necessity of including poorer land in wheat cultivation, and the necessity of turning to wheat cultivation land that has other and more valuable uses. In other words, wheat is produced under conditions of increasing cost. This rise in production costs sets limits to the extent to which America could capture the wheat market of the world, even if unhindered by tariffs. As American output expanded and our costs rose, various points would be found at which it would be profitable for some of the best wheat farms in each of the several countries mentioned to start producing in competition with the American farms.

In the production of automobiles for foreign sale, we could probably expand much farther than in the case of wheat without encountering increasing costs. Even here, however, it is doubtful if all foreign automobile manufacturers would be put out of business by the abolition of foreign tariffs on American cars. Even with automobiles—the classic example of the economies of mass production—costs of production would begin to increase if the individual manufacturers expanded their output far enough.

It should also be noted that it is improper and inaccurate to speak of the cost of production for any product in a particular country in the way that we sometimes see the expression used. What is meant, for example, by the statement, "The German cost of production of aniline dyes is lower than the American

cost"?   If the *average* cost of production of German dye producers is lower than the *average* American cost, this does not
mean that all American dye firms would be forced out of
business by the repeal of the tariff on dyes.   Only the least
efficient and highest-cost American firms might be forced to
discontinue by tariff repeal.   The only circumstance under
which the foreign manufacturers of a product could force all
American firms out of an industry (if tariffs were repealed)
would be the case in which the foreign firms' cost of production was below that of *all* of the American firms and *would
remain below the cost of all of the American firms when the
foreign firms expanded their output to supply the entire
American market as well as their own market.*   It will usually
be found that where free trade exists between two countries,
the effect in most industries is not to force all of the firms out
of the industry in either country, but rather to confine production to the most efficient firms of both countries, thus increasing the general average efficiency of the industry and making
the product cheaper for all buyers.

Another factor that must not be overlooked in this connection is the costs of transportation to the point where the product
is to be used.   In certain products whose cost of transportation
is a comparatively large percentage of the total delivered cost,
it will be found that foreign competitors, even without the
tariff, could make comparatively little inroads upon the American markets.   In some products foreign firms may be able to
compete with the American firms for the business along the
Atlantic seacoast without being able to meet American competition in the markets for the same product further inland.
Thus, for example, when ocean freighters at times charge extremely low freight rates on bricks (intending merely to use
them as ballast rather than to sail light), English brickyards
are able to compete with those along the Hudson for the

business in New York City, but the English producers are unable to ship these bricks even as far west as Syracuse, New York, and still compete with American brickyards.

The Balance of Trade of Goods and Services

We must now turn our attention to the question of the "balance of trade." The first important group of writers on this treacherous subject were "mercantilists." They saw great merit in foreign trade, and alleged that the greatest advantage was to be obtained from what we now call a "favorable" balance of trade (that is, an excess of exports over imports). They believed that one of the most important kinds of wealth which a country might possess was a quantity of gold. Since an excess in the value of exports over the value of imports would bring gold into a country, they advocated measures which would encourage exports and which would restrict or prevent imports. More particularly, since they recognized that manufactured goods have a greater value than the value of the raw materials that are embodied in them, they advocated the importation of raw materials and generous encouragement of the export of manufactured goods.

Adam Smith, the founder of systematic economics, devoted a large part of his book *The Wealth of Nations* to exposing what he considered to be the fallacies embodied in the mercantilistic doctrine. But in spite of him, and in spite of the teachings of the vast majority of economists from that time to the present, many fallacious opinions concerning the balance of trade have persisted as a fund of popular misinformation on the subject of foreign trade. It is unfortunately still necessary to point out the fallacies involved in adherence to crude balance-of-trade criteria of foreign trade. Because of the super-vitriolic nationalism which is rampant in the world today, it is even more necessary to do so now than it might have been twenty years ago.

In the first place, a country's wealth consists not of gold alone but is the sum total of all kinds of goods (including gold) which it possesses. Gold is merely one form of wealth and is not even the most important form of wealth. For example, bread, milk, meat, and a whole list of the necessities and comforts of life might be listed as more important forms of wealth than gold. To see the full implications of this, let us suppose that a crude mercantilist policy were carried to its logical conclusion so that one country managed to get hold of all the gold in the world at the cost of selling all of its other goods. The marginal utility of gold to the citizens of that country would have fallen tremendously, while the marginal utility of the other goods that they had given up would have risen to infinity. What could the people do with the gold? They could not eat the gold. They could not wear it except for jewelry, and gold jewelry would be a pretty poor form of clothing at sub-zero temperatures. Their only recourse would be to try to use the gold to buy back some of the other goods from other countries. But the other countries would no longer have gold standard moneys (they would have been forced off the gold standard as they lost gold). Gold would have "lost its job" as money in the other countries. The gold-owning country, therefore, could not use the gold directly as money in buying back goods. It would have to sell the gold in the commodity gold markets of the other countries for what it would bring, take the proceeds in the money of the other countries, and buy its goods with the money.

International Gold Movements

Not only is a continuous "favorable balance of trade" undesirable between most countries, but it is also impossible. No country can continue for long to have its exports exceed its imports in value and receive the difference in gold unless it is trading with a gold-producing country. In the latter case, exports could continue to exceed imports in the long run only

by the value of the annual gold production of the gold-export-
ing country. If a country is trading with non-gold-producing
countries, its exports to them could exceed its imports from
them only until the gold stocks of the other countries are exhausted. However, if both the excess exporting country and
the excess importing countries are on an effective gold standard, the balance of trade would reverse itself long before the
gold stock of any country was exhausted. This would happen
because the inflow of gold into the excess exporting country
would tend to expand the currency of this country and raise its
prices, while the withdrawal of the gold from the excess importing countries would tend to contract the currency and
lower prices. This would make the country that had received
the gold a good country in which to sell but a poor country
from which to buy. It would also make the countries that had
lost the gold good countries from which to buy and poor countries in which to sell. Imports to the gold-holding country
would increase, exports from it would decrease, and the gold
would flow out.

The return flow of gold to other countries might be prevented for a time by the imposition of still higher tariffs on
imports by the gold-holding country, by a forced contraction
of the currency, or by a law which prohibited the export of
gold. However, to the extent that any or all of these measures
succeeded in reducing the country's imports of goods, it would
also succeed in reducing exports by the same amount, thereby
increasing unemployment in the export trades.

Since the ultimate aim of crude mercantilist policy is un-
attainable, the reader might well raise the question as to why
we are so worried about such a policy. The answer is that
even in attempting to achieve the ends of a mercantilist policy,
irreparable damage may be worked upon the economic structure of the country which adopts the policy. The influence
of tariffs and subsidies will be to induce labor and capital to

be applied to industries in which their efficiency is less than what it would be in foreign countries. Such industries will collapse upon the withdrawal of the tariff or subsidy; the capital in them will be lost and the labor unemployed for some time. The high prices which are induced by the unnecessarily heavy importations of gold cannot be maintained; when the inevitable decline in prices comes, the banking system of the country may collapse with it.

After the gold stocks of the excess importing countries are either exhausted or reduced to that minimum with which the countries will not part, there is one way in which the excess exporting country may continue for some time to export more than it imports: by extending loans to the importing countries to cover the difference between imports and exports. However, the interest and the principal of such loans must be repaid in goods, if it is to be repaid at all. If the excess exporting country continues to maintain or increase its tariffs to prevent the overturn of the balance of trade, such loans can never be repaid. As soon as the moneylenders in the net exporting country realize this, new loans will no longer be made, and the volume of export business which was based on the loans will no longer exist. If the loans are not repaid, as far as the exporting country as a whole is concerned it will not really have sold the goods but it will have given them away to the other countries.

The reader who is interested in doing so may apply the above analysis to the recent economic and financial history of the United States. While no one would assert that the tariff policy of the United States was the sole cause of the recent depression, nevertheless the part which the tariffs of the United States and other countries have played in both increasing the intensity and prolonging the duration of the world-wide depression is one which merits very serious study.

CHAPTER XXII

Foreign Exchange

THE MAKING of a payment to a person in a foreign
country or the receiving of a payment from a person in
a foreign country involves two problems: the transfer of a
means of payment from one place to another, and the trans-
lation or conversion of the means of payment from the money
of one country into the money of another country. To meet
these problems in the most convenient and economical way,
the businessmen and bankers of the world have developed
an instrument for making payments known as the *foreign
bill of exchange*.

The Bill of Exchange

To understand the nature and significance of the bill of exchange we will first give a definition of the bill of exchange
in general which will apply to the bills used in both domestic
and foreign trade. *A bill of exchange is an unconditional
order, drawn by one person against a second person, ordering
the second person to pay a specified sum of money to the
first person, or to a third person named in the bill, or to the
bearer, such payment to be made either on presentation of the
bill or after a specified period of time named in the bill has
elapsed.* It will be seen from this definition that a bank check
is one form of bill of exchange, payable on demand. But
other forms of bills of exchange—the ones we think of most
commonly when we use the term—are those drawn by businessmen against other businessmen.

An example may show us more fully the nature of the commercial bill of exchange. Let us suppose that the Sparrow Shirt Company sells shirts to the value of $1,200.00 to Sam Brown, men's clothier of Keokuk, Iowa. The Sparrow Company wishes to extend credit to Brown for 30 days, yet it would also like to have the money to use in its own business. It may do this by the use of a *time bill of exchange*. Such a bill might be drawn as follows:

$1,200.00   Troy, New York, Dec. 1, 19____

Thirty days after date Pay to the order of OURSELVES

One Thousand Two Hundred—no/100 _____ Dollars

To Sam Brown

     Keokuk, Iowa   *Sparrow Shirt Co.*

The shirt company may take this bill of exchange and sell it to a local bank at a discount representing one month's interest charges. The local bank will send the bill to a bank in Keokuk which will present the bill to Sam Brown. Thirty days later, Sam Brown will pay the Keokuk bank and the bank will repay the local bank in the same manner as if a check had been drawn by Sam Brown on the Keokuk bank and had been cashed or deposited at the Troy bank by the shirt company (that is, through the clearinghouse system).

When the seller of goods does not trust the buyer even to make payment upon the receipt of the goods, a *sight bill of exchange* may be used as a way of selling the goods C.O.D. The only difference in form of the sight bill from the one illustrated is that whereas the time bill reads "thirty days after

date," the sight bill would read "at sight pay to the order of."
If a sight bill were used in our example above, it would be
sent to the Keokuk bank together with the railroad's bill of
lading for the goods.   Sam Brown would have to pay the bill
of exchange at the Keokuk bank before the bank would give
him the bill of lading to get the goods out of the freight station.
In both of these cases, the bank in the buyer's town acts as a
collection agent for the bill of exchange.   If both the bank in
the seller's town and the bank in the buyer's town are parties
to the Federal Reserve agreement to remit at par, there will be
no charge between the banks for this collection service, the bill
of exchange being treated just as another item for collection
similar to a check.   If they are not both members, there will
be a small *exchange charge* for handling the collection item.
Whatever the banks charge their customers for this service is
a matter for agreement between the bank and each customer.

Foreign Bills of Exchange

The most important difference between a foreign bill of exchange and a domestic bill is that the foreign bill is payable
in the money of the foreign country.   We might briefly define
a foreign bill of exchange as: *an order to pay money, drawn
against a foreigner, payable in the foreigner's money, and payable in his country.*   Aside from the difference in the name of
the person against whom the bill is drawn, the only difference
in the form of a foreign bill of exchange from the one we have
pictured above would be that if the bill were drawn against
an Englishman, the amount would be stated in *pounds* instead
of *dollars;* against a Frenchman the amount would be stated in
francs; against a German in *marks;* and so on.

The reader will keep his reasoning about this subject clear
if he always thinks of foreign exchange as *orders to pay* foreign
money and *not* as the foreign money itself.   In the financial
page of the newspaper such headlines as "Foreign Money,"

"English Money," and so forth are really misstatements for the
sake of brevity. The rates which are quoted below these heads
are prices, not of foreign money, but of foreign bills of exchange. The actual money of a foreign country might be
bought and sold in this country; in fact, some small amount
of it is regularly bought and sold. For the purpose of making
or receiving foreign payments, however, foreign bills of exchange are far more convenient and less expensive than the
use of the actual foreign money. For instance, to pay a debt
to an Englishman by buying English paper money in this
country and sending the money to him would mean that I
would have to buy the English money about a week in advance
of the due date of the debt in order to ship the money by
steamer. Thus, I would lose the interest on the money for
that length of time. Furthermore, I would have to take out
an insurance policy to protect me against the loss or theft of
the money while in transit. Similarly, if I wish to travel in
England, it would be better for me to buy a *letter of credit*
(a form of bill of exchange) than to buy English money here
to take with me. If the letter of credit is lost or stolen, I can
have the bank which sold it to me give me a duplicate letter,
since it is payable to me alone. But if I have English bank
notes in my possession and they should be lost, stolen, or
burned, I simply lose the money.

We are now prepared to examine the mechanism by which
bills of exchange are used in making and receiving foreign
payments. We can approach the subject best by means of a
simple example. Let us suppose that the American Electric
Company has sold a dynamo to Robert White, an Englishman,
for 1,000 English pounds. Let us also suppose that the Atlantic
Cigar Stores, Incorporated, has bought a shipment of pipes from
Alfred Dunthorn of London and agreed to pay 1,000 pounds
for them. The American Electric Company has a claim payable in English money but would rather be paid in American

money so that it can spend the money here. The Atlantic Cigar Stores has the American money with which to pay its debt, but Alfred Dunthorn insists on being paid in English money. How will these two payments take place?

The American Electric Company may draw a bill of exchange for 1,000 pounds against its debtor, Robert White. The bill of exchange may now be sold to the Atlantic Cigar Stores for an agreed price, say $4,000.00 (the American Electric Company has thus received payment in American money for its claim). The Atlantic Cigar Stores sends the bill of exchange to Alfred Dunthorn. Alfred Dunthorn will then present the bill of exchange to Robert White and demand that White pay the 1,000 pounds called for in the bill (thus Dunthorn's claim is paid in English money).

This means of handling the transaction has caused the American debtor to pay the American creditor and has caused the English debtor to pay the English creditor. Both debtors have paid their bills in the money of their own country. Both creditors have received payment in the money of their own country. *No money has had to cross the ocean either way.*

The Rate of Exchange

The rate of exchange may be defined as the price paid for bills of exchange. This price is usually expressed, however, not as a price for the bill itself but as a price (quoted in domestic money) per unit of the foreign money in which the bill is drawn. In our example above, when $4,000.00 was paid for an English bill of exchange of 1,000 pounds, the rate of exchange was $4.00 per English pound.

This rate of exchange is a market price determined by demand for and supply of bills of exchange in exactly the same fashion in which the price of wheat, for example, is determined by supply and demand. All that we have said in Chapter VII about an increase in demand tending to raise the price and about an increase in supply tending to cause the price to fall, applies to the price called a rate of exchange just as it does to other prices. The reason for making a separate study of this price of exchange is that the conditions which govern demand for bills of exchange and the conditions which give rise to their supply are considerably different from those which prevail in the markets for goods.

As a guide to clear thinking in the more complicated ramifications of the subject, the reader should keep two rules in mind: (1) *Any transaction which necessitates receiving a payment from a foreign country will tend to increase the supply of bills of exchange on that country, thus tending to lower that country's rate of exchange in our exchange market.* If I wish to collect a debt from a foreigner, I draw a bill of exchange on him and attempt to sell it here. My effort to sell the bill in competition with sellers of other bills of exchange will tend to force the price down. (2) *Any transaction which necessitates making a payment to a foreign country will tend to increase the demand for bills of exchange on that country, thus tending to raise that country's rate of exchange in our exchange market.* If I wish to pay a debt to a foreigner, I attempt to buy a bill of exchange drawn on someone in his country. My demand added to that of others trying to buy those bills will tend to raise the rate.

The reader will also save himself confusion if he confines his attention to the foreign exchange market *in one country* and does not try to jump back and forth from one country to the other. This may safely be done, since the rate of exchange of a foreign country in our market is simply the reciprocal of our rate of exchange in their market. That is, if American debtors are offering *more* dollars and cents per pounds for English exchange, it will be found that in the

London foreign exchange market English debtors are offering *fewer* pounds per dollar for American exchange in exactly the same ratio.

Some of the commoner types of transactions which will necessitate payments being received from foreigners are: export of goods to foreign countries, expenditures of foreign tourists in this country, sales of coal and other ship supplies to foreign ships in domestic ports, purchase by foreigners of American stocks and bonds, sale by Americans (in the foreign markets) of foreign securities previously purchased, and interest and principal repayments on foreign debts to this country.

Some of the transactions which will necessitate the making of payments to foreigners are: imports of foreign goods, payment for freight on American goods carried in foreign ships, American tourist expenditures abroad, payment for insurance policies issued by foreign companies (for example, Lloyds), remittances by immigrants to their relatives abroad, purchase by Americans of foreign securities, the sale in this country of American securities previously purchased by foreigners, and payment of interest and dividends to foreign holders of American securities.

While we have listed the transactions in these two groups as necessitating either the receipt or the making of payments, the first group will not add to the *present* supply of bills of exchange unless Americans attempt to convert their foreign claims into American money *immediately*. The second group will not increase the *present* demand for bills of exchange unless Americans attempt to pay their foreign debts *immediately*. Americans may *postpone* the conversion of their claims into American money by collecting their claims in the foreign country and reinvesting the money in the foreign country. Foreigners may postpone the conversion of their claims by requesting the American debtor to deposit the money to their credit in an American bank, instead of sending a bill of exchange to them. However, unless such investments are maintained *permanently,* the claims will have to be converted eventually into the domestic country's money; meanwhile, the amount of the claim will have increased by the amount of interest on the investment.

Gold Settlements

To the extent that conversion of claims is not postponed by reinvestment, the difference between the total claims in favor of a country and the total claims against it will have to be paid in gold. When a country refuses to allow the export of gold, those who have claims in terms of that country's money have no alternative except to sell their claims at the present low exchange rate of that country or to reinvest them in the hope of a more favorable exchange rate in the future. This may serve to prevent the sale of large quantities of goods to the defaulting country, since sellers know that they will have to accept payment in depreciated exchange. Eventually this may help to turn the balance of payments the other way; but it will be a long and painful process.

Notice that we have said that the difference between the *total* claims in favor of a country and the *total* claims against it will have to be paid in gold. By these totals we mean the total *due from all other countries* and the total due *to all other countries.* It is not necessary that a country's balance of payments be equal with each other country, or with any one country in order to avoid payment in gold. For example, as a result of large purchases of coffee the United States may owe more to Brazil than Brazil owes to the United States. At the same time England may owe more to the United States than we owe to them, because we have sold them automobiles and wheat. Brazilians may owe a net balance to England, because they have bought English cloth. Under these circumstances, instead of sending gold to Brazil we may send the English bills

of exchange drawn against the automobile and wheat customers. Brazilians will be glad to obtain these bills of exchange, since they have to make a payment to England for the
cloth, and they can use the bills to make this payment. Thus
we have a three-cornered cancellation of debts instead of the
two-way cancellation which we had in our illustration of the
American Electric Company and the others.

The Gold Points

When gold does have to be exported in payment for foreign
balances, or imported in payment of balances in our favor, it
is usually not the government but rather private individuals
and banks which do the exporting and importing. We must
now examine how and why these gold movements take place.
When two countries are on the gold standard, the monetary
unit of each is expressed as a certain number of grains of
fine gold, and all legal money of the country becomes redeem-
able in this number of grains of gold per unit. The ratio of
the gold content of the two monetary units is called the *mint
par of exchange.* Before the First World War, a British gold
sovereign contained 113.00117 grains of fine gold, and the
American gold dollar contained 23.22 grains of fine gold. The
sovereign thus contained 4.8665 times as much gold as an
American dollar, so that the mint par of exchange was $4.8665
per pound sterling. This would mean that any American who
had a debt of one pound due from an Englishman could collect
the debt in English money, redeem the English money in gold
at the Bank of England, bring the gold over here, and have a
quantity of gold for which the United States Mint would be
willing to pay him $4.8665. The only disadvantage the Amer-
ican would encounter in collecting his debt in this fashion,
rather than by selling a bill of exchange, would be the cost of
transportation of the gold, insurance on it while in transit, and
loss of interest for the length of time it takes the gold to reach

this country. On very small debts these charges might be high enough so that this means of collection would be avoided whenever possible. On a debt of 1,000 pounds, in ordinary times, the cost of importing the gold might be $20.00 (at the rate of 2c for each pound of the debt). As long as gold redemption is allowed by England and freight rates and insurance charges remain the same, this transportation cost sets the lower limit to which the rate of exchange may fall. To find the amount of American money which the creditor will have after collecting the debt in gold and paying the costs of collection, we deduct 2c from the mint par of exchange ($4.8665), leaving $4.8465. This is the *lower gold point*. Those with claims against Englishmen could realize $4.8465 per pound by collecting their claims in gold. Therefore, they would not sell bills of exchange at any rate below that figure. When the rate would drop to that figure, gold would start flowing into this country from England.

The *upper gold point* was determined in an analogous manner. Americans with English debts to pay could redeem their American money in gold, send it to England, and receive from the Bank of England one English pound for each $4.8665 worth of the gold. If it cost 2c per pound to ship the gold, then a debt could be paid at a total cost of 2c plus the mint par of exchange, or a total of $4.8865. This would be the top price which American debtors would be willing to pay for English bills of exchange, since at any rate of exchange higher than $4.8865 it would be cheaper for them to pay in gold. This, then is the *upper gold point*. With the given conditions (that is, both countries on the gold standard, a mint par of exchange of $4.8665, and a cost of shipment of 2c per pound sterling), when the rate charged for bills of exchange reached this figure, gold would start to flow from America to England.

When two countries are on a full gold standard, the gold points set the limits between which the rate of exchange may fluctuate. This sets limits to the amount of possible losses in foreign trade through exchange fluctuations. If the par and the gold points were as given above and an exporter encountered the worst possible circumstances, that is, if he quoted a price to an Englishman when the rate was at the upper gold point ($4.8865) expecting to sell a bill of exchange at that price and then found when the time came for him to draw the bill and sell it that the rate was at the lower gold point ($4.8465), his total loss through exchange fluctuation would be 4c per pound sterling, only 0.81 per cent. If he had quoted his price to the Englishman on the expectation that the rate would drop to par, his loss would have been only half as much (2c per pound or 0.405 per cent).

Dislocated Currencies

When countries go off the gold standard, these limits to the fluctuation of exchange rates set by the gold points are destroyed; there is no absolute limit except zero to which the rate of exchange may fall, and no absolute limit above which it may not rise. There are, however, certain corrective tendencies which may assert themselves within rather wide and indefinite limits as a country's exchange rate rises or falls. For example, suppose both England and the United States are off the gold standard, gold shipments being prohibited, and the rate of English exchange in America drops from $5.00 to $3.00 per pound. This would mean that Dunhill pipes, selling for one pound in England, could now be bought for $3.00 instead of $5.00 in our money. All other English goods, whose price in English money remained unchanged, would likewise be selling in America for three fifths of their former price in terms of American money. We might thus be induced to buy many more English goods than before, and the increased demand for bills of exchange to pay for the goods would tend to force the rate of exchange upward again. If the $3.00 rate was expected to rise again, speculators might also enter the market and buy up bills of exchange in the hope of reselling them at a higher price. To the extent that they do so, their action will tend to cause the rate to rise more rapidly than it would as a result of the purchases of goods alone.

Note, however, that this increased demand for English bills of exchange is contingent upon the condition that the domestic prices of English goods *do not rise* by an amount which will offset the difference in the exchange rate. For instance, if Dunhill sets the price of a pipe at two pounds, even though the rate of exchange is $3.00, this will mean that Dunhill pipes now cost $6.00 in American money. Therefore, *fewer* of them would be bought than were bought when the English price of the pipes was one pound and the rate of exchange $5.00. Consequently, if the prices of other English goods also rose, the demand for bills of exchange would be still *less* than before, and the rate of exchange would fall still lower. One cause which would bring about such a rise in English prices might be an expansion of the amount of money in England.

Furthermore, when a rate of exchange is falling, if prospective buyers of the country's goods believe that the rate will fall still further, they will do well to wait until the lowest rate is reached in order to obtain the goods at the lowest possible price in terms of American money. Speculators, likewise, will do well to wait for the lowest price of bills of exchange in order to resell them at the greatest possible profit when the rate does rise. If we knew that England was continuing to inflate her currency, for instance, this would be a fairly good indication that the rate of exchange was going to fall still further and a warning to refrain from buying for the time being. Those who bought German marks during the German inflation were either displaying their ignorance of economics or gambling that the German government would reverse its policy and start to contract its currency.

Automatic Corrective of the Gold Movement

In contrast to the above haphazard situation, when two countries are on a working gold standard, not only do the gold points set limits between which the rate of exchange may fluctuate, but also the very movement of the gold itself tends to set in operation the tendencies to reverse the balance of payments which caused the exchange rate to reach the gold point. For example: if England and America are both on the gold standard and the rate of English exchange in America rises to the upper gold point, we have shown how this will cause gold to flow from America to England. The withdrawal of gold will decrease the reserves of the American banking system. The American banks will then contract the amount of deposit credit they are extending in order to maintain their former reserve ratios. This will cause American prices to fall. In England, a contrary action is taking place. Gold is flowing in; British bank reserve ratios are going up and British banks are in a position to extend more deposit credit. The increased credit will cause English prices to rise. Thus, American prices are low, English prices are high. As a result, more American goods will be bought by Englishmen and fewer English goods will be bought by Americans. The supply of English bills of exchange will increase, and the demand for them will decrease. The lower gold point will be reached; gold will flow back again.

Notice that we have said that the two countries must be on a *working* gold standard. This means that they are following what are called "the rules of the game," namely: (1) a country which *loses* gold must *contract* its currency; (2) a country which *receives* gold must *expand* its currency. (Either of these alone would accomplish the reversal of the gold movement; but if the receiving country does not expand currency, the country which loses the gold would have to contract its currency by a greater amount. Or, if the country which loses the gold does not contract currency, the receiving country would have to expand its currency by a greater amount to cause the gold to flow out again. Less dislocation of domestic prices is necessary if both countries follow the rules.)   (3) The country which receives gold must not impose new tariffs on the other country's goods or the expansion and/or contraction in the currencies will have to be just that much greater to offset the influence of the tariff on relative prices in the two countries.

Foreign Exchange Banks

To keep our explanation as simple as possible we have deliberately avoided introducing the activities of bank dealings in foreign exchange. If we have the principles of foreign exchange in mind, we may now proceed to examine the role played by banks. In our previous illustration of payment by a bill of exchange, the debt collectable by the American Electric Company and the debt payable by the Atlantic Cigar Stores happened to be for the same amount, 1,000 pounds. In actual practice this would seldom be the case. Both debts would be more likely a different odd number of pounds, shillings, and pence, so that both debts could not be exactly cancelled by this one bill of exchange.

Here is where the banks step into the picture. They make a regular practice of buying bills of exchange from the exporters. These bills are sent to England and collected in English money. The English money is then deposited to the credit of the American bank in the form of a checking deposit in some English bank. The American bank can now write checks against the English bank for any desired specific amount of pounds, shillings, and pence. These checks are called *bankers' bills of exchange*. The American who used to pay a debt in England might buy one of these checks or bills made out in the exact amount of his debt and send it in payment to his English creditor.

Because there was less likelihood of a bill of exchange drawn against an English bank not being paid than there would be in the case of a bill drawn against a private individual, and because of the superior convenience of bills drawn in any desired amount, the banks were able to sell bills of exchange at a slightly higher rate (usually a small fraction of a cent) than the rate at which they bought them, thus making a profit. Although the difference between the buying and the selling rates is small per pound, when it is realized that some bills call for the payment of thousands or millions of pounds, we see that the total profit per transaction may be large. The banks can also attempt to profit by speculating in foreign exchange; that is, by buying up bills in excess of the amount that they currently sell in the hope that when the rate goes up they will be able to sell out at the higher figure. But a bank that wishes to avoid both speculative profits and speculative losses will attempt to keep its purchases and sales of bills as nearly even as possible.

The banks also have such an advantage over private individuals in the shipment of gold that most shipments are made by banks. Shipping in larger quantities gives them lower shipping costs per unit of foreign currency. Moreover, they can sell a bill of exchange and then ship the gold to be deposited for redemption in the English bank by the same steamer on which the bill of exchange travels. Thus, they lose no interest on the gold while in transit, because they have already sold a bill of exchange to get their money back. It will be found, then, that when the rate of exchange is at the upper gold point people are still buying bankers' bills of exchange and the banks are shipping gold.

Exchange Controls

Practically all the previous discussion that was based on a working gold standard in foreign exchange is now ancient history. From the second time that England left the gold standard until the beginning of hostilities, England, the United States, and France had a foreign exchange stabilization agreement which operated for a considerable time almost as satisfactorily as a gold standard and might have been fully as efficient if the conditions of international trade had been more normal.   Under this agreement each of the countries had an exchange stabilization agency which was empowered to buy and sell the foreign exchange of the other two countries and was entrusted with funds for this purpose. The object was to keep the rates of exchange within the narrowest limits possible. For example, whenever the American rate of exchange in London fell below a certain point, the Bank of England bought dollar exchange, and whenever the rate rose above a certain point, the bank sold exchange. As long as the amounts offered for sale equalled the amounts purchased at the rates set by the control authority, no further action was necessary. In seasonal and short-time movements, any excess amounts offered for sale were purchased by the bank and any excess amounts demanded were sold by the bank from its stock of dollar exchange on hand; or, if it had no such stock, it drew on its balance in the American exchange stabilization fund. The apparent success of the scheme must have been due to very good judgment in "pegging" the rates between which the exchange was allowed to fluctuate very close to the "purchasing power parity" between the two countries.

Exchange Rationing

Argentina and some other countries which used to have heavy export balances to Europe and heavy import balances from the United States adopted the system of exchange rationing. Under this system all foreign exchange was turned over to the government, and importers in Argentina were allowed to have only that amount for payments to each particular country which that country had spent in buying goods from Argentina.   This system was particularly irksome to purchasers of North American goods but, since we were not interested in accepting German blocked marks, it was apparently the easiest way for Argentina to conserve her reserves until we began lending to her through the Import-Export Bank.

Barter Deals

Barter deals were first adopted by Germany to take advantage of the exchange shortage of various countries which resulted from the American tariff policy and British Empire preference. These deals were a straight exchange of goods for goods and hence involved no financing. We ourselves took advantage of one such deal by bartering cotton with Britain for rubber.

These various methods of trading have shown us that it is not at all impossible to conduct some form of international trade between countries which are not on a gold standard. The chief difficulties seem to lie in the restriction of three-cornered trade, and these may be due at least in part to shipping difficulties and war conditions.

CHAPTER XXIII

Unemployment

THE EARLIER chapters of this book have largely ignored the question of unemployment. This omission was occasioned by the fact that in most of our discussion we have been concerned with the analysis of long-run equilibrium conditions. In other words, we have said to ourselves: "Here is a certain set of economic forces; given a sufficiently long period for these forces to exert their full effect (with no change in other data meanwhile), what will be the final result when equilibrium is attained?" Involuntary unemployment of labor (or of any other factor of production) is not consistent with long-run equilibrium.[1] In fact, the existence of involuntarily unemployed units of factors of production is evidence that full equilibrium has not been attained; for these unemployed units, rather than remain unemployed, will underbid the price which is being received by the employed units. This is another way of saying that when unemployment exists, the prevailing price of a factor is not the final equilibrium price. On the other hand, if the price of a factor *is* the equilibrium price, then the presence of unemployed units of the factor (willing to work at that price) is evidence that firms and industries have not yet expanded to their equilibrium output, at which equilibrium output all of these previously unemployed units of the factor will be hired. In any event, we see that involuntary unemployment is a short-run rather than an equilibrium phenomenon.

We must recognize, however, that in the actual world full

---

[1] Under perfect competition.

373

equilibrium is never attained. Usually before full and final equilibrium can be attained under one set of conditions, the conditions themselves change (new inventions and discoveries are made, shifts in demand for products occur, changes in banking policy take place, and so on). These changes call for an equilibrium adjustment different from the previous one; but before this can be fully attained the conditions will change again; and so on. The question of unemployment becomes, then, not a question of final equilibrium, but a question of whether the economic system can adapt itself rapidly enough to changes in conditions so that units of a factor that are thrown out of employment by a change can be re-employed within a reasonable length of time.

Unemployment of labor may be classified under several main causal heads as follows:

1. Seasonal unemployment.
2. Casual unemployment.
3. Cyclical unemployment.
4. Technological unemployment.
5. Voluntary unemployment.
6. Unemployables (personal unemployability).

Seasonal Unemployment

Seasonal unemployment, as the name implies, is caused by seasonal changes in the demand for labor in certain industries. These seasonal changes may be attributed either directly to changes in the weather or to conventional practices. Examples of occupations which are seasonal because of weather are: harvesting, lumbering, navigation on the Great Lakes, work at summer resorts, and so on. Conventional seasons may be occasioned either by the existence of certain holiday business or by traditional trade practices. Thus, the department stores always hire extra help for the Christmas and Easter rushes.

The former practice of the automobile manufacturers of introducing their new models at the first of the year gave rise to a peak demand for labor in the early spring months with a sharp falling off in employment during August, September, October, and November. They have now attempted to remedy this somewhat by bringing out new models in the late autumn, when demand would otherwise be slack. A still better solution, for the purpose of decreasing seasonal unemployment, would be for each manufacturer to bring out his new models in a different month. Such an agreement is not likely to be adopted, however, for fear it would give a competitive advantage to one manufacturer or another. In other industries many methods of reducing the amount of seasonal unemployment have been developed, but much more can be accomplished than has been done to date, particularly by the application of known methods by firms and industries which do not now use them.

Casual Unemployment

Casual unemployment is occasioned by more or less haphazard fluctuations in the amount of work to be done in certain trades. The classical example of casual unemployment has been the work of the longshoremen who load and unload ocean freighters. The irregularity of steamship arrivals results in the need for a large number of workers some days and none on other days. This results in a large number of men "hanging around" in the hope of obtaining work, but actually working only a small proportion of the time. The situation is aggravated in those ports where the longshoremen must report to an individual steamship company's dock, thus keeping an unemployed "labor reserve" for each individual company. In ports where a central "hiring hall" is maintained for longshoremen by either the union or an employers' association, employment fluctuates only with the total number of ships in port rather than with the number at any particular company's dock.

Both seasonal and casual unemployment are partially compensated for by a higher hourly wage than that prevailing in other occupations requiring equal skill but offering more regular employment. This solution, however, is satisfactory neither to the employer nor to a great many of the employees. The employer has higher labor costs than he would have if he could offer more regular employment. Only those employees gain who are employed a greater proportion of the year than is the average expectancy in such an irregular occupation. For example, an oiler on a Great Lakes freighter which starts operation at the opening of navigation in April and continues in service till the close in November or December, may make higher annual earnings than an oiler on a stationary engine ashore. On the other hand, an oiler on a vessel which does not start to operate until late in June and which lays up in early September will earn far less than the man on shore.

Some connection may be noted between irregularity of employment and violence in labor disputes, although the exact causal relationship is not clearly established. It may be that irregularity of employment begets irresponsibility among the workmen; it may be that irregular employment attracts an irresponsible type of man; or it may be that irregular employment prevents the establishment of a disciplined trade-union membership. In any event, strikes in the seasonal and casual trades, when they do occur, are usually notorious for their violence and destruction.

Cyclical Unemployment

Cyclical unemployment is that unemployment connected with those fluctuations in business activity that are known as *business cycles*. A fuller discussion of the causes of the cycle is reserved for a later chapter. For the purposes of this chapter we are concerned solely with the relations between busi-

ness cycles and unemployment. In the expansion (or prosperity) phase of every business cycle, prices are rising.[2] This
rise in prices contributes to cause an increase in wage rates in
two ways: (1) as prices rise more rapidly than costs, opportunities for profits appear, causing old firms to expand and
new firms to enter old industries, thus creating an increased
demand for labor (demand curves for labor in various industries shift to the right); (2) as costs of living advance,
workers are motivated to insist on receiving higher wages and
are encouraged to do so by the fact that various employers
in the same or different industries are bidding for their services (supply curves of labor for individual industries shift to
the left, because opportunity costs are higher). Thus for each
firm we have an increased demand for labor in terms of
money and a decreased supply of labor in terms of money,
both contributing to cause a rise in the wage rate.

At the start of this period unemployment may have existed
(due to a past cycle). As soon as all workers are employed,
however, further increases in wages will not result in a greater
total number of employed workers, but merely in shifts of
workmen from one firm or industry to another as employers
bid competitively for labor services and one employer outbids
another. To the extent that the banking system is creating
bank money (deposit credit) and loaning it to businessmen,
this competitive bidding for labor and increase of demand for
labor in terms of money is intensified.

It must not be inferred from the preceding discussion that
the position of labor in the "prosperity" phase of the business
cycle is as roseate as would appear at first sight. Of course,
the workers who were previously unemployed and who now
find jobs are better off. (They would have been still better off

---

[2] This expansion phase and these rising prices may have been caused either by an
innovation or by expansion of credit by the banking system, or by both. See the
chapter on "Business Cycles."

had there been no previous cycle to throw them out of work in the first place.) Remember that we have been talking about demand for labor *in terms of money* and about *money wages*. To the extent that the costs of living are rising faster than money wages, *real wages* are actually declining. Real wages are the amount of goods that money wages will buy. Thus, in times of rapidly rising prices, a $40.00 a week wage may buy *fewer* steaks and potatoes and shoes than a $20.00 a week wage could buy before the price rise.

It is, however, with the recession and depression phases of the business cycle that we are primarily concerned in a discussion of cyclical unemployment. As we shall point out in the following chapter, if a period of inflationary prosperity is allowed to develop, a deflationary reaction is inevitable. As prices fall below average variable costs, firms find it preferable to close down rather than to continue in operation, and men are thrown out of work. Other firms whose demand curves have shifted to the left, although they may not close down, will find it advisable to restrict output and consequently to reduce the number of their employees. If a previous inflationary prosperity has been allowed to develop, a considerable amount of deflationary unemployment will be unavoidable. The problem is then to care for the unemployed in such a way that the depression will not be prolonged nor unemployment increased by the methods of relief. Some aspects of this problem will be discussed later.

We must not overlook the importance of rigid wage rates as a force which tends to increase the amount of cyclical unemployment which ordinarily accompanies a business recession. High wages prevail at the end of a period of prosperity. But it is only while high prices and large volume of business prevail that business firms can afford to pay these high wages and to maintain the same number of workers employed. As prices fall, some firms are forced to restrict output and others to close down entirely. However, if wages should decline as rapidly as prices, the firms would not find it to their advantage to restrict output so drastically, nor would so many firms be forced to close down. From our discussion of costs we may recall that a firm will continue in operation as long as price is above minimum average variable costs (fixed costs need not be covered in the short run; and a depression is a short run event). A decline in wages lowers average variable costs and lowers marginal costs. Consequently, a fall in the price of the product that would force a firm to close if wages remain high, need not force this firm to close if wages fall along with the price of the product.

We see, then, that the policy advocated by some people in 1930 of "maintaining wages in order to maintain purchasing power" was an economic fallacy. A simple example will serve to make this clearer even in terms of "purchasing power." Suppose that there is a factory employing 10,000 men. Suppose next that to keep wages at $40.00 per week the factory will have to reduce its working force to 5,000 men. Total purchasing power of the men who remained in employment would then be $200,000.00 per week; the other 5,000 men would be thrown on relief. On the other hand, suppose that with a 25 per cent cut ($40.00 to $30.00) all 10,000 might remain employed. Total purchasing power would then be $30.00 times 10,000, or $300,000.00 per week, and there would be no relief burden. Even if only 8,000 could be employed at $30.00 per week, total purchasing power would be $240,000.00, and only 2,000 would be unemployed.

It should not be inferred that rapid declines in wages will be sufficient to prevent all unemployment in periods of business recession. Some industries will have become so greatly overexpanded during the period of prosperity that no rate of wages greater than zero would permit the continued employment of all men in those industries. But no careful student should ignore the possibility that falling wages may tend to reduce the volume of unemployment by a considerable amount. Mr. Keynes advances a contrary argument in his *General Theory of Employment*,[3] but the validity of his argument depends upon assumptions which are involved in it.

Trade-union wage policy should be examined in the light of these facts. All trade-unions find it easier to obtain wage advances during a period of prosperity, both because the employers can afford to pay more and because a strike would be very costly to employers at this time. Some unions are astute enough to agree to voluntary wage cuts in periods of business recession in order to keep a majority of their membership employed. Others are notorious in refusing to cut wages a single penny, even during the depths of the period of depression. When a union insists on maintaining prosperity wage levels, its full membership will be employed only at peaks of prosperity, when prices justify paying such wages. At all other times a greater or less number of its members will be without employment. There is some question as to whether this type of unemployment should be called cyclical unemployment or "voluntary trade-union unemployment."

Technological Unemployment

Technological unemployment is a phrase which has caught the fancy of the public in recent years, and more than the usual stock of misinformation has appeared in the public prints. By technological unemployment is ordinarily meant the displacement of labor by machines, by new methods of production requiring less labor for a given output, by new substitute products (for instance, rayon versus cotton), or by consolidations of existing firms (for example, mergers). The supposed displacement of labor by machines is the most spectacular of these technological factors and has consequently received the most attention, but the other forms fall in exactly

---

[3] Keynes, J. M., *The General Theory of Employment, Interest and Money.* New York. Harcourt, Brace and Company, 1936.

the same economic category and are subject to the same type of analysis.

Before going further into the question we must examine the meaning of the phrase "displacement of labor" more carefully. A casual observer may look at a new machine and say, "Here is a machine that will do the work of 25 men. It will throw 25 men out of work." But if the time of ten men is required—some of them to run the machine, some to keep it in repair, and some to make new machines as this one wears out—the net displacement of men by the machine will not be 25 but only 15 men.

Even so, will the introduction of machinery decrease the total number of jobs available? A careful economic analysis will show us that in the long run it cannot do so. The logic of the situation is as follows: use of the machine (or other "labor-saving" method) must give rise to lower costs; otherwise it would not be adopted. Given this fall in costs, various possibilities present themselves, depending upon the degree of competition which prevails in the industry and upon the nature of the demand for the product. These possibilities are: (1) the price of the product falls by the full amount of the fall in cost, (a) elasticity of demand for the product being equal to or greater than unity, (b) elasticity of demand for the product being less than unity; (2) the price of the product remains the same, and the difference between price and cost goes into a monopolistic employer's pocket. We shall now consider each of these possibilities and its consequences.

1. (a) If the price of the product falls by the full amount of the fall in cost and the elasticity of demand for the product is equal to unity, the same number of men will be required to run the machines producing a larger output (increase in amount purchased is proportional to the fall in price) as was required to produce the former smaller output without the use of the machine. No labor is displaced. If the elasticity

of demand for the product is greater than unity, the increase in amount purchased will be greater proportionately than the fall in price, and *more men* will be required to produce the greatly increased output than were needed by the industry before the introduction of the machine. This is no mere example of "logic chopping" but has been borne out by actual experience when new machinery was introduced in many industries. For example, the Owens glass bottle-blowing machine when introduced was supposed to do the work of 100 men blowing bottles by hand. Yet, with the fall in price caused by consequent lower production costs, so many more glass bottles were used (for example, pickles and olives were now sold in glass bottles instead of in bulk from a barrel) that the industry soon employed many more thousands of men than were employed in the old days of blowing by hand. Henry Ford has introduced one automatic, or semiautomatic, machine after another into his factories, and yet with the steady decline in the price of the Ford car the number of Ford employees has grown from 1,000 to over 150,000. General Motors, which in 1912 employed 16,584 men, in 1937 with much more efficient machinery employed over 200,000. The 1937 figures are chosen so as not to include the effects of war orders. Similar results occurred from the introduction of the linotype machine into the printing trade and from the introduction of machinery into other industries, accompanied by falling prices and elastic demand for the products.

1. (b) If the price falls and the elasticity of demand for the product is less than unity, the public will not have to spend so much to buy the same or a slightly greater amount of this product than it did before. The difference between what the public formerly spent and what it now spends is released as additional purchasing power to buy more of other goods. The workers displaced by the machine may be re-employed in the making of those other goods. It will be a

question of how rapidly they can shift over to the other industries. However, we notice that the total number of jobs available is not decreased.

2. If the employer is in a position to keep the price the same as before and to keep the saving in cost for himself, he will do either one of two things with the extra money: spend it, or invest it. If he spends the money, the solution is the same as was given under 1. (b)—that is, the number of workers displaced by the machine will be required to make the products for which he spends the money. Moreover, the employer who spends the money is quite likely to spend it for "luxury goods." Most luxury goods require more hand labor than a larger quantity of less expensive goods that would sell for the same amount of money. Hand labor or hand finishing is required to give luxury goods their element of "distinction." Luxury goods are also often made to individual order and consequently are not adaptable to mass production. If this is the case, then more labor will be required to make the new goods than was released by the introduction of the machine.

If the employer invests the money, this is just another way of saying that he is spending it for producers' goods rather than for consumers' goods. Workers will be required to build the factories for which the money is spent and to run them.

We have examined all the possibilities and found that, *in the long run,* technological unemployment is an economic impossibility. The steady growth both in total number of employed and in the percentage of total population gainfully employed (women workers in industrial employment and offices were almost unknown prior to 1890) since the Civil War lends substance to this view. In the short run, technological unemployment, if it occurs at all, occurs because the introduction of successive new inventions throws men out of work more rapidly than they can be re-employed in the ways outlined above. Whether this is actually the case at the present time we have no way of knowing, since the Federal Government (regardless of which party is in power) has persistently refused to count the number of unemployed to find out how many there actually are. Recent figures are more accurate, but it is still a difficult question to determine by a census whether workers are voluntarily or involuntarily unemployed. Ordinarily, most of the figures on unemployment that appear in the papers are wild statistical guesses, and many of them are biased guesses. Furthermore, the constant recurrence of the business cycle is an important factor in delaying or impeding the re-employment of workers as machines take their places in different industries. *Much or all of what is commonly called technological unemployment may really be cyclical unemployment.*

Voluntary Unemployment

Voluntary unemployment may be of several varieties. Some people have sufficient independent income to support themselves and do not care to work. These people need not concern us further, although the socialist would say that they are drawing an income from a society to which they contribute no productive services. Another group of people are unemployed because they are waiting for a higher wage than is being offered to them at present. If the worker does not have to remain unemployed any great length of time before he obtains work at the wage he is insisting on, this constitutes no serious problem. Note, however, that the longer he remains out of work, the longer must he be employed at the higher wage to make up the loss occasioned by not working. For instance, suppose a worker is offered $1,500.00 a year but is holding out for $2,000.00. If he has to wait a full year until business conditions improve and he can find a $2,000.00 job, he will then have to work for three full years at $2,000.00 in order to recover the money he has lost by being idle a year.

We must not overlook the influence of too generous relief payments in swelling the volume of voluntary unemployment. If relief payments are $10.00 a week and jobs are being offered at $15.00, there will be many who will prefer not working for $10.00 a week to working at $15.00. Unless relief rolls are carefully pruned and men removed from the rolls when they refuse proffered jobs, the payment of relief may be a serious factor in prolonging a period of business depression.

We have already spoken of voluntary trade-union unemployment, occasioned because a union sets so high a wage that a large number of its members will not be employed. If, under this situation, it was always the same individuals who remained continuously out of work, this condition could not last. The workers who were out of work would either insist that the union fix a lower wage at which they might be employed, or they would leave the union and accept lower than union-scale wages in order to find employment. What really happens in many trades, however, is that instead of half the workers being employed all the time and the other half none of the time, there is a longer interval between jobs, and *all* the workers are employed half of the time. The use of a union "waiting list," on which the man who has been out of work longest is placed at the top of the list and gets a job first, is almost a guarantee that this situation will result. Thus, when the members are unemployed a considerable share of the time, they are likely to place all of the blame on "bad business conditions" instead of attributing part of the blame to the union wage policy. Even if an individual member is aware that the high wage policy is resulting in unemployment, there is always the chance, or the hope, that the next job which he gets will be one that lasts a long time so that he will make good earnings at the high wage rate. Consequently he may do nothing to oppose the wage policy of the union.

Where chronic trade-union unemployment exists, the usual

remedy adopted by the union is to decrease the number of apprentices who are allowed to learn the trade. If maintained long enough, this policy will eventually eliminate the unemployment in the trade; but it has other, more serious consequences. Since fewer men are allowed to enter this trade, there will be more men competing for jobs in other occupations and so tending by their competition to lower the wages of others. Also, the other workers will have fewer goods at higher prices, as manufactured by the monopolistic trade union. For example, the stumbling block in the path of all efforts to provide adequate low-cost housing for the poor has been the high cost of building-trades labor.

By *unemployables* is ordinarily meant those people who are physically or mentally incapacitated for work. It is true that there are some people who are absolutely incapable of doing any productive labor whatsoever. But, except for this class of people, the term *unemployables* should not be used except with reference to a certain wage rate. There may be many partially incapacitated people who are not capable of earning the wage rates that are being paid by industries at present. Some of these may be cared for through the organization of industries to take advantage of what capacities they have (for instance, the industries now run by the blind). Others may find work by working at lower wages to compensate for their lack of efficiency. But if a minimum wage is imposed by law without making some special provisions for this type of worker, it will be surprising indeed if the number of unemployables does not increase.

Unemployment Relief

Our attention now turns to methods of unemployment relief. Public conscience in the more industrialized countries has attained to the point where it will not allow the involuntarily unemployed to starve. Praiseworthy as this attitude is, it should not lead us into a blind sponsoring of all proposed relief methods regardless of their individual merits. It is exceedingly important that the methods of relief adopted should not be such that they will tend to increase the number of unemployed, to make unemployment permanent, or to prolong business depressions. While we have not the time to examine all proposed schemes of relief, if we can develop an understanding of the principles involved, we shall then be able to apply these principles as a test of the economic practicability of such measures of unemployment relief as come to our notice.

In the first place, relief payments are said to "create a volume of secondary employment by putting purchasing power into the hands of the consumer." What is meant by this statement is that other people will be employed to make the goods which the relief recipient buys with the relief money. But is this statement correct; will unemployment be increased? To answer this question, we must know from whence comes the money for the relief payments. If a government obtains money from someone who would otherwise have spent it anyway, his spending would have created just as much "secondary employment" to make the goods which he buys as does the spending of the money by the relief recipient. Only in the event that a government obtains money that would *otherwise have remained idle,* does government spending for relief actually "prime the pump" and provide *additional* secondary employment.

The sources from which a government can obtain funds for relief purposes are few: taxation, borrowing, and the printing of new paper money. If taxes are collected from people who would otherwise have spent the money or invested it (spent it for producers' goods), then obviously no additional purchasing power is placed in circulation. Money is merely taken from the hands of the taxpayers and put into the hands of the relief recipients. The same money is spent, but a differ-

ent person spends it. The same reasoning applies in the case
of government borrowing. To the extent that the people or
the banks who buy the government bonds would otherwise
have spent the money or invested it in private industry, purchasing power is not increased but merely shifted. Moreover,
to the extent that government bonds (with their tax exemp-
tion privilege) compete with industrial securities for the in-
vestors' funds, the expenditure of industrial companies for new
equipment is delayed. It is the so-called "heavy industries"
(manufacturing of machine tools, steel, and so forth) which
make this new equipment. Furthermore, it is in these same
"heavy industries" that the greatest volume of unemployment
occurs during business depressions, and it is these industries
which must stage a recovery if the unemployed are to be "reabsorbed into private employment."

We have said that only in the event that government funds
(obtained through taxation or borrowing) would otherwise
have remained idle will purchasing power increase through
spending for relief. But why is it that funds remain idle?
Ordinarily the only reason why either banks or private individuals retain cash in excess of their normal requirements is
the fear that whatever investments they could make would
turn out to be losses. The flotation of huge government bond
issues may serve to prolong this period of fear. Everyone
knows that sooner or later taxes will have to be raised to pay
the interest and principal on these bonds. The question in
everyone's mind is, then, "Who will be taxed and how much?"
Certain industries which appear to be fields of favorable investment might turn out to be losers if heavily taxed. Other
industries, depending on a luxury demand, may prove to be
failures if heavy taxes on incomes cause people to economize
by not buying their particular goods. In this connection, the
immediate imposition of taxes for relief purposes would be
less demoralizing to the investment market than government

borrowing is, because soon after the taxes were imposed their effects could be noted and investment could then proceed on a basis of sound knowledge.

The third method that we have mentioned—printing of new paper money for relief purposes—is open to still more serious objections than the other two. As the new money finds its way into the banks, it will act as enlarged reserves on which a still greater volume of expanded bank credit can be created, and the subsequent depression will be even more violent than the one which the inflation was designed to relieve.

These considerations do not lead us to the conclusion that relief should not be given. Relief measures, however, should be regarded simply as what they are: relief measures, and not means of stimulating business recovery. Hence the relief measures should be kept to the necessary minimum so as not to interfere with the process of normal business recovery. This points to the superiority of direct relief over work relief as being less expensive. A further argument against work relief may be advanced. Insofar as recovery in the building trades is being delayed by high prices of building materials and by high wages, government purchases of those materials will tend to prevent or to delay the necessary fall in prices, and government hiring of the workers (particularly if "prevailing wages" are paid) will tend to prevent or delay the fall in wages, thus retarding the resumption of building construction by private enterprises.

If we wish to eliminate cyclical unemployment, rather than merely to devise relief measures when it occurs, we must direct our attention to devising ways of preventing the periods of inflationary prosperity which bring business depressions as their consequences.

CHAPTER XXIV

Business Cycles

VARIOUS time series which reflect changes in general business activity are available. These may be single indicators
such as freight car loadings, electric power plant production,
and steel ingot production, or they may be composite indexes
such as the American Telephone & Telegraph Company's Index of General Business Conditions, the Federal Reserve
Board's index of industrial production, or the Cleveland Trust
Company's index.

Any of these time series, after seasonal movements within
the year and long-run trend have been eliminated by various
statistical methods (as they are removed in the composite in-
dices mentioned above), exhibit a more or less regular wave-
like movement when plotted on a chart. This wave-like movement we call the business cycle.

Usually a business cycle has four phases. Writers on business cycles call the phases by different names. J. A. Estey calls
them expansion, recession, contraction, and revival.[1] Some
other authors call them recovery, prosperity, recession, and
depression. A fifth phase, that of financial panic, may ac-
company some cycles and not others, and when it does occur,
it is not always in the same position in the cycle.

After some originating force, variously identified by the different theories of the cause of business cycles, expansion starts.
This phase is characterized by increases in the volume of bank
credit and its rate of circulation, increases in employment, in

---

[1] Estey, J. A., *Business Cycles*, Prentice-Hall, Inc., New York, 1941.

profits, in wages, and by changes in the demand for capital equipment. Since the greatest additional employment in this phase is in the "heavy industries" or capital goods industries, the wages spent are apt to cause the prices of consumers' goods to rise more rapidly than other prices.

Estey defines the recession as the turning point during which the forces that make for contraction finally win out over the forces that make for expansion. Costs have already caught up with profits in some lines and passed them in some others. There is unloading in the stock market, strain and some contraction in bank credit. Prices start to decline. Production may continue for a while, but much of it is on a variable cost rather than a total cost basis. Whether there will be a panic depends upon the nature of the preceding rise, partly on market news items and the way they are played up, and partly on the banks themselves.

Contraction is characterized by a rapid decline in output and employment. Capital goods suffer the worst and consumers' goods the least. There is a fall in average prices, caused partly by liquidation of inventories, partly by reduction in bank credit, and partly by postponement of buying in the expectation of further decline or fear of loss of employment. Costs and price relationships are distinctly out of line.

Revival is characterized by leveling out of previously falling prices. As inventories are gone and must be replenished at levels that cover costs, the motives to price cutting cease. Consumers' durable goods are wearing out and need replacement. Some costs begin to fall. Union wage rates may be cut actually if not nominally by less insistence on working rules. People begin to buy "to avoid the rise" and revival is under way.

There are a great many theories of the causes of business cycles. These may be roughly classified into groups:

1. Real causes.
2. Psychological causes.

3. Monetary causes.

4. Underconsumption theories.

5. Savings and investment.

Under each of these headings may be found anywhere from three to a dozen theories by different authors. Merely to give an adequate brief digest of each of these theories would take up most of this book. Such books have already been written by Professor von Haberler and Professor Estey. I shall therefore confine myself to a discussion of only two theories, which I have selected because I think that they are among the best and because they fit well together.

The business cycle represents a departure from equilibrium conditions. Therefore, if we are to find a cause for the business cycle, we must take as our starting point an assumed condition of complete equilibrium in the economic system and then explain how this is disrupted by the cause or causes we find. To start our analysis in a period of depression, with unemployment and unused resources on hand, would only cause us to reason in a circle. Depression, unemployment, and unused resources are the result of a past cycle. We cannot take them for granted but must explain how they came to be.

In our economic system as described in the earlier parts of this book, every departure from equilibrium conditions should merely give rise to a new set of equilibrium conditions to which the economic system should more or less rapidly adjust itself, and each disturbance should carry with it the seeds of its own readjustment. For example, if the price of a particular product is too high, resulting in a rate of returns which is higher than that to be obtained in other lines, additional competition will be attracted into the field. This competition will affect the situation in two ways: first, by lowering the selling price due to the increased supply of the product; second, by raising the costs due to competitive bidding for labor, for raw materials, and for loanable funds. Rising costs and falling selling prices would then bring about a situation in which the rate of earnings in this industry is no higher than in others and further expansion should cease.

Before starting a new firm in an industry, intelligent businessmen will attempt to take into account the effect which their own addition to the supply and that of their competitors will have on the market price. Their guide, then, is not present "quantities demanded" in physical units (as some writers would seem to imply) nor even present prices. It is forecasted future selling prices. This allows room for errors of forecasting as an explanation of the business cycle. However, such reasoning would ignore the second element in the situation which we have mentioned. Rising costs, by decreasing prospective profit margins, should discourage further additional firms from entering the industry, long before the product of the first additional firms comes to the market to depress the selling price. Each new firm which enters the industry (and each expansion of productive capacity by old firms) should thus cause estimates of future prices to be revised downward, and should cause an *immediate* rise in costs. Under such a situation, some slight overproduction might result in a few lines because of errors in forecasting, but certainly nothing like the violent disturbances which we know as business cycles.

In the business cycle, however, we are confronted with a situation in which disturbances from equilibrium, instead of leading to rapid readjustment, give rise to further deviations from equilibrium; in which price rises lead to further price rises; in which large numbers of commodities advance in price at the same time; in which periods of abnormally high prices, instead of being followed by equilibrium prices, are followed by periods of abnormally low prices. Where are we to find the explanation for this? It may be found in two elements which were ruled out by our assumptions in the supply and demand discussions of previous chapters—in innovations, and in the changes in the quantity of money, and the maintenance of artificially low interest rates by the banks.

Innovations

An innovation [2] may consist of: (1) the introduction of a new product; (2) the introduction of a new method of production for an old product (either by new machinery or by a previously untried method of organization of the factors of production); (3) the opening of a new market; (4) the development, or acquisition, of a new source of raw materials; (5) a substantive change in the organization of business (for example, the organization, or breakup, of trusts or cartels).

These changes give rise to substantive changes in the data on which businessmen base their calculations. Until the innovation has had time to be absorbed into the economic system and the system has adjusted to it, the old rules for adjusting production to consumption will no longer work. Instead of being able to take costs and selling prices as given data and adjusting output to them, businessmen find that costs are changing continually, rapidly, and often without notice. Instead of a single shift in the demand curve to which output must be adjusted, they are confronted with a succession of shifts in the demand curves for their product, and with little indication of what the final position will be.

To understand this better, let us trace the course of an innovation, say, the introduction of a new product. Remember that we start from an equilibrium position with no unemployment and no unused resources. (The effects of unemployment and unused resources will be considered later.) First of all, the new industry must have plant and equipment. To make this plant and equipment, labor and other resources will

---

[2] The innovations theory of the business cycle as explained here is that of Professor Schumpeter, but he should not be held responsible for my statement of it.

be withdrawn from the old industries where they have been employed. This will tend to increase the costs of the old industries. It will also decrease the amount of the old products, since the labor and resources are no longer employed in making them. To obtain the labor and the resources, the founders of the new industry must have money capital. Moreover, they must pay more for resources and for laborers than these factors have been earning in their previous employment in order to attract them away from the old industries and into the new one. Let us assume that the new money capital is provided by the creation of credit by the banking system.[3] The demand in terms of money for the old goods will now be greater than before. (The workers who are building the new plant, and the owners of the other resources, will want the same goods that they formerly purchased and will have more money with which to buy them.) Thus, supply of the old goods is decreased and demand is increased, both tending to cause the prices of the goods to rise. There is no reason to expect that the increases in demand and in costs will be felt equally by all the old industries. Those old industries, the demand for the products of which rises more rapidly than production costs, will thus be making an abnormal profit and will themselves be motivated to expand. To the extent that they borrow from banks in order to do this, the inflationary effect upon prices and the bidding up of costs in order to obtain resources is magnified.

Once the first firm in the new industry has demonstrated the possibilities of the new product, a host of imitators will enter the new business, eager to take advantage of the possibilities for profit in the making of the new product (for instance, one company brings out an electric refrigerator, and

---

[3] If innovations were financed out of real savings, their rate of introduction would have to be far less rapid. Furthermore, without the inflation caused by created credit, the disturbances of the price structure would be far less severe than they are.

other companies, seeing how well it sells, bring out competing refrigerators). The effect of the actions of these imitators will be to magnify the disturbing effects of the innovation as indicated above. A period of "prosperity" is then in full swing.

What happens next? As the factories are completed and the new product starts to appear on the market, it competes with the older goods for the consumers' dollar. To the extent that the public buys the new product rather than old ones, demand for the old products is decreased. As the innovating firms start to repay bank loans out of profits, quantity of money is decreased, making for a deflationary effect upon prices, and decreasing the demand for goods in terms of money still further. As the old firms find the demand for their products decreasing, they will lay off workers and use the money to repay bank loans, rather than to renew the loans and keep the same number of workers. The unemployed workers will not buy the same quantity of goods that they did before, and so demand for goods is still further decreased. We are in the "vicious spiral of deflation."

Business Depressions

The depression can best be understood as an attempt of the economic system to readjust itself to the new equilibrium conditions caused by the presence of the innovation. The new product must be incorporated in the economic system at an equilibrium price and output; hence the older industries must become adjusted to new equilibrium prices and outputs based on the presence of the new product in the market. The depth of the depression is not conditioned by the disturbances caused by the innovation alone, but is more attributable to other causes that vary in intensity from one business cycle to another. Some of these causes are:

1. The extent to which the innovation is introduced before the previous cycle has run its course and before readjustment to

the previous cycle has been accomplished. Thus, if the innovation is introduced in the depression phase of the previous cycle (before full equilibrium has been attained), many firms that are doomed to eventual extinction will be given a new "breathing spell." Those prices which should have fallen to bring about readjustment will be prevented from falling. The shifts of labor from one industry to another required for equilibrium adjustment will not yet have been completed. For these reasons, the "premature" appearance of a new period of prosperity involves not only its own maladjustments but also carries over to the next period of depression some of the maladjustments which should have been corrected by the previous depression.

2. The extent to which bank credit has been expanded in the period of prosperity. The greater the expansion of bank credit has been, the more rapidly some prices will have risen relatively to others in the period of prosperity, and consequently the greater the amount of readjustment that will be necessary to bring prices into line with each other again. Furthermore, the greater the amount of speculative overbuying that has been financed by bank credit, the greater the possibility that these loans will not be repaid as prices fall, and consequently the greater the dangers of bank failures and financial panic.

3. The nature of the competitive impact of the innovation. If the demand for a new product is at the expense of a decreased demand for all other products in general, then the loss of demand felt by each of the old industries will be comparatively mild, and the readjustment may be easily accomplished. (Only one or two firms need leave the industry for equilibrium to be restored; or perhaps excess capacity can be reduced merely by curtailing maintenance expenditures and not replacing some capital goods as they wear out.) On the other hand, if most of the competition of the new product is confined to a very few of the old industries, large numbers of firms in these indus-

tries will have to go out of business with consequent heavy losses of invested capital. Moreover, to the extent that the old industries losing business are concentrated in particular localities, the unemployment of labor due to labor immobility will be more serious than if it had been spread thinly over the entire country or the entire world. Likewise, to the extent that unemployment is concentrated among workers of the same specialized skills, it will be more difficult for them to be reabsorbed than if the unemployment was diversified among workers of many different skills.

4. The longer the construction period required by the innovation, the more violent is the necessary readjustment likely to be. When the plant and equipment for the innovation can be built fairly quickly, the new product will start to appear on the market and force readjustment before extreme maladjustments have had time to develop. When, however, the equipment for the new industry requires a long number of years to construct (for example, a railroad), the whole economic system tends to become adjusted to the temporary demands of the construction period. Then, when the construction period has ended and the shifts in demand occur, a far more extensive readjustment will be called for.[4]

5. Closely allied to Point 1 above is the factor which has been so well explained by Professor Schumpeter, that of improper selectivity in the granting of bank loans in the period of depression. If the banks follow their usual procedure, two classes of firms will find it easiest to secure loans in the depression period: those that have a large proportion of their own capital invested in the business; and those that have the best

---

[4] Professor Schumpeter has developed an interesting theory of the connection between "major innovations" and "long waves," and "minor innovations" and "short cycles." However, it is one of the virtues of Professor Schumpeter's theory that, while it can explain such periodicity as does exist, the theory itself is not dependent on periodicity for its validity.

reputation for repaying their loans in the past. But some of these may be the very ones that will eventually be forced out of competition by the innovation. If these firms are tided over the period of depression by the granting to them of bank loans, their failure may be delayed until the next depression period, to the severity of which this delay in adjustment will contribute. In a period of depression following an innovation, it may be extremely difficult for the banks, or anyone else, to determine how much of a firm's loss of business is purely a depression loss which will be recovered when general business conditions improve, and how much is a permanent loss due to competition of the innovation.

The Additional Credit Theory

An alternative, although not contradictory,[5] theory of the business cycle as developed by Professor F. A. von Hayek runs in terms of monetary causes, and changes in interest rates.[6] We found in the discussion on distribution that one of the conditions of equilibrium is that the marginal products of factors of production must be equal to their prices. In the case of money capital, another way of stating this principle would

---

[5] Professor Schumpeter makes credit creation an integral part of his theory. He would, however, insist that deliberate lowering of the "market rate of interest" or expansion of currency as a political fiscal policy comes under the heading of "non-economic causes." Professor Hayek, while recognizing innovations as one of the most important causes of changes in the "natural rate of interest," would hold that innovations cannot explain the cycle without a substantive monetary explanation, and would insist on the importance of declines in the market rate of interest as a sufficient originating cause of a cycle *sui generis*. There are many other differences in exposition which may be considered more than mere differences in emphasis. Nevertheless, the two theories are not irreconcilable but are both important contributions to the understanding of a difficult subject.

[6] The statement of the theory which follows is an oversimplification. For a full statement of Hayek's views, see *Monetary Theory and the Trade Cycle*, Harcourt, Brace & Co., New York, 1932, and *Prices and Production*, George Routledge & Sons, Ltd., London, 1931. His article, "The Paradox of Saving," *Economica* No. 32, May, 1931, besides being a masterly criticism of the fallacies of underconsumption theories for the business cycle, will prove an aid in the understanding of the thesis of his two books.

be to say that the rate of return [7] which is being earned by invested funds must be equal to the market rate of interest. This equilibrium may be disturbed by either (a) a *rise* in the rate of return on invested capital (the most probable cause of which is innovations) or (b) a *decline* in the rate of interest charged by lenders (the principal lending agencies being, of course, the banks). Whether caused by (a) or (b), this discrepancy between the rate which can be earned by using capital in business and the rate which must be paid for its use is a motive for business expansion involving both an increased demand and higher prices for capital goods, and an increased demand for funds with which to purchase the capital goods and with which to finance their manufacture.

As we have seen in the chapter on interest, if the increased amount of loanable funds were obtainable from savers only, the rate of interest would have to rise to compensate for their increasing rates of time preference and their consequent increasing reluctance to loan greater proportions of their incomes. If the market rate of interest did so rise, the expansion would be curtailed very quickly and a new equilibrium point would be reached because (a) the increased prices of capital goods and the increased interest charges would soon bring the cost of *using* capital goods up to the point where it equalled the expected rate of return, and (b) the higher interest charges and higher labor costs (necessary to draw workers away from consumers' goods industries) would soon bring the cost of *manufacture* of capital goods up to the point where it was equal to the higher prices of capital goods.

As we have seen in the chapters on money and banking, however, the amount of loanable funds can be expanded by *created* bank credit, and in the usual course of events this is the case. When this occurs, it is not necessary for the rate of

---

[7] *Cf.* Hayek's *Monetary Theory and the Trade Cycle,* p. 209, for a discussion of the natural rate of interest.

interest to rise as rapidly as it would if new savings were the only source of credit. In the competition by the banks to make use of their idle lending capacity,[8] the rate of interest they charged will rise very slowly, if at all, during the early part of the period of expansion. Furthermore, the cash balance theory teaches us that this expansion of bank money will result in disproportionate price rises which will in themselves be the motivation for overexpansion and speculative activity in many lines.

During all the period when interest rates are kept artificially low by the expansion of bank credit, many projects are undertaken which would not be advisable at higher rates of interest. But these low interest rates cannot be maintained forever. Eventually a drainage of cash will force the banks to take heed of their reserve ratios. New loans will be discouraged by a higher rate of interest and old loans will not be renewed. The demand for capital goods which was motivated by low interest rates and financed by bank credit will now decline. Capital goods manufacturers will curtail output or close down, and the spiral of deflation will begin.

Forced Saving

Since *forced saving* plays an important role not only in the theories of Schumpeter and Hayek but in the writings of many other modern theorists (for example, D. H. Robertson and J. M. Keynes), we will do well to understand it thoroughly. We can grasp the nature and significance of forced saving best by contrasting it with "voluntary saving." When you save voluntarily, you do so by not spending all of your income on consumers' goods. Thus, you save both money and goods. For yourself, you save the money you did not spend; for the community, you save the goods you did not buy. Conse-

---

[8] Remember that expansion of credit by one bank provides a basis for expansion of credit by the others, so long as they "keep in step" in expanding credit together.

quently, when you lend the money to someone who uses it to hire workers to make producers' goods, the workers take the money which you did not spend and spend it for the goods you did not buy. There is thus no tendency for the prices of consumers' goods to rise. To state the proposition in a different way: the withdrawal of workers from the making of consumers' goods in order to make producers' goods decreases the supply of consumers' goods. But the fact that you refrain *voluntarily* from buying consumers' goods means that the demand for consumers' goods in terms of money is likewise decreased. Decrease in supply is offset by decrease in demand, so that prices do not necessarily rise. Furthermore, as long as you and other people continue to save the same amount (and lend it), the demand for producers' goods will remain unchanged and there will be no need for the producers' goods factories to shut down (as we found to be the case when bank credit was curtailed).

What is the situation under forced saving? The banking system lends created credit with which to buy or manufacture producers' goods. Workers are withdrawn from consumers' goods industries, and the supply of consumers' goods is decreased as before. However, since we presume you are not saving voluntarily, your demand for consumers' goods will not have decreased. On the other hand, the increased quantity of bank money placed in the hands of the workers will mean an increased demand for consumers' goods in terms of money. To the extent that you and other people have fixed incomes, you will be deprived of goods by the higher prices. This is what is meant by "forced saving." You do not save money but, although you spend the same amount of money, the higher prices of goods prevent you from consuming as much as you did before. These goods (or rather the services of factors of production) which you involuntarily refrain from consuming are then available for consumption by the workers who make producers' goods. This is not an equilibrium situation. As soon as possible, you and the others who have been deprived of goods will attempt to secure an increase in your incomes (when contracts expire, higher salaries will be insisted on; when leases expire, higher rental will be demanded; and so on). As your incomes increase, you will try to buy the goods of which you have been temporarily deprived by the high prices.

This increased demand will cause the consumers' goods industries to bid competitively for workers and raw materials, thus raising costs in the producers' goods industries. Still more important, as the limits of bank credit expansion are approached, interest rates will rise rapidly. Thus, the longer the productive process before goods can reach the consumer, the greater will be the burden of increased costs imposed by the higher interest charges. In the face of higher interest charges, possibilities for profit will exist only in the making of consumers' goods by the shortest means possible. New projects requiring a long time for their completion will no longer be undertaken, and work may even cease for a time on partially completed projects. The construction, machine-tool, and similar industries, feeling the decline in demand for their products, will start to lay off workers. The loans granted for many long-term projects will prove to be unsound, and banks will start to contract credit in a struggle for liquidity. In consequence, workers will be released from the producers' goods industries faster than they can be reabsorbed by the consumers' goods industries. The unemployed workers will buy fewer goods and the consumers' goods industries in turn will suffer from reduced demand, although not so seriously as the producers' goods industries. Recession and depression ensue until different prices and costs can be readjusted to each other on a workable basis.

To complete another phase of our analysis, let us return to

the situation under voluntary saving. When the producers' goods (the construction of which has been financed by voluntary saving) are completed and start to yield a result in the form of consumers' goods, the increased amount coming on the market will tend to cause the price of consumers' goods to fall. However, since no distortion of the price system through the expansion of bank credit has taken place, such a decline in price would have been anticipated before the construction of the capital goods was undertaken. Businessmen would have taken into account the effect of a lower price for a larger output, and would not have ordered the capital goods unless the lowering of costs would be sufficient to offset the expected decline in price. This sort of decline in price would thus be merely a required equilibrium adjustment and not a serious disturbance to the economic system. Indeed, the virtues of improvements in production which lower costs, and of the consequent competition which lowers selling prices, are extolled by all of the orthodox economic writers.

Stabilization of the General Price Level

Now, however, suppose that these prices are falling owing to decreased production costs. The authorities of the banking system, noticing the decline in the average or "general" price level, say to themselves: "A falling general price level is bad. It will discourage business. We must keep the price level up. To do so we must expand the currency. The easiest way to expand the currency is to lower discount rates, which will encourage borrowing and put more bank credit into circulation." What happens if this policy is adopted? The lowered interest rates will encourage the production of still more capital goods, resulting in a still greater output of consumers' goods, again starting to cause a fall in the price level, so that a still greater expansion of credit is required to keep the price level from falling. Obviously this process can be continued only until the absolute limits to bank credit expansion are reached. Meanwhile all of the disproportionalities, which we discussed under forced saving and in the chapter on money, will have developed. Thus we may see that the maintenance of a stable price level when costs are falling is really a form of concealed inflation.

It is only in these terms that the situation in the United States from 1923 to 1929 can be understood.[9] We had an extraordinarily stable price level from 1923 to 1929, but the collapse of 1929–33 demonstrated the tremendous amount of unsound credit on which it was based. Whether we have learned anything from the experience and whether it will be politically expedient to put our knowledge into practice, only time can demonstrate.

---

[9] From a statistical point of view, the inflation was even more "concealed" than we have indicated. It was to be found mainly in the increase of "time" rather than of "demand" deposits, although demand deposits did increase by a considerable amount. During this period, because of the lower reserve ratio required on time deposits, many banks urged their customers to transfer their idle demand deposits to time deposit accounts. When the idle demand deposits were then replaced by active demand deposits, the increase in "velocity of circulation" was considerable. Moreover, since the requirement of 15 days' notice before withdrawal of time deposits was waived by most of the banks, the time deposits themselves became in effect demand deposits for many purposes.

Index